Enjoy!

Madam

Prostitutes, Punters and Puppets
Memoirs of a very British brothel

For Gill
Happy reading

Linda Dunscombe

Becky Adams &
Linda Dunscombe

Madam Becky

♡ xx

Cover design: Chloe Rush Amethyst Design
www.amethyst-ds.co.uk

Photography: Karen Boyle
www.karen-boyle.co.uk

British Library Cataloguing Publication Data.
A catalogue record for this book is available from the British Library

ISBN 978-0-9571489-0-1

Magic Beans Media
59 Buckfast Ave
Bletchley
Milton Keynes
Mk3 6ND

www.magic-beans-media.co.uk

Tel 01908 366428

This book is dedicated to all those who have shared my outward journey, and to Dilly the brightest star who illuminated my road home.

Photography: Karen Boyle

BECKY ADAMS is an Author and Toastmaster who lives in Buckinghamshire with her small dogs and horses. She has two daughters and a grandson.

In her previous life as a Madam she spent twenty years involved in the British sex industry. During that time she featured in ITV's Personal Services Series and her exploits graced most of the tabloids. She has appeared on the Trisha show as well as BBC and SKY news.

She was also the founder of Scrubbers Topless Carwash, Madam Becky's Gentlemen's Clubs and FooFoo adult shops.

LINDA DUNSCOMBE is a Writer and Tutor with an MA in TV Scriptwriting from DeMontfort University, Leicester.

Acknowledgements

I'd like to say thank you to Sarah and Faith at All Ears Events for getting me going on my book writing journey and to Linda Dunscombe for her tuition, editorial input, support and keeping me focused when my mind and body wandered off to find cake. Not forgetting Richard Fitt and his ladies at Authors on line who knew all the answers.

Big thanks to Darren for the hot dinners and daily assistance. Nourishment of body and soul.

Lots of love and gratitude go to my daughters Abi and Emilia who've been ignored for a year whilst I've been typing and my dear old mum who has supported us all as always in every way possible. And my dad who just thinks I'm bonkers.

Wormy kisses to Dogbaby, Precious and Pug my sofa companions through endless cups of tea, gingernuts, re-writes and edits.

If I can do it anyone can.

CHAPTER ONE

'Good evening ladies and gentlemen. Thank you all for coming.' I took a deep breath and smiled saucily. 'I must say, that it makes a nice change to be able to say, '*Thank you for coming…*'at the beginning of a booking.' They laughed tentatively, unsure how to respond.

Pausing briefly, I made a show of peering out from the stage into the audience although the spotlights blinded me, making seeing anything impossible.

'Blimey! It looks like I've managed to make some of you come twice.' I waved, pretending to greet people I recognised. 'At my age, with my ovaries making anyone come at all is something to be proud of.'

The crowd roared with laughter and relaxed. I breathed a sigh of relief. It was going to be a good evening.

'My name is Becky Adams, but you can call me Madam.'

Prostitution is a difficult taboo subject, and listening to someone openly discuss sex work and bizarre fetishes makes many people feel uncomfortable and squirm in their seats, even with some moody lighting and a few glasses of vino.

I love public speaking. Sharing the ups and downs, in and outs of two outrageous decades spent running brothels in the leafy suburbs of the Home Counties. Stories of me and my naughty ladies being hounded by the authorities; vilified by the neighbours; dressing middle-aged men as babies; counting blow jobs and avoiding jail.

Strangely though my audience was often more nervous than I was. If they had never heard me before and had no idea what to expect, then generally they expected the worst. Most assumed I'd be a raging nymphomaniac who'd followed my dirty obsession with sweaty sex and genitalia into a seedy world of vice and hard-core filth. But here I was, blonde, polite, and just a little old fashioned with a love of small dogs and confectionery. Mother, grandmother, business woman. The product of nature, nurture and circumstance just like everyone else.

Over the last few years I've been invited to address many women's groups and business clubs. Sadly some members would boycott the evening refusing to come and hear me for fear of embarrassment. Some would be angry that their club allowed a person such as me, a former Madam, a purveyor of prostitutes into their midst. But those who did suspend judgement and came to listen were surprised, entertained and intrigued - subsequently recommending an evening with Madam Becky to their friends.

I've been told I don't look like a 'Madam'. I'm not really sure what a Madam is meant to look like, but I've been blessed with some long-legged and small-waisted genes. Throw in a good education and some cosmetic procedures and in my mid-forties I'm still looking pleasant enough if a tad plumper than I had been.

I don't arrive to speak clad in rubber or with my knickers on show. Although admittedly for a comedy turn at a rugby club I would wear my infamous PVC cat-suit, but that was more for practical purposes than titillation. Rugby club annual dinners always seem to end in a food fight. Dressed in PVC I could be wiped down with a damp cloth and chauffeured home minus the inevitable coating of mashed potato and black forest gateaux.

I genuinely like people. I'm open and honest, but never crude. I would never knowingly upset or embarrass anyone, that's not my style. I'm more Benny Hill than Ben Dover, maybe with a touch of the 'Carry Ons' and a sneaky Sid James laugh.

Telling my massage parlour tales to a large group of people is a way to help remove stereotypical ideas about the sex industry, not to crack a cheap smutty joke at the public's expense.

Sensibilities and maiden aunts are safe with me.

My eager listeners that night were all journalists and TV types who'd been writing all sorts of nefarious gossip about me for years. Some of it true, most of it wonderfully hilarious and creatively invented by the editors. According to one red top I'd been busy spanking members of the royal family, and frightening spaniels by having sex with the aristocracy during pheasant shoots in the Chalfonts. As a lover of tweed and waxed moustaches, it sounded smashing, and wonderfully sporting but sadly not true. The real truth was stranger than anything the tabloids could make up.

Prostitutes, politicians and footballers are always fair game for the newspapers. When you run massage parlours and escort agencies for a living you spend your working days with a variety of members from all three groups. The fact that I had a convent education, was a bit posh and outspoken, always happy to poke my head over the parapet and appear on the telly to defend sex worker's rights had made me a popular media target. I was happy to play along with the game.

The spotlights were blinding, but as I glanced sideways I saw a seven foot image of myself projected onto the screen behind me. It was the vision that used to greet clients as they opened the door into my large and legendary gentlemen's club, 'Madam Becky's' - provincial brothel and shagging HQ in Milton Keynes. A younger, slimmer me, in the skin tight, barely zipped, black PVC cat suit with huge bright pink lettering, WELCOME TO MADAM BECKY'S.

Feigning a shocked backwards stumble I looked up at myself.

'Well, I say. That was a few cakes ago.' I laughed with my audience. 'And as a lady of a certain age, I am going to have to stand in this corner, where the lighting is more flattering, whilst I tell you about the different people who have frequented my various premises over the last twenty years.'

The audience were silent, willing to listen.

'This evening I'll be telling you about the changes I've noticed in the punters who visited my establishments, and how ordinary girls now decide to be escorts as a career choice, rather than out of any perceived poverty, desperation or coercion. As you'll appreciate, there won't be a power point presentation.' I chuckled. 'No photographic evidence as we have to protect the guilty. So tonight ladies and gents, you'll just have to look at me, either pre-cake Madam Becky,' I pointed to the slim, PVC projection. 'Or...' undulating my hand down my body like a magician's assistant, '...the post, several years of Victoria sponge cake, matronly Madam Becky.'

So then chaps, on with the show.

'In fifty percent of countries across the world prostitution is legal. In fact, prostitution is perfectly legal in the UK. You're allowed to sell sex, or buy sex. What you get sent to prison for is helping others buy it or sell it. Being a Madam is very illegal. My job of chatting on the phone, arranging teapots on trays and folding towels carried a sentence of up to fourteen years.'

'It's estimated that at least two and a half million men in the UK pay for sex, and that number is doubling every decade.' I let those surprising figures sink in. I could almost feel the women in the front rows look sideways at their men and wonder if they ever had, if they ever would, visit a lady of loose morals.

'I know nothing about street girls and drugs; all my premises have been very middle class, middle market. Quality and value for money was my business ethos. Nice friendly ladies, expensive bubble bath, a cup of tea and a ginger nut.'

'I provided my girls with a life coach, savings plans and private health cover, but despite paying my taxes, and ensuring the girls paid theirs, I was hounded out of business, and in September 2009 I hung up the cat-suit, and closed the bordello door for the last time.'

I looked into the spotlight spangled darkness.

'To be honest, since selling 'Madam Becky's' I've enjoyed not looking over my shoulder, always checking to see who was watching me, who was following me, or who was waiting to beat me over the head with a stick and run off with my immoral earnings. I've been arrested for kidnapping a pair of oversized pants, pole dancing in slippers and dispensing cold beer and salted peanuts. It seems ironic and unjust to me that the law states that I had to pay income and council tax from my illegal operation. Money then used to fund the police and local authorities to come and close me down. I'd rather they just invoiced me every time they raided us. That would seem more honest somehow.'

They laughed in all the right places. When I became serious and talked them through my belief that the internet and satellite TV was responsible for de-sensitising kids to sex causing them to have totally unrealistic and sometimes damaging sexual expectations of themselves and others, they listened intently.

'We have school children dressing like prostitutes, and prostitutes dressing like school children. The Murdoch industries condone this and you as journalists need to take some of the blame.' I could hear the awkward shuffling of chairs.

My fears about the over sexualisation of children isn't a laughing matter, and I could hear from the murmurs of agreement that others, the parents amongst them, shared my concerns.

'When I started my first escort agency in the early nineties it was almost impossible, and very expensive, for a client to find two ladies who'd work together in a realistic lesbian way. Even just a decade ago sex was still seen as something slightly mysterious and treated with a modicum of respect. Now, in massage parlours across Britain, we have girls of eighteen and nineteen who are happy to have intimate relations with men, women, soft toys and vegetables for a basic fee. In fact, this type of shenanigans is part of a normal weekend of binge drinking for many of today's young people, so it stands to reason that they'd have no problem doing it at work for money. Being bi-curious is now widely discussed in teen magazines as almost a fashion statement. Girls snog other girls and their friends' dads on early evening TV shows, watched by impressionable small children nationwide. We are becoming gluttons for cheap tasteless sex like we've become gluttons for cheap tasteless food, devouring all, with no thought for the long term consequences for the individual or humanity.'

I paused again for the mutterings of surprised acknowledgement to subside. I'm a mum and a granny, and it may sound like double standards, but to me there's a big difference between providing a professional sexual service for consenting adults in a controlled environment, and society going into a shag-happy, knife-wielding free fall with the feminists and Government blaming everyone but themselves.

'Let's face it,' I said grinning and lightening the mood after my political rant. 'The tabloids run stories of girls having sex with Premier League players and getting paid three grand for a few hours partying. Most of the girls I know would have sex with a footballer for a cheese sandwich. Why would you go and work for the minimum wage when you could fiddle with an athletic boy, drink champers and get paid four months' salary? Personally I'd rather have a cheese sandwich and a nice sit down. Fit boys, overflowing with testosterone are too much like hard work at my age, but that's just me.'

I stood on the stage and thought back over my twenty years in knocking shops, and remembered with a smile the hundreds of girls and thousands of clients that had walked over my well-vacuumed carpets to recline on the well-made beds.

'The clients have changed as well over the years...' I mused. 'Previously they'd been mainly pleasant, management types who could afford one hundred and fifty pounds per hour. Now with the opening of our borders, student debt, cheap lager and the UK being the most promiscuous society in the western world, the prices have tumbled and everyone's at it.'

'At 'Madam Becky's', which was a very smart, well run brothel with educated, attractive ladies and male escorts for men, you could get full sex for twenty minutes at the bargain price of forty English pounds. Sounds ridiculous, but it's the going rate most places.'

'Clients these days are fussy. Not grateful, like they used to be. Not delighted and fascinated to find a smoothly mown lady garden under a racy pair of panties. With all types of porn just two clicks away from the under twelve's, most boys seem to grow up not realising that girls even have pubic hair or small deflated breasts. Young girls compare themselves to surgically enhanced half-starved stick insects and feel ugly and outcast.'

'People want it all now, they want it cheap and they want it quick. It's no surprise to me the world's going mad, and we're losing control of our kids with their search engine based perception of sexuality.'

'An escort's clients expect quality and value for money like they would from any service. At 'Madam Becky's' we even had a loyalty scheme where you had your card stamped, and after ten stamps you got a free go. Unfortunately we got closed down and I ran off to France to hide from the police and pickle walnuts before we started competing with Tesco and adding vouchers for cheap petrol to our special offers and BOGOFs.'

I knew my time with this crowd was nearly up and on cue one of the organising ladies was signalling from the side of the stage. We had to allow a few moments for questions and answers, and there were always plenty of those.

A huge round of applause and enthusiastic whooping filled the room before the first hand went up. The spotlights swung briefly away from me and into the crowd. A man stood up and an assistant handed him a microphone.

'Madam Becky, have you ever been asked for anything that has really surprised you?'

'Well, to be honest,' I said, 'half a lifetime assisting fetishes in bawdy houses means even the bizarre quickly becomes normal. We had a guy who liked being rogered hard up the bum for an hour with items from the fridge's salad drawer, and no, I don't mean a wet lettuce. He then recovered from this exertion with a nice mint tea and a freshly sliced if slightly soiled cucumber sandwich!'

I let the image sink in, and listened to the inevitable shrieks and moans of disgust. 'Another chap had a dental torture fantasy, but we soon sent him packing with his pliers and bleeding gums.'

I did a fake shudder at the memory. Funny old business.

The lights deserted me again and swept around the room. Lots of hands were up. It was always the same, so many questions. But there was one that always, always without fail got asked.

The spotlight beamed down on a smart attractive lady. She stood up and took the mike. 'Madam Becky,' she said, in a soft Irish accent. 'You had a God fearing expensive education. How did you make the leap from convent school to selling sex? How on earth did a girl like you end up opening a brothel?'

A murmur went around the room. It's always the big one. I waited for the lights to settle back on me and I smiled down at the audience.

'Ah,' I said. 'Like all the best adventures, it started quite by accident, a very long time ago...'

CHAPTER TWO

Nobody wakes up one day and thinks, 'I know, I'll run a brothel!' Nor was 'Madam' on the list my school careers adviser gave me. It was more a case of stumbling, quite by accident, into the profession. I suppose to even begin to understand you have to start right at the very beginning.

To say that my relationship with my mother was difficult is the understatement of the century. Looking back I realise that she probably thought she was doing the right thing. Babies don't arrive with a detailed list of care instructions. And I don't think myself or my brother were what she expected from her offspring, especially as we grew older.

I think it all started out happily enough. My mother and father were living with my Dad's parents when I was born, saving hard for their first home. From a family of tambourine shaking Welsh Salvationists, Mum stayed true to her roots, and chose to deliver me, within the sound of the Bow Bells, at Clapham Salvation Army hospital, making me officially a cockney.

Forty four years on, my mum has still not forgiven my father for arriving to meet me that first day of my life, roaring drunk, and ricocheting at gathering speed along the hospital corridors into the ward, scattering nurses and dispensing trolleys as he went.

'She looksssshhh like a ssshhkinned rabbit,' he drunkenly announced to his shocked, newly delivered wife. 'When it'sh the weight of ten houssssshe brickssssss, then I'll pick it up.'

Good to his word, rather than nurturing children he concentrated his efforts on building a successful architectural practice and chose to over indulge himself in car racing, partying, and other amusing but self-centred behaviour that was a delight to everyone but my struggling mother.

The rapid growth of his business allowed us all to move to a large, four-storey house in Hertford when my brother Matthew was born a year later. It also paid the outrageous private schools fees for us both from the age of three. As well behaved, angelically blonde, middle class infants, we were sent to attend a prestigious and very expensive prep school run by uncompromising Irish Ursuline nuns. Currant buns my small curly haired brother called them.

Several years of piano, ballet and elocution lessons followed and although not a Catholic, I was left with no doubt what was expected from me by the Holy Trinity and my parent - obedience, courtesy and a deeply ingrained study ethic.

My mum was a strong, intelligent feminist from a poor but proud Welsh mining community. She was determined to mould her offspring into the shape she wanted us to be. Sadly for her we had ideas and identities of our own. Whilst easy to control in our younger years, we both became increasingly unmanageable and vile as we grew older.

My mum had freed herself from the poverty of the Valleys with education. She'd gained a grammar school scholarship, and then clawed herself through a variety of nursing, midwifery and health education qualifications. Meeting my father had introduced her to a strange and crazy world of artistic, flamboyant, party animals with far more money than sense.

I adored my father and his wild friends, but we saw very little of him, for which Matthew, my only sibling, seemed quite glad for some reason. I thought my father was utterly wonderful.

My mother took it upon herself to oversee the family with a similar method of discipline as had been dispensed by the terrifying nuns at my school - the same harsh, unyielding household regulations she'd grown up with in Wales during the difficult days after the war. Hardly applicable we thought for the 1980s.

As rebellious teens, we called her the Ayatollah, and would chant a song at her about prayer mats and dictatorship to the tune of the Oaky Cokey, complete with a full range of hand gestures while she swiped at us with a wooden spoon.

Rules in our household were plentiful and rigid, and non-compliance was always dealt with harshly. Little wonder it caused such rebellion as the years progressed.

I first ran away from home when I was about five years old. I don't remember what my mother had done to upset me, but I packed some tins of tuna and a packet of hula hoops into my leather school satchel and planned my departure. Pulling the hood of my anorak over my head, leaving my arms free, I peddled off to meet my destiny with my coat flying out behind me like a bat cape.

It felt, to my skinny, waif-like body that I'd biked for miles and I must have travelled a fair distance, as eventually I ended up on a dual carriageway. Startled by the traffic, I skidded to a halt in a gravelly lay-by. Huge, noisy lorries raced past me and dust and debris flew up into my face. I sat down on the rough, grimy grass bank and bravely fought back my tears. Opening up my bag, I pulled out the can of fish in brine and examined it carefully. My tummy was rumbling and it was starting to get dark. The first realisation to hit me was that I had forgotten to bring a tin-opener. The second realisation was that I was in fact only five with tiny hands, and had no idea how to use a tin-opener even if I had one.

Big fat raindrops landed on my cheeks and mingled with the tears I could no longer contain. Terrified by the constant roar of vehicles coming at me from both directions, fear and panic overwhelmed me. I wasn't enjoying the freedom of the open road at all, and needed to go home for my tea.

Putting the impenetrable fishy tin back in my bag, I shoved a handful of hula hoops into my mouth, picked up my bike and with my gangly legs working as hard as they could, I set off back the way I'd come. Of course this meant I was peddling wildly the wrong way down the dual carriageway into an oncoming stream of agog, ashen faced motorists. Amazingly nobody stopped to assist or even abduct me, and even more amazingly I made it back without being flattened like a hedgehog under a juggernaut.

I arrived home, cold and wet, my anger only slightly muted by the horror I'd encountered on my great escape. Clenching my jaw and preparing to defend my actions from my mother's wrath, I was greeted by a total nonchalance and disinterest in my mutiny by my parent who looked me up and down, passed scathing comment on my bedraggled appearance and continued reading her book.

Clearly, if I wanted her attention I would have to up the drama.

My father's business continued to expand: the Ritz hotel and the subsequently besieged Iranian Embassy were added to his design portfolio along with various airports, fancy wine bars and trendy nightclubs. His group of friends now included pop icons, formula one racing drivers, actors and politicians.

In the 1970s the wealthy, groovy people were migrating out of London and buying foolishly large houses in the country. When I was maybe six or so, my dad bought the family a swanky new house, as a statement of his success. He moved us, my beloved kitten Fuzzy and Haggis the Cairn terrier to Wales, whilst he continued being creative and flamboyant in the City, unencumbered by a wife and kids. I missed him dreadfully, but I had Fuzzy the cat's small, square ears to whisper my feelings of loneliness into, and that always helped.

The Wales we lived in was not the dirty, desperate coal face and slag heaps of my mother's childhood. We were on the English boarders near Hay on Wye, a stunningly beautiful place of gentle countryside and meandering rivers - a gathering point for the flaky, sensitive types from the sticking and gluing arts and crafts world. Hay on Wye boasted its own literary festival with resident lovies and a trans-sexual celebrity. It was all very racy and contemporary for the seventies.

Farmers exercised their prize winning Hereford bulls along the country lanes, leading them on a rope clipped to a ring through a big damp nose, whilst London stockbrokers tried to squeeze past in Lamborghinis, keeping the revs low so as not to startle the muscular beasts... or the bulls.

We were now happily ensconced in a rambling country mansion, surrounded by acres of rose gardens, ornamental rockeries and paddocks. My brother Matthew and I continued to study pianoforte and the odd pas de deux. I also added the pony club, learning songs about cuckoos in Welsh and sheep bothering to my list of childhood activities.

My father and his architectural associates were still busy building a reputation in central London and going to all the best parties. He would commute to Wales at the weekends, often bringing with him a houseload of the most bizarre friends. Meeting up at Marble Arch on a Friday evening, his chums would fill their Ferraris and Bentleys with bottles of champagne and merlot, then drink and drive their way two hundred miles up the A40 to the finish line at the Three Cocks Hotel in Glasbury - a charming village, just over the welsh border near the banks of the River Wye and just a short booze sodden drive from our house. A case of vintage port would await the first triumphant motorist, and my father in one of his several Aston Martins was often victorious.

The Three Cocks Hotel was owned by a delightful but utterly bonkers Frenchman from the legendary Heinz family and it felt like my second home. The weekend Wacky Races continued until a merchant banker chum purchased a helicopter. It could just about be landed at a jaunty angle in the field behind the hotel's restaurant. I don't think Jimbo, the landlord's horse, thought much of the arrangement, as he stood in his stable, vibrating from the rotor blades.

Fast living, coupled with high speed and alcohol, meant that the game and its participants gradually died out over the next few years. My father suffered a massive heart attack during one visit home at the age of thirty six. It nearly killed him. I wasn't aware of anything at the time; the panic and disaster somehow hidden from my brother and me. My dad made a slow but full recovery in secret. Sadly, it was something else that made me furiously angry with my mother years later when I eventually found out.

I was always so excited about my dad's weekend visits. Every Friday evening I would bolt down dinner, get quickly bathed and ready for bed. Then I'd sit on the bottom of the large carved staircase that swept through the centre of the house into the grand entrance hall. My feet, freezing from the slate flagstone floor, would be pulled tight up under my nightie as I waited expectantly to hear the throaty roar of a hot DB6 engine throbbing up the drive. Hopping from foot to foot, squealing with delight, competing with a leaping dog, I'd hurl myself at my dad the moment he pushed open the heavy oak front door, twittering and demanding hugs before he'd even put down his bags and drawn breath.

Exhausted from the journey, and smelling of leather upholstery, he'd fight his way past excited pets and my incessant chatter into the piano room to see my mum. I'd be cunningly dispatched to make him a whisky and water and hunt down some Bombay mix while he collapsed exhausted onto the large sofa in front of the fire. Dashing back from the kitchen, performing high speed skids on the polished corners, I'd return to him as fast as I could. Then I'd tuck myself into my special cubby hole, the space behind his knees as he stretched out and relaxed. We'd start our weekend of fun and foolishness lying on the couch singing a duet of the Westminster chimes in cat noises and writing silly poetry for the dog.

My weekends with my dad, tweaking the Bobby Dazzler, the fastest go-cart in Wales, and eating crisps in pubs always ended too soon. Sunday evening would find me sobbing, with my little seven-year-old arms clinging as tightly as I could around his legs as he shuffled slowly towards the front door and the road back to London. Trying to impede his exit, I was dragged wailing across the hewn slate floor, scraping my knees, howling with misery. The scabs would take until Thursday to heal, be picked off and flicked at my brother. As a desolate, heartbroken child, the blood and tears were acceptable collateral damage to have delayed his leaving me for even one more minute.

Friday would find me bathed and fidgeting at the front door again waiting impatiently for him to come back home for a few more enchanted days.

My dad carried on enjoying his fast, crazy living whilst my childhood unfolded with years of horse riding, building dens in the woods and playing Ben Hur with Fuzzy the cat who seemed content to sit in the Bobby Dazzler go-cart-come-Roman chariot as I raced her around the garden. Fuzzy, the British Blue, amiable round-faced cat, was my closest companion throughout my early years. One day as we drove the thirty miles school run home from Brecon Convent, Mum glanced casually over her shoulder at us kids in the back of the car and said, 'oh sorry, but Fuzzy's dead. I got old Mr Snelas to bury her in the vegetable patch near the greenhouse.'

I was only about nine when my cat died, and I'd loved Fuzzy more than anything in the world. She had survived busy town living at our old house in Hertford only to be flattened by a car in the tranquil Welsh countryside. Several shocked seconds after Mum had broken the news, all hell broke loose. I became hysterical in the true medical term, and by 6.00 pm, in desperation, the local GP was summoned. Given a sedative injection, I lay in bed for days, shouting, praying and begging for Jesus to bring her back, gagging and vomiting on my snot. I'd spent my entire school life with Jesus, and I couldn't understand why he wasn't arranging a resurrection; he'd done it before, on a much grander scale and the nuns at school always told me how much he loved me, so where was he now?

Several times a day I was fed sleeping tablets hidden in strawberry jam on a spoon, until eventually I'd calmed down enough to leave my room. Six months later, just as I was coming to terms with Fuzzy's entry into pet heaven, Matthew, my dear brother, told me he'd dug her up by accident whilst planting lettuce seeds with my grandfather. He cruelly informed me that she was still alive under the ground half a year after being run over, but he'd buried her again because our mum told him to do so because she hated me.

Nine years old, and utterly bereft, more hysterical than I had been on the day of her death, I spent the whole night with a spade in the vegetable garden racked with sobs trying to find her again to save her.

Life went on but nothing lasts for ever. Change is inevitable, and it was about to come knocking.

My dad had separated from his more sensible business partner, and a few bad deals had seen us fall on harder times. He often joked about money. 'It talks to me,' he'd say, insisting it told him to buy sports cars and expensive whisky. 'Easy come, easy go,' he'd laugh as the bills piled up. 'There's plenty more where that came from.'

But when I was almost thirteen, the money only had one more word for my dad which was 'goodbye' and off it went for good. The bank foreclosed. We lost our house. My mother was devastated and Matthew and I were suddenly homeless. Nothing would be the same again.

Coming down to earth with a bump, the plan it seemed was we were to be moved from private education and a grand house in Wales, to a comprehensive school and a small rented house in North Devon that came with my mum's new job.

I'm a person who forms very strong attachments to the places I live. Maybe even more than to the people I live with, and to me Wales was my home. Somewhere I loved very much. I'd spent years happily wandering alone through the fields with my dog, talking to myself, eating hazelnuts off the trees, and playing ponies. My friends from the convent were mainly boarders and lived at school during term times, so I rarely saw them socially, but I didn't mind, I was always happiest on my own in the countryside untangling sheep from barbed wire and poking fledglings back into nests.

Whilst I understand now that financially it was impossible for my world to continue as it was, nothing was ever discussed or explained to my brother and I, and a feeling of helplessness, betrayal and anger grew steadily inside me. I was out of control of my life, irrelevant in the minds of adults, with no input into what happened to me, or where I lived. No one wanted to know how I felt or what I needed to be happy. No one listened, so I stopped talking to them, and communicated my seething disapproval with silence and glowering, staring hatefully out of the car window as I was forcibly taken places I didn't want to go.

My mum, as tenacious and hard working as ever, was desperate for this new job and a new start. She was excited about the move to Barnstable in North Devon, and enthusiastically talked about it to the side of my insolent head as the answer to all our problems.

'I don't want to go Mum,' I said, fighting back the hormonal teenage histrionics. 'I'll never see my friends again. It's a million miles away.'

'For Christ's sake,' replied my mum, 'there are other people in the world. You'll make new friends.' She started to walk away, 'we're going and that's all there is to it.'

'I don't want to leave Fuzzy,' I cried out after her, as my eyes filled with unstoppable tears.

She paused, turned and stared at me. 'What? You're thirteen, that bloody cat has been dead for years. What the hell are you rattling on about you stupid child?'

'Fuzzy's body,' I said, determined now to defend my love for my cat, dead or alive. 'I don't want to leave Fuzzy's body. Someone might dig her up.'

She stiffened, bracing for a fight, or even worse - my emotional melt down. Emotion was a rude word in my mother's vocabulary and we were not permitted hysterical dramas.

Of course the grown-ups didn't care about Fuzzy's remains being left behind to be dug over by the new owners of our cabbage patch. We moved as planned to Devon, sadness and distress ignored. Friends, human and furry, alive and dead, were left behind.

CHAPTER THREE

Dedicated as always to expanding our educational horizons, Mum forced her love of learning repeatedly down our throats. My brother and I, now surly, miserable, displaced teenagers, spat it back out at her. We turned our music up and slammed our bedroom doors on her near constant tirades of anger and frustration at our ingratitude and foul manners.

In a bid to make peace and cheer me up, my mum had agreed to let me look after a little grey pony called Smarty and took me to the secondhand dog's home and allowed me to adopt Samson the Wonder Dog, a disgraceful looking Yorkshire terrier, with one ear that stuck up like a flag, an overshot jaw and severe epilepsy, who'd stolen my heart at the first wag of his tatty tail. Samson, a small, useless, no good dog proceeded to yap, fit and convulse his way through the next ten years.

Leaving Samson the Wonder Dog home alone practicing his separation anxiety and shrieking through the window, Matthew and I occasionally attended our new comprehensive school which we saw as an undisciplined free for all. A social event, to be visited infrequently and only when it was too wet or cold to skive off into town, or wander aimlessly along the North Devon coast.

We were regimentally pushed into open rebellion by a change of circumstance and my mum's desperate attempts to keep control of us and her own sanity. We responded by lavishing mockery of everything she tried to achieve and believed in.

'Well,' the pompous and disgruntled headmaster would announce when he caught me snogging in the corridor, bedecked with Siouxsie Sioux eye makeup. 'You wouldn't have behaved or looked like that at the convent would you young lady?' Tutting, he'd shake his head dramatically. 'You're mother must be so disappointed. All that good money spent on your education. That you should become such a wastrel in my school, it breaks my heart.'

I'd just shrug my shoulders and slouch away.

Matthew, Samson the Wonder Dog and I spent many a damp night sleeping rough on a bench in the park or in Smarty's stable. We'd been thrown out of the house by our mum for not washing up or for looking at her funny. And sometimes we'd stay away simply because we didn't want to go home to get chased with a wooden spoon and thrown out again.

Often we camped out in a ramshackle old caravan that crouched like a hibernating beetle under many years of rotten leaves and mould at the bottom of my boyfriend Sid's garden. Only slightly dryer than the park bench, the caravan lacked the benefit of a through draught, but we were safe from the local singing wino who liked to serenade us at 3.00 am over a bottle of meths. Sid, my first boyfriend, then thirteen and a year my junior, was known to his mum as Nigel. Re-christened by his chums in honour of their Sex Pistols hero, Sid was too nice really to be a proper punk. He did his best with some safety pins and slightly offensive badges pinned dangerously on his custom ripped lapels, but he was never entirely convincing.

Terrified of waking an aviary of neurotic budgies and alerting his dad, Sid would bring food and blankets out to us as we hunkered down for the night on the strangely moist, smelly, dralon caravan cushions. He'd sneak on tiptoe, going the long route through the broad bean canes, preserving the secrecy and silence. In the morning, after his parents had left for work, we would race, shivering , starving, and dying for a wee, up the path and, sod the canaries, into the house to thaw out and raid the biscuit barrel before school.

The pivotal wooden spoon moment happened when I was about fourteen. I'd done something to unleash my mother's anger and she was hissing and spitting at me while I cowered in a corner. Wooden kitchen implements, hairbrushes and Hoover pipes were her weapons of choice, and at the beginning of any disagreement my mother would rush into the kitchen to find some gravy stained gadget to batter us with. That particular day, observing her unbridled fury from between hands I held in front of my face to protect my ears from being boxed or my cheeks slapped, something snapped. Something deep inside me changed.

'How dare you,' she shrieked. 'Get to your room. I wash my hands of you,' and then she started to count. 'One...two...three!' I knew what was expected of me. On the victorious count of three, if I hadn't scampered crouching up the stairs whilst she swiped at my legs, I would be hit repeatedly and hard with whatever was at hand.

But that time I didn't run.

'No.' I screamed back at her, surprising us both. 'That's enough!'

I decided at that moment that yes, I did dare to have my own opinion, and yes, I did dare to make my own decisions. I wasn't going to be a victim. Nobody was ever going to bully me and tell me what to do and how to think again.

I stopped cowering. I stood up straight. I pulled the wooden spoon out of her hand and I hit her with it. Full force. Recoiling backwards in horror she looked at me in shocked disbelief. I had a new-found confidence after that day and my mother found it increasingly difficult to control me or my brother with physical force.

Of course, looking back I'm sorry, I wish I'd found another way. But then I also wish that she'd been a more accepting and understanding parent. Neither of us got what we wanted or needed from our relationship. She was always disappointed and I was always a failure.

My childhood fights with Matthew, my brother, intensified from sitting on top of him pinning his arms to the floor whilst slapping his face, force feeding him grass, spitting on him and other common sibling games, to full blown fisticuffs. His spiteful destruction of my Motorhead posters in my bedroom resulted in me beating him enthusiastically with a tennis racket. Falling backwards onto my bed, protecting himself with his surgically-booted flat feet, he lashed out at me for all he was worth and kicked me square in the face breaking my nose. Running downstairs in search of first aid, blood soaking the front of my clothes, bones at a comical angle, I was greeted by a look of disinterest from my matriach.

'Sodding well serves you right,' she said, turning her back on me. I was left to my own devices. No sympathy and no trip to A&E.

Matthew had discovered Crazy Colour hair dye and was sending our mother into states of apoplexy with bright red and magenta new romantic droopy fringes. One sunny morning, sitting in the back of her bright yellow

Mini Clubman estate, he announced to the back of her head he had just had his ears pierced.

We were driving down Pilton Street, a steep hill into Barnstaple town at that precise moment. My mum gave up on the driving and turned around to attack her son. The little lemon car veered dangerously towards the curb.

'Mum!' I screamed, as I grabbed the steering wheel. We were hurtling along, gaining speed and running completely out of control - the car and my mother's temper. She was hanging over her seat battering Matthew with all her strength - a frenzied punching fit on any part of him she could reach.

'I will not have my son looking like a fucking Christmas tree,' she raged into his smug, grinning face. His long giraffe legs and fallen arches deflected most of her blows.

Somehow I managed to keep us in a straight line and by yanking up the handbrake I slowed our decent enough to avoid smashing into the shops at the bottom of the hill. Returning most of her attention to driving, but still cursing between gritted teeth, she uttered the faithful old threat of 'just you wait till we get home and I ring your father.'

Only when we did get home my brother didn't wait for the anticipated ranting or beating. He clumped upstairs and packed a small bag, taking himself off, back into town. Looking to teach Mum a lesson, he marched briskly into the police station.

'I want to make a complaint against my mother,' he said to a rather stunned desk sergeant. 'She assaulted me.'

He then demanded they deal with her outrageous behaviour and ideally remove him from the family, for his own safety, and the safety of future hair do's. They unfortunately took him at his word and he was taken into care, assigned social workers and a police liaison officer to keep an eye on him, which somewhat cramped his style.

I visited him a few times in the children's home where he was staying. It seemed quieter and tidier than our house, which was a good thing. I remember being so frustrated that no one would listen to me. I realised that children have no voice and no control over what adults do or say and it really pissed me off. Despite all the authorities' well-meaning assistance, nothing improved our relationship with our mum, and life went on.

Matthew didn't stay in the home long. He re-dyed his hair, pierced his nose and made a bid for freedom by hitch-hiking from Devon to London, where the streets are paved with gold sequined lamay and hair colouring is a human right.

Penniless but finally happy, and just fifteen, he moved into a squat in Islington. His flat mates were a pre-op trans-sexual, a rent boy and an obese fire-eater called Gill. Sadly Gill killed herself, but Matthew and his gay friends, who later included Boy George, Leigh Bowery and Steve Strange, went on to create the now legendary and much reminisced eighties London nightclub scene, about which bizarrely, my mother is now very proud.

Just after I'd finished my 'O' levels, (that means different things to me these days, and are normally charged as an extra) my mum had a promotion at work.

'We're moving to Aylesbury,' she announced, as though it were a done deal and I had no say or input into the decision at all.

'It's for the best,' she added, walking away from me.

'I can't. I won't,' I shouted at her departing back. 'What about Sid?'

She shrugged her shoulders as though the name meant nothing.

'And Smarty,' I cried, unable to stop the tears falling. 'Who'll look after my pony?'

Reluctantly she stopped and turned to face me again. 'There's not a man on earth worth crying over and certainly not a bloody horse,' she said angrily. 'You're being ridiculous.'

Despite my tearful protests she moved us again from our North Devon coastal home, my borrowed pony and Sid, my first love, to Aylesbury. She'd decided a move nearer to my wayward father, who was living in Soho, would add another 'firm hand' to the task of controlling my equally wayward brother who was still squatting somewhere in the capital with his chums How she thought anyone could have a 'firmer hand' than her own, I had no idea.

We moved into an unpleasant seventies house in Stoke Mandeville - emotional outbursts and any mention of misery banned. I would stand for hours staring out of my bedroom window, lonely tears pouring down my face, playing Pink Floyd's album 'The Wall' over and over again. I missed Smarty my pony desperately; I'd only borrowed him, and he'd been returned to his owners, but I was afraid they'd not care for him properly or love him like I did.

You can never replace the bonds you form through school, or the animals you've told all your secrets to and left behind. I felt so far away and lost. Matthew, the serial escaper, was being dragged on a weekly basis, at Mum's insistence, from his squat in London back to Stoke Mandeville by my dad. Angry at my parent's interference in his new life, Matthew encouraged me to run away, and hitch with him from Aylesbury back to Devon for a laugh. It took us nearly three mirthless dreadful days, raining all the way. I was so happy to see Sid and Smarty, but it re-broke my heart when eventually I admitted defeat, said goodbye all over again and boarded a coach home.

CHAPTER FOUR

Back home in Stoke miserable Mandeville, ordered by my mother, I reluctantly enrolled at Aylesbury College to study for my 'A' levels. ('A levels' are a speciality service that earn ladies lots of money, but that's for later) I towed that line for several surly, dreary weeks, and then abruptly left, much to her chagrin, announcing my decision to train as a riding instructor.

'You're planning to do what?' she yelled. 'Over my dead body are you.'

I gave her my best withering look. 'Yeah well, I'm sure that can be arranged' I snarled. 'You may find there's a queue of candidates to cut your moaning, frigging head off.'

The insult bounced straight off her.

'You need to finish your 'A' levels and go to a good university,' she demanded. 'Not ponce around cleaning up after bloody horses all day. Where's that going to get you eh? You're ridiculous.'

She paused and folded her arms. 'I forbid it,' she added, doing her usual trick of walking away when she'd said her final word. As far as she was concerned that was the end of the matter.

'Forbid all you like,' I screamed at her departing back. 'I've made my mind up. I'm working with horses. I'll pass my riding instructor's exams and you and uni can go to hell.'

For several years I put up with her disapproval and worked hard at a smart dressage yard, studying with a stern and grumpy, international dressage judge. Sadly my high hopes of being a top-notch horsewoman were crushed by judgemental, condescending attitudes of the Pony Club mums. Despite passing all my qualifications and my slightly plumby accent I never really fitted in with the headscarved upper echelons of the British Horse Society.

Eventually I got a wonderful job running stables for a 'Riding for the Disabled' charity, helping the most amazing kids gain independence and confidence through their love of ponies. It's a fabulous feeling to wake up every morning with a happy heart, delighted to go to work. I thought I'd discovered my perfect career.

Once a week, I caught a packed commuter train from Aylesbury to London, getting off in Seer Green, the heart of leafy Buckinghamshire, for my day release at horsey college. Sitting quietly in a cramped rail carriage wearing my full riding regalia, I felt all eyes on me. With my jodhpurs, white shirt and tie, I tried to be inconspicuous whilst bankers peered at me enquiringly over their morning copy of 'The Times'. Awkwardly embarrassed in my tight, black, fitted jacket, leather gloves and whip, I cringed into my seat, ignoring the glances of the stuffed suits and Thatcherite yuppie go getters. It was 1985; I was seventeen, leggy and slender with long blonde hair. I thought my shiny leather boots, skin tight breeches and spurs were being viewed with scorn. It was only years later when I resurrected this highly popular outfit for our 'speciality services' that I realised the saucy truth behind the close, focused scrutiny of my fellow male travellers on the eight fifteen to London.

On one of my days off from the stables, I walked into Aylesbury to do some loitering. Whilst engaging in nonchalant teenage wall leaning, I spotted a shaven-headed, Dr Martin clad, bovver boy exiting a phone box.

In an act of rebellion towards my mother who hated all men, especially the badly behaved, tattooed variety, I concluded I may have found a kindred spirit in this troubled seventeen year old. Only just released from a Young Offenders Institution the day before, Gary seemed perfect boyfriend material.

Gary and his best friend Alan were busy but unaccomplished petty criminals, with a very poor success rate. A situation made all the worse by the fact that Gary's estranged father was a DI in regional crime, and had to keep arresting his own son, and explaining the weakness of his genetics to his superiors.

For my controversial, parent-hating, teenage mind, it was great. Gary was my ideal man. I realised however, I would have to do something about Gary and his chum Alan's inconveniently frequent prison trips.

Alan's criminal career peaked dramatically when he staged an armed robbery on a local post office, and troughed swiftly afterwards when his stolen Honda

CX 500 getaway motorbike got stuck in a field. He had to be prised from three foot of mud by a helpful farmer, who then instantly recognised him later in a line up. Having stashed the loot under Gary's mum's bed, and considered it a job well done, Alan then went off to the pub to boast about his cheeky audacity. After his speedy arrest, he was easily identified by the post mistress as the nice young man who had reliably done a paper round for her several years previously.

Luckily, some may say, Gary and I were in Spain whilst this adventure was unravelling into farce. But we knew from Gary's infuriated mother that the police had raided her home and discovered the money and stolen bike helmet under her divan. When we flew back into Luton, my parents, never fans of Gary, were waiting to collect us, and so were the police. With some ducking and diving and hiding behind fellow travellers we managed to avoid the latter and make it to my father's car with our liberty.

Unable to bear anymore botched jobs, I appointed myself to the role of crime co-ordinator and set about getting them organised. Well, Gary, as Alan was now doing a ten year stretch for his foolishness.

Gary and I moved to Milton Keynes in 1988, and our daughter Abigail was born in March 1989. Travelling Europe, Gary was busy stealing things and having fun with a collective of professional football hooligans.

At home alone, I tried to do a normal job selling double glazing whilst bringing up our baby and dispensing epilepsy tablets to Samson the now middle-aged and stinky Wonder Dog. When Gary was around, our relationship had become increasingly volatile, and once again I was desperately unhappy and lonely. Very easily riled, Gary was prone to hypocritical jealousy, especially when fuelled by vodka and an England defeat, and our fights would be vicious and destructive.

I have always been teetotal; having suffered from debilitating migraines since a small child, I was terrified of dizziness and nausea. With a clear, sober mind I would bait and taunt my boyfriend, mentally running rings round him as I waved proverbial red flags. I always won the arguments by jumping onto the moral high ground, from where I would goad him further as he charged at me in a drunken fury, before I kicked him in the face.

As difficult and violent as he was, I was horribly miserable but unable to see a way out of the situation. I was trapped in a self-destructive spiral and feeling as out of control of my life as I had as a kid.

One night, after celebrating a work colleague's birthday with friends and a quick orange juice after work, I drove home, wishing I had somewhere else to go. As I slowed the car to park it, Gary suddenly leapt out from behind a bush. He pulled the driver's door open and dragged me from the still moving vehicle by the throat. I don't remember screaming. A bit hard to do when you're being strangled. It might have been the noise from my unmanned auto as it slammed into the wall, but something alerted the neighbours who called the police.

Two officers pulled into the car park in the nick of time, and Gary released his hold on my throat, just as I was starting to pass out. I collapsed to my knees as the policeman stepped between us.

'My baby's in the house on her own,' I managed to gasp to a WPC, 'I need to go to her.'

The policewoman helped me up and together we went towards the house, leaving Gary shouting about me being a bitch and gesticulating to the other officer.

'You ok?' she asked, putting her arm around my shoulders. 'What's going on here?'

I started to cry, partly from frustration but mainly because she was being so kind.

'It's always like this.' I said through the tears. I wasn't badly hurt; I was used to fighting with Gary. I often started the trouble just to get a reaction or a conversation out of him, so I wasn't going to complain when he reacted. Fighting with me seemed to be the only time he took any notice of me these days. But I'd had enough now. I sat at the bottom of my bed, looking at the sleeping baby in the cot. She was thankfully oblivious to her dysfunctional family.

I looked at the WPC. She was late twenties, pretty and with soft, caring eyes that seemed full of compassion. It was all too much for me; I couldn't hold it all together any longer.

'How old are you?' she asked gently.

Ignoring her question the tears fell and I poured my heart out.

'He leaves at 5.00 in the morning; I lie in bed and hope that he'll be killed in a car crash.'

The shock showed in her eyes.

'He drives way too fast, like the idiot he is,' I added, as though it were some justification. 'He'll kill himself one day. I wait for a knock at the door, hoping that one of your lot will be standing there, telling me he's dead. I hate him so much.'

'How old are you?' She asked again.

'Twenty three in May,' I replied, feeling much older than my years. 'What a mess. Poor baby, thank god she's asleep. He just left her in here on her own.'

'I don't understand?'

'He was hiding in the bushes waiting for me.'

'How long had he been outside?' she asked.

I shrugged. 'It could've been ages, he's such a dick. I hate his guts.'

I wasn't surprised by her confused expression. How could I explain the destructive madness that was our relationship?

'But why? Why hide in the bushes?'

Her guess was as good as mine.

'He likes hiding in bushes.'

It was strange but true. He could hide in shrubbery on a stakeout for hours.

'Why do you stay?' she wondered aloud.

I sat in silence. I had no answer to that question. I really didn't know why. It wasn't because I was in love with him. I couldn't stand him. Fear maybe? Better the devil you know and all that.

'I suppose because of the baby; I've got nowhere else to go. My mum's not speaking to me. She hates Gary and won't forgive me for getting pregnant.'

'Is there no one else who can help you?'

I shook my head. 'I stayed in a squat in London with my brother for a while when I was pregnant, but we fell out. Then I got ill and started bleeding so much I came back here to be near my doctor.'

She stood up and leaned over the cot, touching Abi's sleeping face softly with the back of her finger.

'Would you like me to call the women's refuge? See if they've got any room for you both?' she asked.

'I'm not really a battered wife,' I replied, surprised.

'He had his hands round your throat when we arrived, I think that qualifies. What would have happened if we hadn't turned up? How far would he have gone?'

I didn't want to answer that one. Was he capable of really hurting me? Why not? I wanted him dead. No surprise then if he felt the same. 'I don't even know what his problem is. I only went out for an hour after work.'

'Maybe you just need some space, some time to think, and work out what's best for you both.' She looked at Abi. 'Well, all three of you.'

Suddenly I was so tired of it all, and I could feel hot tears fighting to escape again. 'Ok,' I said to her obvious relief. 'Thank you, but what about the dog? I can't leave him, he needs his tablets.'

I knew if I went then, with the police, whatever possessions I left behind he'd chuck out, which would include Samson the world weary Wonder Dog. The constable waited while I quickly threw the most important bits for the baby and me into a black bag and tied the top to make it easier to carry.

'I don't want to walk out past him.' I was worried he'd start again and get himself arrested. I did feel a bit stupid, as if siding with the police was a betrayal. But him leaving the baby alone, to sit in a bush for god knows how long for god knows what reason was pathetic. It was time to do something about it.

The WPC radioed for another car to be sent to the next street, and while Gary was still being detained by the other officer, we made a dash for it through the back door.

The hostel was warm but noisy and smelled strongly of old cooking and cigarette smoke. Children ran up and down the hallway, and I heard someone shouting at a crying infant somewhere up the stairs.

Sitting shell-shocked in the office whilst they took my details, I tried to listen as someone explained their rules of confidentiality, rotas for cooking, washing and countless other things. I couldn't keep the dog with me and sadly had to leave him with a friend from work. I was lucky to have a room to myself, and before I was taken to my new space to settle the now fretting baby, the kindly copper said her goodbyes and wished me well.

When Abi finally dozed off, I crawled into bed and cried myself to sleep. I woke up barely an hour later to the sound of another baby howling next door. That's when I started to get really pissed off with myself and the situation.

I had spent all my early life being pushed around by my mother; my teenage years battling first with her and then with Gary. Why was my life like this? I started to realise as I lay there, that fighting was part of my nature. I wasn't a victim even though I felt like I was. I had got myself into situations because

I refused to be ordered around and told what I could and couldn't do. People who wouldn't listen to my feelings reminded me of my childhood and made me difficult and defensive. This wasn't the life I wanted for myself and my child. I wanted more, and I wanted it to be about me. I lay awake all night thinking hard and making life changing decisions.

The next morning I was up early and, with Abi in my arms, I went in search of a better future. I found a flat to share and negotiated deposit free rent and moved in with my daughter, a sad little bin bag of belongings and my tatty old mutt. I was determined to turn it around.

It was my life and I was in control.

No one was going to push us around again.

CHAPTER FIVE

The double glazing company I worked for had kindly let me use one of their little vans to get to the office. Things were looking up, and as the months passed, with the help of a hundred percent mortgage and some hard negotiation, I managed to buy a run-down Victorian terraced house in Bletchley with a splendidly large garden. I've always been keen on horticulture, back then in the sense of cultivating my vegetables and later in the sense of cultivating fallen women - both tasks requiring endless patience and careful hoe handling.

In 1989 I was looking forward to getting stuck into my herbaceous borders when not working ridiculously long hours or cleaning out Abi's new rabbit.

My boss, a stereo-typical home improvements sales manager, was a stroppy and somewhat fag stained dwarf. Almost circular, he sprouted a strange arrangement of ginger hair that sparrows could nest in, but would chose not to on health grounds. He had a bit of a thing for me, and after the incident with Gary word soon got around that I was living alone and working hard to get back on my feet.

One day, Old Red called me into his office. I wasn't worried; I didn't think I was in trouble. If anything I thought he was just going to ask if I wanted to run the new telesales project. He had been wonderful letting me use the van, and I was so grateful.

'Thanks again for the use of ...' I started to say as he closed the door and sidled up to me.

He was invading my space, but the penny didn't drop. I stepped backwards politely.

I was still trying to work out what the hell was going on when he stood up on his toes and shoved his hand down my top. 'Come on love, you scratch my back and I'll scratch yours...'

Shocked, my mind tried to catch up with the unfolding events. I backed away further, but he threw me hard against the door. 'Come on love you need me.'

Yeah like I needed syphilis I thought.

'That's my front you're scratching, not my back,' I retorted angrily, the red mist descending 'and if it needs scratching I'll do it my sodding self.' I pushed him away as far as I could. He stumbled but kept his footing.

He sneered at me, his piggy, bloodshot eyes squinting. 'Come on love, otherwise it's goodbye van, goodbye job.'

'Well, it's goodbye job then you shitty, wretched, little man.'

Rushing towards me at incredible speed on such stunted legs, within a second he was too close to hit. As he groped me, his hot onion breath blanketed my face. Furious now, I freaked. Unclenching my fist I pushed the palm of my hand flat into his face with all my strength and body weight. His head snapped upwards from the force of the impact, my fingertips thrusting and gouging into his moist eyes.

With a shout of pain and alarm he lurched backwards across the room, clutching his head in his hands. 'Bitch!' he yelled at me. 'You fucking ungrateful bitch.'

'Maybe I am,' I spat at him, 'but I've not gone through all that crap these last few months just to be groped and threatened by some over-weight pygmy.' I paused at the door. 'Oh, and if you want the van back, you'll need these.' I jiggled keys invitingly in front of him 'so you'd better go and get them.' The bunch and fob sailed majestically out through the open window he'd been using as an ashtray, and into the prickly vegetation below. Perfect aim. A lucky throw!

Turning my back on his tirade of abuse, I raised a middle finger in a farewell salute and marched from the room slamming the door behind me.

A short lived triumph. I had a long walk home.

Penniless, jobless and van less, with a scary mortgage and barely any furniture, I threw myself on the mercy of the state, and signed on. After hours of waiting and pleading I was grudgingly handed a twenty pound crisis loan to tide me over until my first week's benefit arrived. I found a milkman who I could pay at the end of the month, so at least the baby would eat, even if I couldn't.

Happily, I also discovered that despite having an empty bank account my debit card would still work at Sainsbury's, but why, and for how much longer I had no idea.

I needed help, I needed some good luck, and I needed a friend.

Pete was one of the sales reps from the window company, a nice bloke with a good heart. Visiting for a coffee and a chat, he told me the hilarious stories of my abrupt departure that were circulating the offices. We laughed about it, but he became very concerned when he realised that I was barely managing to feed Abi. He lent me fifty quid and told me a confusing story about a lady he knew who used stolen credit cards to make money.

'She might be willing to help you,' he said. 'She got my mum a lovely joint of beef last week.'

Pete carefully explained that to get cash back from supermarket tills with a stolen card these people needed to buy baskets of food to look like genuine shoppers, moving on to the next supermarket and repeating the process, often visiting up to twenty stores a day. There wasn't enough room in the get away vehicle for dozens of bags of groceries, so they binned it as they went. It seemed to him like a lot of much needed sustenance was being wasted.

'If I tell Sue how skint and desperate you are, I'm sure she'll fill your fridge...'

'That would be amazing Pete, if I had one.'

He looked shocked. 'No fridge? How can anyone not have a fridge?'

I shrugged at him.

'Ok well your cupboard then. It's gotta be better than just dumping the food in the street when you and Abi are going hungry.'

I was still totally confused, and didn't really understand what he was telling me. To my poverty stricken mind it seemed extraordinary that anyone would be throwing their shopping away.

'Come on,' he said 'what have you gotta lose?'

He had a point. It probably was worth a try. So off he went to talk to Sue.

Looking back I don't really know if I was naive or desperate or simply didn't care. It didn't feel like I was skirting on the edge of criminality. I'm not sure I considered anything beyond the means of getting my daughter something to eat for her dinner.

Sue turned up the next day with carrier bags full of the best quality Waitrose goodies. A veritable feast. She wasn't shifty or shady or any of the clichés that seemed to suggest a hardened criminal. She was a few years older than me, slightly plump, well dressed and, declining my offer of some coffee she'd just brought me, got straight down to business.

'This is how it works,' she said. 'Ever had your purse or handbag nicked?'

I nodded. I had, a few years back in London. It had been a right pain, but aside from the inconvenience I hadn't suffered any hardship from it.

'We buy bank cards from kids who've nicked handbags. We change the signatures and then use the cards to buy bulk cigarettes which we then sell on at half the price. We get cash back from the supermarkets, and buy electrical items with the cards to order like stereos and videos - that sort of thing.'

She grinned. 'We offer a service, a bit like a catalogue. Show us what you want and we'll get it for you. Cheap.'

I must admit I liked the sound of it. 'Like a fridge?'

'Sure. Easy enough to get you one. You just have to choose the right stores. All shops are different, they have different security measures and some are easier than others.'

Sue went on to explain that Sainsbury's tills were not linked to the bank at all, which explained why my card still worked even though I was penniless. Basically they just printed a receipt. If only I'd known. I could have gone into Sainsbury's and with the switch card from my utterly empty bank account, bought the makings of a smashing Sunday lunch, got some cash back to put towards my mortgage arrears and stopped struggling to survive.

I was utterly astounded. I hadn't eaten properly for days, and this just sounded so easy. Surely too easy.

'It's safe? I mean nobody gets caught?'

Sue looked confident and sure of herself. 'As long as you do as you're told and don't get too cocky. Avoid Tesco's, they have bang up to date tills. I've heard that the big entrance doors can be locked from the checkouts. Then you've had it. Trapped inside with security until the police arrive.'

I was listening carefully. It seemed I could go out and raise some cash on my own card. It would give me food and solve my immediate problem. But with my own card and my own signature on it, clearly at some point I would have to repay the debt to the bank. Not a big fan of banks, I didn't like the sound of that bit.

Sue was watching me closely as if trying to read my mind. 'I'll teach you how to use the stolen cards if you like.'

At that moment I knew I was in. I needed food, I needed a fridge and I had a mortgage to pay. Any qualms I had quickly disappeared as she explained that you had three days to use a card after it had been reported stolen before it registered on the system. After that you had to chop it up and throw it away, normally down a drain in the road. Removing the signature from a card and a driving licence, Sue assured me that as long as it was obvious to the banks that fraud had been committed, then the card holder would be reimbursed for all their losses.

I could live with that. Whilst I didn't want another family to go short because of me, I was always happy to stick my fingers up at the banks.

So the deal was done. Sue left and I knew I was ready to dip my toe into the world of credit card crime.

The big DIY shops were the perfect fraud training grounds, and used by most new recruits for their MasterCard maiden voyage. A mixture of poor cameras, lax security and dozy teenage cashiers, greatly improved the odds for the criminal. Trouble was, I was now a pedestrian, so I talked Pete into being my getaway driver for my trial run.

'Are you sure you want to do this?' he said, clearly worried as we drove into the car park.

'Pull over by the exit,' I replied, focusing on the job. I had enough second, third and even fourth thoughts of my own. I couldn't be dealing with his as well.

'I could try to lend you some money until you can get another job,' he added. 'Honestly Becky, I just thought that Sue could get you some shopping, not that you'd want to get involved.'

'There,' I said, ignoring his concerns and pointing to a perfect place to pull over.

'If you get caught it'll all be my fault and I'll never forgive myself.' Worry was written all over his face.

I took a deep breath and glanced back at the entrance.

Pete was gripping the steering wheel like he was about to bugger off without me any second. I knew if I didn't calm him down I would be making my escape on foot.

'Pete, please don't feel bad. The way I see it is... it's just the banks that are getting ripped off. With the people's signatures wiped off and the cards reported stolen, the banks can't make these people pay for what gets bought by me.'

Poor chap, he really did look miserable.

I smiled at him. 'Truth is I'm happy to steal from the banks. They sent my dad outa business when I was a kid, took our house and broke my mum's heart. They're bastards. They deserve everything they get as far as I'm concerned, I'm just kinda... redressing the balance as it were.'

To my young eyes all those years ago in Wales, it seemed that the bank manager who'd had us kicked out onto the street must be the devil himself. They had such power and caused so much pain. I had no qualms about taking a bit back. Sod them.

'I see it as my public duty to piss the bastards off as much as I can. Besides I'm sick of going hungry, and having other people controlling my life and affecting Abi.'

I looked at him and made myself smile in what I hoped was a reassuring manner. 'If I get caught then it's my fault not yours. I want to do this.'

He nodded, he looked a little happier, although he was still clenching the wheel and his teeth, face and knuckles were as white as if he'd just hit black ice.

'Just stop here and I'll be as quick as I can. Ok?'

I opened the door, his hand shot out to grab my arm.

'Becky, be careful.'

I had every intention of being very careful. I climbed out of the car and hurried into the store.

Standing in the DIY warehouse with the stolen credit card burning a hole in my bag, I felt like everyone was staring at me. The original signature had been melted off in a bath of anti-freeze and acid, and after several hundred practice scribbles, I'd re-signed it with my fraudulent version of the name on the front.

I stood in the shop, and had no idea what to buy. It needed to be smallish and easy to carry just in case I needed to do a runner. I gave myself a hard mental slap. I was being stupid. What was I thinking? If it 'came on top' (the official term for getting rumbled apparently) I needed to leave my purchase and run for my life - not try and take it with me. No point in going to jail for five litres of magnolia paint and some quality sand paper.

Ok, here we go.

I repeated the name on the card over and over in my head. So I didn't forget who I was meant to be. I wandered guiltily around, convinced that THIEF was tattooed on my forehead for everyone to see. My mind was so occupied with remembering how to do the signature properly in the right name, I couldn't focus on choosing an item, and my feckless loitering was beginning to look suspicious. I considered a beautiful pot of newly flowering violets. But I was afraid if I had to run for it I'd drop the pot and damage the flowers, and I couldn't let that happen. Eventually I just picked up a large, long tube of ultra strong contact adhesive. If the worst came to the worst, I could always use it as weapon - sort of a DIY light sabre. Hoping that The Force would be strong with me, I crossed over to the dark side, and headed for the nearest check out to commit my first fraud.

It was busy. Two people were ahead of me in the queue. As nervous as a long-tailed dog in a room of rocking chairs, I held the card in my hand. My eyes flicked compulsively from the signature, to the exit, then to the security man who was now chatting to a lady handing out leaflets at the conservatory display.

I chanted my new name over and over in my head - Don't forget, don't forget. Would I be able to do it right? Would it look the same as the one I'd scribbled on the back of the card?

Now was the time I'd find out. I moved forward to the cashier, one eye scanning the car park looking for Pete and his car, hoping he'd be up to the job, and hadn't got out to buy six mini ring doughnuts for a pound, or worse still hadn't bottled it and buggered off.

The boy at the till smiled at me. He rang in the price.

'Five ninety nine please.'

I handed the card over, my hand was trembling. He nonchalantly swiped it through the terminal in front of him, and laid the printout before me to sign. He handed me a pen.

Shitting hell, I'd forgotten. My stupid mind was blank. Nothing. I had no idea who I was meant to be. I looked at the white square of paper, back to the cashier, back to the paper. It felt as if hours were passing... as if I'd stood there for half a day!

He smiled at me. 'It's five ninety nine,' he said again. 'Is something wrong?'

I panicked. I picked up the pen and in a mad rush of confusion, I just scribbled my own name across the receipt.

'Thanks,' he chirped, and without even comparing my scrawl with the card slid the docket into the till.

With arms numb from adrenaline, I snatched up my no nails light sabre, and my mouth too dry to bid him good day, I scuttled away towards the exit.

'Miss.'

Oh no! That's it. Busted. He was calling me back. I froze. Should I turn? Should I run?

'Miss?' he called again. 'Excuse me! Lady with the glue!'

Almost paralysed with terror, I turned slowly.

'You might need this,' he said with a grin, waving the stolen plastic at me.

I took the card robotically and managed a sharp nod in thanks. He returned to his till and I made another attempt for the exit.

'Hi Becky!'

Jesus Christ! What now? Who was that?

The lady handing out the double glazing propaganda of my former employers stopped talking to the security guard and waved her pamphlets at me. I'd not recognised her until then.

'I heard what happened to you!' she chirped excitedly, drawing attention to us both. I reluctantly acknowledged her. 'Good on you girl, he had a right pair of shiners,' she enthused. 'Wish I'd seen you thump him. Slimy sleaze ball. Don't reckon you'll be wanting one of these leaflets then?' she laughed.

'No thanks,' I heard myself reply as if in a dream, pointing my glue at her. 'I'm just gonna hold the old windows together with this stuff.'

The doors to freedom slid open. I resisted the almost overwhelming urge to sprint headlong to safety. Ignoring the palpitations, I faked a casual saunter to Pete's car and threw myself breathlessly into the seat as a wave of euphoric joy and relief washed over me.

'How'd it go?' he said as he pulled away.

'I forgot my name,' I laughed. 'But it was amazing! Wow what a buzz.'

My excitement must have been contagious, Pete started laughing. 'You're crazy Becky. Completely frigging crazy!'

'I thought I was fucked. That sodding Liz woman was working on the window stand just by the door, chatting up security, and she recognised me. I thought I was toast.' I poked him in the arm with the nozzle of my illegally obtained fictional glue weapon. 'My work here is done Obi Wan'. He looked at me quizzically. 'Come on, put ya foot down and take me shopping. Let's get this show on the road, I've got a new Visa card, and I'm bloody starving.'

Laughing at my audacity, I headed off happily into my new world of organised crime.

CHAPTER SIX

In my mid-twenties I had been single for quite a while, and having wonderful fun.

I'd found Abi a lovely childminder, and at the weekends she was spending time with her dad Gary the hoodlum and his new wife. Gary and I were getting on great since we'd split up, and I was happily feeding his new family with my excess groceries from my Delta card trolley dashes.

I earned thousands a week from the cash back, reselling fags and buying TV's to order. We travelled across the country, hundreds of miles a day - a supermarket circuit. It was hard dreary work and put me off shopping for life.

My expensive elocution lessons came in handy at last. If you spoke like the queen and knew a poem about cormorants in Latin, shop assistants would happily accept unauthorised cheques for large amounts of money. Five hundred pounds worth of overpriced shoes and handbags were often purchased in one transaction, and then sold cheap to my friends. Just goes to prove that a quality education is never wasted.

Never that motivated by money, it wasn't long before I bought only what I needed to fulfil orders then left the cards unused. Off I'd go to the gym to do my deep knee bends and star jumps, preferring to tone up my long legs and chat up boys rather than traipse around the shops stealing more and more money. I was berated by my team for wasting the optimum three days I had to use a card before it registered as stolen on the system. Working nicked Visas all day everyday just because you had them in your handbag eventually just felt like having a job, and got very repetitive and dull. I had a fridge and furniture now and didn't see the point in endlessly stuffing my pockets with tenners.

I had a nose job paid for with 'cash back', to correct the bump that young Matthew, my brother, had given me with that kick in the face in my teens. I was slim, trim and as frisky as a ferret. I thought I was totally indestructible and irresistible and I was having the time of my life.

Then Cupid fired an arrow out of the blue, and I fell head over heels in love with Dan, a cute boy I'd spotted on the treadmill. He was stunning, and he blew my socks off. With his pale skin, jet black hair and blue eyes, he looked like Disney's version of Snow White crossed with Arnold Schwarzenegger - huge buffalo shoulders and a waist like a teenage girl. My lust made him appear strong and silent, but my friends saw that he was in fact vacuous and slightly dim, and they teased him and me mercilessly. I defended his honour and fell out with a few of the nay-sayers, including Pete, who drifted away from me as I slid deeper into my life of crime.

How I adored Dan. Friends called him my puppet and laughed at the way I controlled him and bossed him around. He lived in the normal world, worked with his mum, and paid his direct debits. He even had a car that he'd bought with real money earned from gainful employment, rather than the dodgy stolen cars we all drove and filled with nicked petrol. It was never wise to break the law in a vehicle that could be traced back to you in any way, so swapping number plates was part of my morning routine, after making tea and poking some lettuce into the rabbit. Dan's clean living was a bit of a novelty.

Polar opposites, I wonder if part of my initial attraction to Danny boy was his normality - a strong family unit and the loving, supportive relationship he had with his mother. Something I'd never had and it fascinated me.

Eventually, I persuaded him that there was no need for him to waste his life working, and spending so much time with his mum. Giving in to me, he handed in his notice and became a reluctant accomplice. A bit like a sulky magician's assistant, only with us after we'd made things disappear, the members of the public and the banks never got them back again.

Being arrested was an occupational hazard and I took it all in good stead. A game - us versus the Old Bill, but it frightened Dan enormously. I understood that I would go to prison eventually, and I accepted this as an irritating but unavoidable consequence of being a public inconvenience. But the love of my life was having second thoughts. We kept getting nicked, but nothing much happened to us apart from suspended sentences and the odd probation worker wagging a finger. But no matter how much we pushed our luck, the police just asked us loads of questions which we refused to answer, fed us strong tea and chips then let us go.

'You're very calm about this Becky,' the arresting officer from the fraud squad said as he led me from my house and folded me into the back of an unmarked car.

'Well,' I smiled. 'We live in the UK. What are you lot going to do? There's very little you can do. When they bring back hanging, then I'll worry.'

He looked shocked.

'Seriously, what can you do to me?' I continued. 'You'll lock me up for a few days. I'll do a thousand sit ups, read the Bible, catch up on some sleep and then come home. No problem really. Same as always.' And that's how it was. It's not right but that's the British judicial system for you.

The only time we were foolish enough to use Dan's beloved car was returning from a hearing at Windsor Magistrate's Court. We stopped for a bite to eat, paid with pilfered plastic, and were captured immediately. This resulted in his parents' house, at which the vehicle in question was registered, being over-run with coppers in the early hours of the morning. It was ransacked by a full uniformed team, in view of his mum's friends and neighbours as they headed off to school or work. Embarrassed and distraught, with no understanding of what was happening to them, his parents were taken to the police station and questioned endlessly throughout the day. I seemed to be the only one who saw the funny side.

Dan's family accused me of bewitching him and ruining all their lives. They'd stopped speaking to me, although I'm sure they were talking about me. Now I had him all to myself and could manipulate him at my leisure.

Looking back, I think I was oblivious to my disgraceful behaviour. I was out of control and running wild. I'd had no contact with my mum and very little with my brother for years. There was no one to question me, ask me what I thought I was doing. Everyone I mixed with was as bad if not worse than I was. I was enjoying myself.

The end of the credit card road came in the shape of a petrol station. My mentor and original partner in crime, Sue, had a hearing at Aylesbury Crown Court. She went to appeal for the return of her seized cash back and forty thousand fags the police had selfishly confiscated during a raid on her house.

Unwilling to spend real money on petrol for the drive to court, she asked me to fill her car up with the American Express I was using that week. This sadly was all caught on camera, and it wasn't long before there was a knock at the door and I was carted off to the cells. Unluckily for me the handbag contents that I had been merrily wafting around a garage forecourt had belonged, in its previous life, to a local magistrate who didn't see the comedy in the situation, and wanted me beheaded.

With a huge turd now in the swimming pool of my life I was on bail for over eighteen months and back to being poor. I needed a plan.

I knew I was looking at a prison sentence, so I needed to create an image of hard work and good deeds to present before the disgruntled judges to mitigate my circumstances. I needed to be able to say I'd learnt my lesson; that I employed people who'd lose their jobs if I lost my freedom. I had to appear repentant and humble, to throw myself at their feet and plead for my liberty.

A wiser person might have opened a school for autistic badgers, become a nurse or organised a charity cycle ride to Peru dressed in tweed, winning the public vote. Sadly, under pressure, my anti-establishment chromosome which seems hard wired into my DNA came surging to the surface. In a moment of self-obsessed contemptuous stupidity, I took off my clothes, covered myself in bubbles, and opened 'Scrubbers' - a saucy, topless car washing business, causing the most controversy and public outcry seen in Milton Keynes since the battle over the placement of the concrete cows. By the time of my court hearing I was public enemy number one and vilified throughout the Shires as a disrespectful, non-conformist hussy.

My nearly nude car washing crew were featured nightly on the BBC and regional news; the powers that be were demanding my public flogging. In the words of a parish councillor - 'These women are standing almost naked, dampening down see-through singlets so their attributes became more apparent and causing a hazard to passing motorists. Something needs to be done about it, and quickly, before someone is seriously injured.'

Appearing semi-naked in the tabloids, I drove happily around Milton Keynes in a huge van with 'The best Hand Job in Town' painted down the sides in day glow pink. I really couldn't see what all the fuss was about.

My first ever Scrubbers customer was a self-made marketing guru of about my age. Mr Pip, as I'd decided to call him, had chosen to travel on the opposite life path to me, and had focused all his abundant skills on becoming successful rather than just being pointlessly annoying. His interest in Scrubbers was more the branding and business concept than the topless ladies, and he became one of my best ever friends. He's a 'love him or hate him' kind of a guy, and almost as many people hated him as hated me, so we had that in common. Rude, arrogant and accepting of nothing but genius from his staff, he was a hard task master and has played devil's advocate throughout my colourful career. He saw the potential in franchising Scrubbers, and tried to help me overcome my self-destructive tendencies. Sadly, my will was stronger. He was always there in the background doing his best to save me from myself, but failing miserably.

My boyfriend, Desperate Dan, had convinced his parents to lend me a few thousand pounds to set up Scrubbers, then they lent me more money to re-furnish the house in the hope I would stay on the slightly more straight and narrow. This money quickly ran out as the five other Scrubbers and I spent most of their investment going out to lunch and eating cake. The poor boy then sold his much loved car and donated that money as well to my hopeless cause, so determined was he that I stayed away from crime.

After spending his every penny I chucked him. He was devastated; I thought I'd been really wonderfully clever. I'd not signed anything, so I wouldn't be paying the money back, and I'd kept the furniture. Dan was lodging with his friend Pissy Jason, jumping through hoops to get me back.

I tortured him emotionally for another month or so. I'd promise to have him back if he bought me things, then I'd slam the door in his face when he came to deliver them. Literally sometimes. But then life slowly started unravelling.

I had a pre-sentencing court appearance, and usually full of it, this time for some reason I was losing my nerve.

'Jesus Becky, it's 6.30 in the morning, what's up?' Mr Pip wasn't impressed by being woken up by a ringing phone.

'I'm in court at 9.00. Will you come with me? My brief says I need a character witness.'

'Why me?'

'You're the only proper person I know who's still speaking to me. All the rest of my friends spend more time in court than the magistrates.'

'You ok Becky? You sound worried. Not like you to give a damn about being in the dock.'

He was right, or at least until that moment he had been. But something had changed, something deep inside of me and I was afraid.

'I've just been in and watched Abi sleeping. I've just realised what it'll be like for her if I get sent down,' I sighed. 'I'm such a crap mother. I wanted to be different than my mum, but I'm worse. At least she always provided security and stability. I just spend my whole life selfishly fucking about.'

'Blimey!' I could hear him sitting up in bed. 'That's a turnaround from the girl who's papered her loo with arrest warrants and summons, and told me she's looking forward to checking out the gym in Holloway. You told me that all the exercise and solitude in prison will be like going to a down market spa for a long break.'

Did I really say that? Fear and the reality of the situation myself and my child were in had replaced my destructive arrogance with lightning speed. I was beginning to see what an arse I'd been.

'Well, like you keep telling me, I can't be a wanker all my life. I've woken up fretting. I've got a bad feeling about this. Will you come?' I must have sounded desperate.

'Of course I will. The way I see it, organised crime is almost the same as being an entrepreneur. If you used as much skill and effort in a proper business as you do nicking cards and avoiding the filth, you'd make a fortune. A legal fortune that they'd let you keep and spend.'

'Thanks Mr Pip, but then I'd have to pay tax. I wouldn't like that much.'

He groaned at my dedication to feckless bad behaviour. I was just relieved that he was coming. 'I'll see you in court,' he said and ended the call.

Obviously I was found guilty, despite Mr Pip doing his best as a character witness. My sentencing date was set and my solicitor told me to be prepared to be sent to jail for three or four years. My lack of regular money meant my house was about to be repossessed. One of my good friends died from cancer and I needed a hug from someone who really loved me.

Nothing seemed quite so funny anymore.

'I'm so worried about Abi,' I confided tearfully in Mr Pip. 'She can't really go to her dad's if I get locked up; they're overcrowded in his flat anyway now they've had the new baby.'

'What about your mum?'

I looked at him shocked. We'd parted on very bad terms the last time I'd seen her.

'She wouldn't help me. She hates me.'

'I doubt she hates you,' he said. 'She's just like us normal people; she's sick of you being a dick.' He looked at me with a stern glare. 'You're very difficult to like much Becky, but I'm sure she still loves you. I know she loves Abi.'

Was he right? I didn't want to ring my mum and I certainly didn't want to ask for help. But what choice did I have? I looked at Mr Pip. 'OK,' I said.

'You'll call her?'

'Yes,' I said, knowing I had to change. 'I'll admit I need her help. For Abi's sake. I'm so sick of being a dick too. Look where it's got me.'

My mum, who had barely spoken to me over the past few years, arrived from Wales where she'd recently moved to help pack up my house and take three year old Abi, and her rabbit, home to the land of my grandfathers. She saved my little one being taken into care, and Flopsy being made hutch-less. Luckily for him, Samson the Wonder Dog had shuffled off his mortal coil a while ago, so at least he didn't have to relocate to the valleys.

At home alone and miserable I really, really needed some loving support and someone to take it all out on. So I summoned Dan, and around he came, like I knew he would. I was genuinely pleased to see him. I smiled and went to hug him and be comforted, but he turned from me and went upstairs.

'Ah, missed me too have you?' Clearly I was about to get a really good horizontal hugging. Always easily distracted from a crisis by a decent shag, I loosened my buttons and followed him up to my bedroom. But when I got there he was packing the last of his belongings into a sports bag.

'Dan?'

'I'm outta here,' he said.

He was leaving me?

As he hauled his bag off the bed I saw a large love bite on his neck. I laughed at him spitefully. 'Mmm, classy. Run into a rope did you? Piss off back to whoever it is then,' I shouted as I shoved him down the stairs.

At the door he paused and looked back at me with hate in his eyes.

The love had gone, I'd killed it.

But even then I couldn't halt my destructive downward freefall. I was missing Abi; I was angry with myself; I was still fighting the world. I'd been doing it for so long, and I just couldn't see how to stop.

I had the locks changed and headed out to tell all my friends what a wanker Dan was. Arriving home later that day, I discovered that undeterred by the new locks, my now ex- boyfriend had taken out my entire front window, and removed all our new furniture through the opening. A note lay in the middle of the carpet that read simply – 'I've had enough of your shit…'

I tracked him down to his friend, Pissy Jason's house. I sat outside in the freezing dark night, warmed by my hatred and fury. When Dan was still out at 5.00am, presumably with the lady of the love bite, I kicked my way into Jason's house and stomped up to the bedroom he rented. With a knife, scissors and my teeth, I sliced, cut and chewed my way through every item of clothing I'd ever bought for him with other people's money - every shoe, shirt and cashmere jumper. The room looked like a giant hamster nest when I left just before dawn.

I went home and collapsed.

I was literally physically and emotionally finished. That was the grand opening night of a breakdown that would successfully run for two years with an all singing all dancing suicide attempt during the interval.

Lying on the floor in my empty sitting room I sobbed, snotted and gagged through most of the next day.

Mr Pip told me off for being a prat as usual, and somehow got me cleaned up and into bed. I stayed there until my final court date several weeks later. Never a drinker, I downed a bottle of Jack Daniels and several packets of painkillers, genuinely wishing to die. Instead, I awoke refreshed from the best night's sleep I'd had for weeks and into the hell of another day.

I cried constantly. I put myself into counselling, but they couldn't do anything with me, and suggested I tried getting angry. That was hopeless as I was so full of guilt and remorse about the way I'd treated everyone. I had no idea why I'd behaved like I had, and I was so very sorry. I tried to pay Dan's family back, but they wouldn't speak to me. I discovered he was seeing someone else; she was sweet and good to him and they were in love. I was heartbroken, but glad for them both.

I'd lost him because I was so vile, and it served me right.

It was a lesson learned. A lesson I've always remembered. No matter how much someone loves you, if you piss them off enough, they'll eventually leave you, and be glad that they did.

I truly believe in the laws of karma. If you take something that is not rightfully yours, you'll lose that which you hold most dear.

I spent years taking from others, being a total arse, and laying down some serious karmic rakes, which I had now stood on - every one of them hitting me full in the face.

I lost everything, even things I didn't think I cared about. I lost my daughter, my home, my relationship, my business and my marbles. There was nothing left for me to do but face myself honestly, and deal with my bizarre personality traits.

I started to study astrology, in a bid to understand my selfish motivation. I did regression therapy. I lay down in a field surrounded by crystals, white feathers and tufts of herbs, chanting at the sun. I had needles stuck in my elbows and gazed at tea leaves. I went to church and clapped and sang to Jesus. I asked him to help me and make me a sunbeam. I walked for miles on my own and in silence, watching as nature continued through its cycles, and tried to have faith that this pain in time, would also change.

I knew the arrogant, defensive and destructive person I had been hadn't kept me safe. Hurtful, selfish behaviour and thoughtlessness is not the way to happiness.

My ego had been burst in that night of the long knives and shredded shirts, like a balloon popped with a sharp pin, and I had nothing to replace it with. I volunteered with the Samaritans, and worked on their telephones. I knew I would have died if Mr Pip hadn't been there for me, and I knew not everyone was lucky enough to have someone to turn to. My spiritual journey and personal development started then, and it has been a big part of my life ever since.

Scrubbers, the topless carwash, collapsed under the weight of tear-filled hankies, and an English winter, just as a franchise agent was about to give me huge amounts of money to buy the rights from me. I let it all go to concentrate wholeheartedly on my woe and my misery.

Eventually I was sentenced to several maximum terms of community service for my sins, two years in total. Not much really when you think of the mischief I'd been getting into. I found great healing and wisdom in the elderly people I was assigned to work for as penance. I helped them dig their gardens, plant their marigolds, and carry their grow-bags. In the winter, in a weird twist of fate, coming full circle back to my roots, I was sent to the Salvation Army charity shop to help sort clothes and serve customers.

They were wonderful people. I would stand behind the counter, wearing the best bits of my morning's rummaging all at once, making them laugh; mixing multi-coloured layers of knitted jerkins with hats and aprons, and, if I was lucky, some horn-rimmed specs, a fur muff and a nice pair of gentlemen's brogues. I chatted to the old ladies about their families and small dogs, and thought myself the luckiest person in the world.

Abi was back with me having spent a while with my mum in Wales, and had started at a nursery to allow me time to serve my penance. I was desperate to be a better mother; it was so nice to have Abi back at home and I was determined to make her feel safe and loved. I'd made friends with a really nice lady, Debs, one of the chatty, friendly mums I saw every day in the playground. She had a good solid marriage and had dedicated her life to her children's stability. Over coffee one day I told her my story. She didn't really understand why I'd done what I'd done, but was non-judgemental and worried about Abi being so small and having to cope with so many disturbances in her young life. I was still a random weeper, bursting into tears for no reason, but I was on the mend.

I had been to the gates of Hell, and peered in. I had been forced to look at myself in the mirror and see the truth. I hated who I was. But I was lucky. I had a second chance, and I was determined to take it. I knew I could and would be a better person.

Not a saint, maybe not even a sunbeam, I was still me. But I wanted to be a 'me' that I could like.

The new Becky was done with taking. I wanted to give back, to help others and re- balance my karma. If you believe in re-incarnation, it makes sense to learn your lessons quickly, or you'll just have to do it all again next time. One lifetime like that was enough for me, thank you very much. I was the only person who could change it - if not for myself, then for Abi.

CHAPTER SEVEN

They say time mends all wounds, but when you've lived with pain and desperation for so long, even if it's self-inflicted, you don't notice the healing process gradually mending your broken heart. It creeps up on you slowly whilst you're busy believing all is lost and that you will never be happy again.

I would measure the passing of each miserable month by menstrual cycles, and each time my lady problems arrived I thought, 'well, that's another four weeks without Dan.' Life dragged on and although optimistic by nature I wasn't expecting it to improve much. Mr Pip took me on a week's holiday to try to cheer me up.

'If you put as much effort into doing something properly as you put into being a pain in the arse...' Mr Pip would lecture me from under his signature patronising raised eyebrow as we sat in the Spanish sun, 'you could achieve anything you wanted.' I'd shrug him off, but I knew he was right. 'Why is it only me who sees how much potential you have?' he'd ask.

'You just can't be a wanker all your life Becky.' He had a point, and I was doing my best, but it was so hard and I was still so forlorn.

'I think it's because you think you can't achieve your goals in the real world, so you're afraid to try. You cover your fear with all this stupid crap you keep getting involved with. You won't let yourself be successful...'

I knew he meant well, but it was hard to hear, so I moved my sun-lounger and stopped listening. It's hard to be motivated when you're utterly miserable.

It was Debs, my new friend, the mum from Abi's school, who became an altogether less demanding and judgemental friend. Sensible, and in her early thirties, Debs could usually be found preparing meals in her kitchen with her leggy brunette side kick Tasha, an attractive lady a few years older than both of us. They were a happy, patient pair who'd spent long periods of time with me when I was heartbroken and dreary, just being there, getting me through each day, listening to the endlessly repeated stories and guilt-filled monologues about Dan, the one I'd loved and lost. They didn't tut at me, complain or roll their eyes. At least not to my face, I was pitifully hard work. They stoically sat there, mug of tea in hand, fag in the ashtray, and calmly allowed all my waves of unhappiness to wash over them day after day. It must have been woefully tedious for them but they stuck with it and eventually things started to look up.

Driving to Debs house for a cuppa and some company on a warm sunny afternoon, I was forced to slow down for road works. Whilst manoeuvring my way through the cones my attention was drawn to a well-muscled chest and fabulous pair of arms handling a jack hammer in a very manly way. Doing a double take, I nearly veered off the road. I laughed at myself, and made a mental note to drive home that way for a second sneaky look. I was surprised by the realisation that if I'd fancied random ground workers maybe I really was cheering up and moving on. It was time to start living again.

Feeling as if I'd turned an emotional corner, half full of the joys of spring, I dashed into Debs' house keen to describe the roadside biceps in all their rippling glory. Debs was perched on the edge of the sofa in floods of tears. Tasha, kneeling on the floor in front of her, holding her hands, looked up at me with a grimace. The sea of used pastel tissues that surrounded them indicated the situation had been going on for quite some time.

'Ian's left me,' was all she managed to say before renewed sobbing utterly overwhelmed her.

Happily married we all thought for sixteen years, with four delightful kids, her husband had just walked away. No real reason Debs could understand or Ian could explain. No evidence of anyone else, no big fight. Just all over in an instant.

'Why?'

'He said he needed space,' she sobbed. 'I don't understand what I've done.'

'What a wanker....' I squeezed in next to her on the sofa and pulled her into my arms.

'Ian said he needs to find himself,' Tasha sneered, making inverted commas in the air with her fingers as we boiled the kettle to make Debs a cup of tea. 'He'll find himself in a shallow grave if he doesn't give her any money for his kids,' she added.

It was heart rending to watch my friend so lost and in such a desperate state. I knew what she was going through, and my heart bled for her. I tried to comfort her and tell her that eventually it would all make sense but she was too hurt to listen. Truth was it didn't make sense, not to any of us.

The weeks dragged slowly by, the tears flowed, but the money never arrived. We both lent Debs what we could, but it was never enough. I hadn't been working due to being driven officially mental by unrequited love and Tasha only did a few part time hours to fit in around her two boys, so our funds were limited. Mr Pip took her shopping on a few occasions and dispensed advice whilst she wearily pushed her trolley and distractedly bagged up loose veg. Debs was grateful, but she needed a permanent solution and some financial peace of mind.

'He's not paid the catalogue,' Debs said furiously, holding out a letter, the payment demands written in blood red across the top. 'I really hoped he would. It was the only way I had left to buy new school shoes.' The tears of frustration and confusion started to flow again. 'Why is he doing this to us? How can he do this to his family?' she cried, despair and betrayal rising up like a tide, threatening to pull her under again.

We had no answers for her. All my months of meditation, contemplation and navel gazing didn't seem much use in this situation. I had no nuggets of wisdom to share. I'd lost my man because I was an arrogant, thoughtless egomaniac and I'd paid a high price. Debs was kind and sweet and had totally worshiped Ian, she didn't deserve this. There seemed to be no way to win with romance, it was a total mystery.

'I've just bought some tarot cards from the market,' Tasha stated, as if this was the obvious solution to the problem. 'Let's see what they say about it all. Here Debs, you sit your bum down. Becks, stick the kettle on. Let's see if there's anyone out there! Knock once for yes, twice for nooo!' and she rapped twice on the small round dining table, giggling as she pulled up a chair and got comfy.

'How does it work?' Debs asked, looking at the box of cards suspiciously.

'I'm not sure,' I said. 'I've been seeing some funny stuff in my head when I've been meditating, and some weird things have been happening, but I've never used the tarot.'

'Why did you start meditating?' she asked me as Tasha gnawed her way into the tight cellophane wrapping on the colourful cards with her teeth. Debs sighed sadly, talking to herself, not waiting for my answer. 'I wish I could meditate, my mind won't shut up. My thoughts just go round and round all night. I can't tell you when I last slept properly. I'm gonna die of exhaustion if we don't all starve to death first.'

The cards were spread on the table, looking bright and friendly - sweet-smelling like the shiny paper in expensive books. Debs touched them gently, picking them up one at a time and looking at the pictures.

'I bet I get the Death card,' she said morosely. 'Just my luck.'

'Death doesn't always mean you're going to snuff it, I know that much.' I tried to reassure her. 'It can be about starting again. Rebirth, that kind of thing. Meditating helps me understand why I do stupid stuff, so I can stop myself doing it.' I smiled at her. 'Hopefully.'

'Will my secrets come out?' she asked, tracing the bright intricate pattern of magic symbols with her finger.

'Secrets? What, like you're really a big black man with a three foot willy? We've known that for ages,' I quipped. 'Why do you think Tasha likes you so much?'

Laughing, Tasha took a swipe at me with the instruction book she'd been trying to understand. But Debs wasn't laughing.

'No, like I'm going to join an escort agency.'

'I'm the clinically loopy one,' I offered, not really taking her seriously. 'I'm the one who's secretly still in love with some bloke who hates me.'

'That isn't a secret Becks,' Tasha laughed and threw the balled up cellophane at me.

'Listen please,' Debs said very quietly, staring at a card she was holding, her eyes welling again with tears. 'I've already been to see someone, an agency, and they've taken me on.'

Slowly she raised her eyes and looked at us both. 'It's the only way I can feed the children and pay that bloody catalogue off.'

We both stared back at her in stunned silence.

'Escorting? What like going out to dinner and weddings with rich business men?' Tasha asked. 'You'll have to fill a doggy bag up for the kids. Hey, maybe you can take them with you.' She laughed at her own absurdity. 'That'd be a shock for him. Tell the client you will only go out to dinner if it's KFC or McDonalds and you need to be home by seven on a school night.'

I looked from Debs, who was now staring blindly at the table, to Tasha. 'I think we're talking more about staying in for the evening than going out Tash.'

'Eh?'

Debs remained quietly studying the cards as though they were the most absorbing things she'd ever set eyes on.

'Escorts don't escort men to weddings, more escort them to bed,' I added.

'Bed?'

'Come on Tash! Escorting is a fancy name for being on the game. It's not dinner and dance, it's bonking and blow jobs. It's murder and mutilation if you're not careful. Selling sex. Having sex for money with stinky old men and nutters.'

Debs burst into tears, jumped up from her chair and ran out of the kitchen.

'Well done Becky,' Tasha said acidly as she followed her out.

I just sat there in disbelief, shocked. Saddened I pushed the cards back into a pile. I tried to work out how to make it all better. I hated seeing my friend suffer. Life could be so shit, so unfair to the nicest people. Following them into the front room I balanced miserably on the padded arm of a chair. 'I'm sorry,' I said. 'I'm not judging you; I'm just scared for you. There must be another way.'

'What other way?' she asked through a renewed bout of crying. 'The rent's late. My bank won't give me a loan, I've asked. I've got nothing left on my credit cards.'

They both gave me a look at this point. 'And I'm not using any stolen ones. I wouldn't have the guts to do what you did,' she said referring to my flirtation with organised crime. 'And you can't keep asking Mr Pip to buy my food.'

I nodded. My venture into crime had taught me it wasn't a life I'd wish on anyone. Great short term gain but like everything, there was a price to pay. She blew her nose on a tatty, slightly used hanky I handed her from my pocket.

'Benefits will take weeks to sort out, and I need money fast. Proper money. I can't afford to go back to work. I've looked for jobs, but child care will cost more than I'll earn. My skills are outdated and I've no qualifications. What choice do I have Becky?'

I had to concede, she had a point. 'My brother's got a few friends who're escorts,' I said, thinking aloud. 'I'll ask him how it works.'

'Aren't they all gay?' Tasha asked.

'Yeah, gay or trans-sexuals, ' I said agreeing, 'but surely it must be the same principle?' Looking at my watch I said, 'It's almost 3.00pm Debs, Abi's at her little friend's today, do you want me to walk down and get your kids, I'm in no hurry? You can stay here and chill out a bit. Have a fag.'

She looked relieved. 'Thanks Becks.' But then the phone rang and a look of terror crossed her face as she stared at it.

'What?' I asked. 'You want me to get it? Tell them you're out?' I offered, thinking it must be a debt collector. I remembered avoiding the phone when my house was being repossessed, hiding in the kitchen holding my breath when the bailiffs were knocking at the door. Relentless bullies, no matter how many times you hung up on them or pleaded with them, they just kept hounding you.

Debs shook her head, sheer panic on her face. 'It may be the agency,' her voice barely a whisper. 'They said they might call. They've got a regular client who might want to see me.'

We all stared at it. The ringing continued. The pressure got to me and I grabbed the receiver. I looked at Debs who nodded, I silently handed her the phone. She listened mutely, and then rummaged for a piece of paper and with trembling fingers she wrote down a name and address before hanging up.

We stood dumbfounded for several seconds until Debs breathed out sharply, straightened her shoulders and announced, 'I'm going to do it, I've got to.'

She'd made the decision and we all knew there'd be no changing her mind.

'It's at a hotel,' she said, strangely calm. The tears and trepidation were gone. 'It's in Milton Keynes at 3.30 so hopefully I should be back by 4.45pm.'

'Yeah hopefully,' I said, unable to share her new found tranquillity, and feeling myself getting wound up.

'Are you still ok to get the kids from school Becky?'

Fighting the urge to scream, to grab her and refuse to let her go, I folded my arms around her slight frame. I was wrong, she wasn't as ok as I'd thought, she was trembling and terrified. 'Sure, of course I will. But you need to sort yourself out girlie, you've got eyes like piss holes in the snow. Arrive like that and he'll be demanding his money back.'

She checked herself out in the mirror above the mantel piece, then wiped her eyes, blew her nose and dashed upstairs.

I left her to it, whatever 'it' was, and headed off to round up her offspring. Worried sick, I prayed to every god I could think of that it wouldn't be the last time I saw her.

It occurred to me as I walked anxiously down to the school that no-one had copied the address of the hotel and I had no idea where she was going. Nor any idea what the agency was called.

Sitting in front of the telly contentedly munching through their after-school snacks, noses to the screen, Debs' kids were oblivious to my mounting terror. This was the early nineties and mobile phones were still in their infancy. As a stay-at-home mum, Debs definitely didn't have one any more than I did. I was furious with myself for not checking the details. What kind of friend was I? I'd let her disappear into such a potentially dangerous situation with no backup plan or protection.

I'd made myself a cup of tea, but it had gone cold and scummy as I leant on the worktop watching out of the window down the front path. I saw Tasha walking up with her two boys. They were nice, dark haired lads of twelve and thirteen. She let herself in and sent her sons to watch telly with the others.

We decided between us that if Debs wasn't back by 5.30pm we would call the police. We wouldn't be able to tell them where she'd gone or who she was working for but we knew it was a hotel in central Milton Keynes, and we felt better for having a plan. I was sure escorting was illegal and that she would get arrested if we involved the police, but I'd been arrested many times and it wasn't that bad; certainly better than being kidnapped or hacked to pieces I figured.

I checked my watch for the hundredth time. It was 4.15pm; this was the longest afternoon of my life. Tasha, desolate, sat at the kitchen table where this adventure had all started a few short hours ago, worriedly drawing glasses on Kylie Minogue as she pouted from the cover of the TV Times. We heard the front door bang open and a second later Debs, wearing a huge grin, came into the kitchen and flopped down noisily into a chair.

'How easy was that!' she said dramatically kissing a large pile of ten and twenty pound notes before slapping them onto the table.

'You ok Debs? What happened?'

She looked ok, in fact she looked better than ok. She was beaming.

'I sure am ok!'

'Debs, tell us what happened for God's sake,' I demanded, still needing reassuring.

'A hundred and seventy quid! And I was only there for half an hour,' she said laughing. 'And only, you know - 'at it'- for about three seconds. Two pumps and a squirt! He was really nice, bless him and young. Not at all smelly. He even gave me twenty quid tip as well. It was amazing. So easy.' She pushed three tenners to one side. 'I have to give the agency thirty, but that still leaves me one forty. I can't believe how easy it was. Seriously look,' she tapped her watch, 'I've hardly been gone an hour.'

She was babbling with excitement. Tasha and I just looked at each other. While we'd been through the seven levels of Hell and back, imagining all kinds of twisted perverted horror, it seemed she'd been having a high old time with some cute boy.

'And I didn't even shave my legs.' She jumped to her feet. 'Kids ok? I can go shopping now. Get some decent grub for dinner.' Animated and smiling she went to check on her family.

Tasha looked at me. 'Bloody hell,' was all she said.

'Mmmm, bloody hell indeed,' I agreed.

Debs didn't go shopping. She took us all out for a pub supper. I protested, but she told me not to worry, she'd just see another client tomorrow and go shopping with that money instead. She was happier than I'd seen her since her husband left.

'That'll serve that bastard right,' she announced with a big smile to a slightly confused waitress as she happily handed the client's money over to pay the bill for the meal. 'And that fella earlier was a better shag than my shit-bag husband. Ex-husband,' she quipped spitefully as the waitress walked away. 'All three seconds of it.'

We joined her in the sisterly mocking of Ian, but I was feeling really nervous about the whole thing. I took Abi home to get her ready for bed, but almost as soon as I got through the door my phone rang. It was Tasha. Her and her boys were back at Debs minding the kids. The agency had called with another booking, and Debs or 'Mandy' as she was now calling herself had driven off to see her second client of the day.

It looked like she would be going shopping tomorrow after all.

CHAPTER EIGHT

Over the next two weeks Debs was averaging three bookings a day. It was because she was new the agency told her. Clients get fed up seeing the same girls repeatedly, so new girls were always busy at first. I couldn't get used to thinking of her as Mandy, but she explained all escorts used a false name, and so did the punters. 'John' was the default name for most men who used working girls. Mandy was her sister's name, which meant it was easier to remember than something sexier picked at random.

Pocketing over a thousand pounds a week and an element of marital revenge had cheered Debs up enormously, so when at the end of her third week bonking customers her period arrived she was devastated.

'What do other girls do when they have their lady problems?' I asked.

She shrugged her shoulders. 'I've never met any other girls, I don't know. Stop for a week I suppose.'

'Can't you ask the agency?' Tasha questioned.

'No, I'll sound really stupid. Anyway, I don't like the bloke. He's seriously creepy. I try not to speak to him apart from getting booking details. I'm sure he'll ask me for a freebee soon.' She shuddered dramatically pulling a face. 'Whenever he comes round to pick up his fees I pretend I'm going out or that the kids are here so he can't come in. I don't think the clients like him much either as it goes. He's rude to them and they say he lies about the girls, what they look like, how old they are. Stuff like that. Apparently he sends out some real shockers. It pisses clients off big time.'

'You could probably do with a week off anyway,' I said, thinking that I could do with some time without the worry. 'You're looking knackered, literally shagged out, even with your new hairdo and tan.'

'I'll do it for you,' Tasha announced suddenly. 'I'll do your bookings.'

'Tasha!' I shrieked, genuinely shocked.

'You don't drive though, and you don't look like me,' Debs replied, not at all surprised that Tasha was casually volunteering to become a prostitute. Clearly they'd already discussed this possibility.

'I'll join the agency and I'll get a taxi.'

I shook my head. This was becoming surreal. So much for my week free from worry.

'Taxi drivers round here know everyone,' Debs pointed out. 'You'd be busted in no-time Tash. If that ex of yours ever found out he'd be worse than Ian I reckon. He'd try to take the boys off you, you know he would. It'd be the perfect excuse to fuck you over and fight for custody.'

'Doesn't the agency have someone who can take you?' I wondered. 'When I spoke to my brother about it, he said that the good set up's in London provide a driver for the girls or boys. It helps keep them safe, as someone always knows where they are, and the customer knows the driver's outside waiting.' I looked from one to the other. It made good sense to me.

'The girls pay the drivers about fifty quid from their money,' I explained. 'Although obviously they charge more per job in London.' I looked at Debs, 'That lot you're working for really don't give a shit. You're going to get chopped up and made into cheap sausages one day if you're not careful.'

Debs shrugged, but Tasha looked troubled.

'Seriously,' I added, 'it only takes one problem to mess up your life forever. You're not much use to your little ones dead are you?'

We all sat silently. Debs lit up a cigarette and inhaled deeply. Tasha sipped her tea. I was thinking hard. I didn't want them doing it, but it was pretty obvious that it would happen with or without my support or assistance.

'I'll do it! I'll drive you...' I blurted out suddenly in a eureka moment. 'You can give me a few quid for each job to cover the petrol.' I was making it up as I went along, but it seemed like a cunningly good plan. 'I'll sit outside and keep an eye on you. If I get a mobile phone you can call me when you get into the house and let me know you're ok. Any funny business we can have a code word or something and I can call the police and chuck bricks through the windows.

Or just kick the door in screaming and embarrass them into letting you go.' I grinned, 'you know me, always up for a scrap. I'd be more use doing that than sitting here babysitting.'

The kettle was flicked on again, and we sat around the table like the three witches from Macbeth hatching our plan. Tasha got the tarot cards out and I shuffled them and asked the ethers if they thought me becoming an escort deliver service was a good idea.

Tasha was studying the booklet and reading aloud. 'I think the spirits are in favour. But there are more changes to come.'

'Like what?' Debs asked.

'No idea,' Tasha replied.

'Well you're a useless soothsayer,' I said as I gently flicked a corner of biscuit at her. She made no move to avoid it and it stuck in her hair. 'You didn't even see that coming'.

We ate more custard creams dunked in tea and tried to come up with a stage name for Tasha and her prostitution debut.

The three of us had spent a comical afternoon trying to invent fabulous new names for her, most of which made her sound like a small pony or an exotic fruit. Delilah, Honey, Tallulah, Pammy... The harder we tried the more bizarre it became, and we laughed uncontrollably until we were in danger of wetting ourselves.

Tasha AKA Sadie was never really comfortable with escorting. Nervous and always on the verge of fleeing, she'd grill the agency receptionist endlessly about the clients they were sending her to. Were they a regular? How old were they? What were they like? Often the girl who'd taken the booking wouldn't know the answer; they were just voices at the end of the phone. They really weren't interested in Tasha's fears. If she saw clients Debs had seen previously she was more relaxed. But Tash wasn't a natural like our friend who'd taken to whoring like a rat at a pork chop, wanting to shag and make money day and night. Debs was gleefully hording her winnings in a shoe box under her bed and arranging to take the family on holiday to Spain at half-term.

'I think we've created a monster Dr Frankenstein,' I half joked to Tasha as we watched Debs happily trot down the path to her car to see her fifth gent on a particularly busy day.

'You're not bloody kidding,' said Tash. 'But she's done this herself remember, we did try to stop her. Best to just let her get on with it I reckon.'

I was much happier being the driver than I had been sat at home feeding various children cheese puffs while my imagination sent me insane with panic, so when a booking came in for Tasha/Sadie, on the far side of Northampton I was ready to go. It would be almost a four hour round trip, Tasha paid a babysitter and off we went.

He was a new client to us. It was a long, slow drive, and tricky to find, so Tasha was anxious as she got out of the car and tottered unsteadily down the street. She knew to phone me as soon as she was inside and the chap had paid her. Always money upfront. Those were the rules. I would give her five minutes to say hello and get organised before I expected the call to come through saying all was well. Hearing her heels clattering fast towards me not two minutes later, I was out of the car in a flash. She was shaking and had tears running down her face; she almost hurtled straight into me.

'He doesn't want me. He shouted at me, he's really angry. He wants stuff, but I don't understand what. Oh Becky take me home please. I can't do this. He wouldn't even let me into the house.'

How dare anyone treat my friend so badly?

'Get in the car,' I told her, 'and lock the door. I'm going to sort this out.'

'Leave it Becky....let's just go home.'

I could hear her shouting at me as I marched determinedly up the pavement to confront the man who'd frightened her. She might be ten years my senior but I always felt older if not wiser than her and Debs.

Banging hard on the door, the wood vibrated under my fist, I was seething. Who the hell did he think he was speaking to her like that, just because she did what she did to earn money? He was paying her after all, so how could he pass judgement on her. She was a kind, sweet girl. How could he make her cry like that? I was incensed, and I was planning to let him know exactly what I thought.

The door opened eventually and I was faced by an irate, but attractively shirtless man in his early thirties with a towel round his waist.

'We have a problem,' I said, fixing him with my sternest look. 'The girl you've just made cry is sitting in the car with my security man,' I bluffed, 'and you're bloody lucky it's not him standing here dealing with you.'

'Let me in please,' I demanded as I pushed past him into his front room. I was surprised to see a stunning, mixed-race girl with legs like Red Rum and a thick mane of dark cascading ringlets. She walked through the kitchen door, giving me an enquiring stare. She was dressed in stockings, a leather basque and had a dog's collar and leash fixed on her lovely neck. The two little black pointy ears attached to a velvet headband confused me further. She gave me quite a start I must say. I wasn't quite sure where to look.

'You lot can sod off,' the client said after overcoming his surprise at having a tall, stroppy, blonde girl arriving from nowhere and shouting at him. 'You're useless. Don't say I didn't warn you this would happen.'

'I'm not from the agency,' I said. 'I work with the girl's security. I have no idea what you're talking about. Sadie's safety is my only concern.'

He folded his arms across his chest in a defensive pose. 'So what's the problem then? I've not touched her, she's totally safe. I just told her to leave.'

'Why? What's wrong with her?'

'Nothing. Everything. You do it to me every time I call up to book a girl. You send me the wrong type of bird. I don't like English women, the agency knows that. Three times now I've paid the girl money for nothing. She's not brought the right equipment, and she looks all wrong. I'm not doing it again. You can tell that bloke in the office that he's lost my business.'

He really did seem genuinely upset. My own anger was beginning to dissipate. It didn't seem to be a personal attack on Tasha.

'Oriental girls are the only ones I want to see,' he added as if reading my mind. 'Thai, Chinese, Japanese, whatever, but not English. The booking is for me and my wife,' he gestured to the dog-lady…'and I'd pay the girl extra to use a strap-on with us both.'

I had no idea what a strap-on was, but I nodded my head.

'I'd rather go without, or have a wank and save myself a hundred and fifty quid. And you're late. I told them it had to be before 3.00 as we've got to go out and see my wife's mother.'

Let's hope she gets changed out of her Crufts outfit first I thought, looking quickly at the lady with the puppy ears and studded collar, unless her mother's Barbara Woodhouse. I felt like I'd skipped into another reality. I was totally baffled. I had no knowledge of what a strap-on was, where and how you strapped it, or what it did when it got there. I played along. I did understand that he obviously hadn't got what he'd wanted, and that the customer should always come first. This chap wasn't getting the chance to come at all, and that seemed like very poor customer servicing.

'Ok,' I said, 'fair point, but as I've explained, I'm not from the agency, and I'm not responsible for the office being useless, I work for the girls freelance.'

I was also shocked that any agency had girls who would have sex with other girls, and the idea of doing so with a husband watching seemed strangely wrong and very European.

'I'm really sorry; it's not acceptable that you're not ….erm….,' I blushed a little, 'satisfied. I'll explain to Sadie and tell her it wasn't personal. In her defence, the bloke in the office never stipulated a time, or your...' I struggled to find suitable words... 'your interesting preferences. It looks like they've wasted everyone's day. I really am sorry.'

'We've just moved from London,' Lassie explained, toying with the dog leash fixings at her throat. She had a lovely voice, soft and sultry, I'd half expected her to yap at me. 'We never had a problem filling our requirements there, and this is most unprofessional.'

Sighing, I said, 'we are a still a little backward out here in the countryside, we've only just mastered the art of shaving our armpits and navigating roundabouts.'

'You have plenty of those in Milton Keynes,' Lassie smiled.

'What's your name?' the husband asked, softened somewhat by my apologies.

I really did understand why he was annoyed, even if I didn't understand what he was asking for and how he planned to achieve it.

'Becky Adams and it seems to me that as an escort agency customer you should be treated the same as a customer in any other business.' I was thinking aloud really, the stirrings of an idea worming into my brain. 'Just because you're buying sex... of a sort. The customer is always right at the end of the day. You should expect to get what you ask for at the very least. No strap-on, I agree it's shocking. Most unsatisfactory.'

'Well, Miss Adams, if that's how you feel, then maybe you should find some girls, open an agency and do it properly.' He seemed quite cheered up, and sidled next to his wife and started caressing her waist.

'What's your name?' I asked.

'John,' he said unsurprisingly, with a small smile.

'Well, John from Northampton, maybe I will open an agency, and if I do, and I have any strap-on carrying Oriental ladies may I give you a ring?'

'Please do,' he said, opening the door to show me out. He picked up a pen from the hall table and scribbled a number onto a piece of paper. 'I'll look forward to it, Becky.'

I walked away, his number pushed into my pocket, a strange feeling of euphoria seeping through me. Was I really thinking what I thought I was thinking?

Happen I was, and it wasn't often I managed to shock myself.

'How difficult can it be to run an escort agency?' I wondered aloud as Tasha and I drove back to Milton Keynes. 'I would never do that to my clients.'

I slowed down behind a van and glanced at Tash. I was buzzing with the possibilities, but she didn't seem to share my enthusiasm.

'I think you should be honest with people,' I said, putting my foot down to overtake the van and a tractor that was causing the hold up. 'I think if you haven't got the type of girl they want, then you shouldn't lie. What's the point of sending them someone you know they won't fancy?'

'Oh yeah. Thanks for reminding me,' she snapped.

Surprised, I looked at her. I'd been so excited by my own thoughts it never occurred to me that she wouldn't share my excitement. I'd assumed she was upset because she hadn't been paid. But it seemed John from Northampton had ruffled her feathers and hurt her pride. I really should have been more sensitive.

'Hey,' I said taking my eyes from the road to smile at her. 'You're lovely Tash. It's just that he wanted some tiny Japanese girl that would sleep with his wife,' I grinned. 'You're almost six foot and as English as fish and chips. Besides...' I paused and winked at her, 'you have no idea what to do with someone else's fanny. Do you?'

'No way would I!' She screwed up her nose and shook her head violently. 'Was he gonna watch? That's gross.'

Was it? I really wasn't sure how I felt about it. I'd been surprised, maybe even a bit shocked when I first saw his wife and learned what they wanted. Not that I really understood what they'd wanted. But actually I was more interested in the business opportunity it offered. Were there lots of Johns out there? All disgruntled, frustrated and let down because the industry that was supposed to service their needs (however unusual) was too lazy, incompetent and uncaring to do the job properly.

'The agency should never have taken the booking,' I said. 'He reckons it happens all the time.' I prattled away, thinking aloud. 'He said if I opened an agency and had any Thai girls that I should call him.'

I glanced sideways. Tasha was listening to me now. 'What do you think we'd need to get us started?' I asked her.

'You can't be serious Becks?'

She appeared alarmed by my ramblings. In fact, she looked like she was about to resign before we'd even started.

'I'm sure if we all worked it out together, we could make it happen.' I stopped at traffic lights and glanced at her. 'You ok Tash?'

She shrugged. 'Do you think there are lots of men wanting weird stuff like him?'

I looked out of the window. We were at pedestrian lights in the middle of a small town on the edge of Milton Keynes. Shoppers were busily going about their business unaware of my scrutiny. I pointed to a middle-aged guy who had just come out of the bank. 'Him for sure,' I said. 'I bet he has all sorts of strange fetishes.'

Tasha giggled and craned her neck to watch him as he crossed the road behind us. 'Like a strap-on?'

The car behind me beeped impatiently. The lights were green. I pulled away and glanced back at the man in my mirror as he disappeared round the corner. 'Definitely a fan of the strap-on,' I said with confidence and authority.

'So what the hell is a strap-on?' she asked.

I smiled and shook my head. 'I haven't got a clue. It must be something you fix or stick onto somewhere using straps. I've never heard of one.'

'What.... like those luggage things you strap onto your car when you go camping?'

'I doubt it Tash, but I don't really know. Might be.'

We both laughed at the absurdity of it all. At least Tasha was in a better mood now. If I was serious about starting up my own agency, I would need her and Debs on side. The agency the girls were working for took a thirty pound fee from every job, which seemed like a rip off. They only answered the phones, and passed the girls a name and address. I was sure I could do it, and my brain started whirling with a plethora of sexy words and enticing company names for a new business. I'd made up my mind, I was opening an escort agency.

CHAPTER NINE

'*Treacle Tarts Upper Crust Delights*' was born. My first out-call escort agency. This later became abbreviated by all the randy residents of the Home Counties to just 'Treacle's'.

Mr Pip disapproved of my career choice, and didn't want to help with designing the logo for my harem, so the first step was to get the art department of the local rag to design me an ad.

A saucy postcard-type sketch of a buxom wench in a short pinny, coquettishly holding a fruity tart aloft, seemed to do the job and into the paper it went. Favourable tarot cards were turned. Mr Pip tutted. We were on our way.

The calls started immediately. I foolishly thought that the normal business procedure would be that the phone would ring, I would answer, and a man would request a lady. He'd make a booking. I would despatch the object of his desires and a good time would be had by all. A process hopefully repeated at least ten times daily, turning a nice profit. I had not been aware of the need to factor in the endless silent callers, heavy breathers, wankers, panters, grunters, time wasters and hoaxers that would block the lines and drive me to the very edge of reason. For the first two days, I gave each caller the benefit of the doubt. I went through my whole sales spiel. Prices, descriptions, company ethos, blah blah. But by day three I was recognising voices and scenarios. I was utterly amazed at why any person could be bothered to call a number up to twenty times a day and ask exactly the same questions. And why did the phantom thrusters call a company who sells sex and try to shock them by pretending to be having sex? It's like phoning a dog groomers and barking. No-one's impressed. By day four I was saying 'I think you may have phoned us before sir, I believe you have all our details. Good day.'

By day five I was telling them to fuck off, and by day six I was just sighing and hanging up within the first five seconds of their performance. Several of these very same gents made the very same calls daily for all of the next twenty years that I was running agencies, parlours and brothels in Milton Keynes. Very odd.

Alone in the office (my kitchen table) in the early 1990s whilst Abi was at nursery, I took a call from a softly spoken gentleman asking for a lady. He sounded about twelve, bless him, but I had no one available. Debs was giving one of her regulars some afternoon delight and Tasha was having her corns trimmed at the chiropodist. They were still my only girls, and the phones were getting busier every day, but not busy enough to turn away clients.

Promising I'd get a lady to call him immediately to arrange an appointment, I started panicking. There was no one to send. Not prepared to lose the money, I decided to go myself and alone, breaking all my own rules about security and safety. We only had one driver and he was delivering Debs, hot and fresh to Leighton Buzzard. But I was determined. If my friends could do it, then so could I.

I called the client back and pretended to be someone else, younger with more experience. The deal was done. I scribbled down the address, switched on the answer machine and headed off.

I kept telling myself it was business. He was a customer and I was offering a service. No big deal. It just happened to be a personal service.

The address I'd been given turned out to be a local Chinese takeaway and I was met at the door by a tiny pocket-sized Oriental man in his twenties. My first thought was *'I wonder if he knows any Thai girls for John in Northampton.'* But that question was soon replaced by confusion as he lead me through the kitchen and motioned for me to perch myself on a little shoe rack under a hanging rail in the cloakroom.

Silently he handed me a wad of notes and whilst I sat and counted out the money surrounded by boxes of menus and coats he proceeded to undress. He then sat snugly beside me, his pale skin glowing in the dim light, and stroked my safely trousered knee.

I waited nervously for things to get down and dirty. But they didn't. We just sat there side by side, balanced precariously on a thin sliver of shelf in silence as if we were strangers sharing a bus seat. Embarrassed and uncomfortable, I

67

guessed that as the supposed professional it was up to me to take the lead and get the balls rolling. I'd noticed some mucky magazines on the floor under our little love bench and in desperate need of some assistance, I picked one up.

'You like these ladies?' I asked him in my most suggestive phone answering voice, trying to sound sensual and appear as if I knew what I was doing.

He nodded and started to play with himself while I flicked through the pages looking for the horoscopes. Within minutes, it was all over. I'd not touched him and he'd not touched me. But he seemed happy enough. One satisfied customer and one bemused novice escort. I was still fully dressed with the money in my hand. What now I wondered?

'You like spling roll an fizzy olinge?' he asked me politely, picking up a bottle of brightly coloured pop.

I declined, feeling totally bewildered as I scuttled out and back to my car. Was that it? I'd just been handed a hundred and fifty quid for sitting amongst some anoraks looking at tits and bums, whilst a nice young man abused himself half-heartedly. There was no gruesome sweaty intercourse. There was no sizzling action amongst the deep fat fryers.

I called Debs to ask what I'd done wrong. She started laughing down the phone at me, making me feel even more of a failure.

'Chinky Charlie,' she said when her laughter finally stopped enough for her to talk. 'He like ten minute wanky wanky.'

I wish I'd said 'yes' to the spring rolls. I was starving and strangely elated, like I'd been initiated into some club or secret society. But I knew truthfully that the 'hands on' side of the work wasn't going to be for me. I was happier running the agency, answering the phones and swearing at perverts, but it was obvious that I needed more staff.

How do you go about recruiting prostitutes? I had no idea, so I placed an ad in the paper and surprisingly girls called up for a job.

One of them was Victoria. She was a career courtesan, an expert, who had plied her trade all over the world on land and the high seas. In her late forties, smart, almost attractive, utterly financially ruthless, Victoria arrived armed with suitcases of sex toys, lacy lingerie and off shore bank accounts. She'd married three of her wealthiest punters, left them, but kept the houses and money, and was now stalking her fourth.

The girls and I sat in front of her transfixed, like children being told ghost stories. She was the fount of all carnal knowledge; she taught us what men really wanted and how to charge extra for it.

OWO was an abbreviation for oral sex without a condom - when a gent wanted a blow job minus the Johnny. CIM was 'come in mouth', the end result of the preceding oral without a condom. Victoria tersely pointed out that most of the clients knew what these abbreviations meant, and the fact that we were sitting there stunned with our mouths hanging open in shock was outrageously unprofessional.

I don't think any of us liked her; in truth I was a little intimidated by her. But I knew that if we were going to survive and thrive in the world of fornication for a fee then we had to wise up. And she really had seen it, done it and wiped up the spunk with the Tee-shirt.

The next shocking revelation bestowed upon us was that John from Northampton's mysterious strap-on was in fact a dildo or vibrator in a little harness that ladies attached to themselves - strapped on, just as the name suggests, then used as a pretend penis to poke up mens' bums, or up other ladies in any orifice.

'No!' Tasha squealed, clearly horrified. 'Well I'm not doing that. It's disgusting!'

I sat there mesmerised as Victoria talked us through her bag of tricks and demonstrated how to do a perfect blow job on a lurid pink rubber willy.

So enthralled were we, watching her gratuitous genital handling, that when the work phone rang we all jumped. I stretched over to answer it, with one eye fixed on the dirty demo, only half listening to the enquiring client.

'Pardon?' I asked the caller. Waving at Victoria, I silently asked her to pause her show. 'Maybe you should call us back nearer the time sir, when you're feeling the urge?'

I looked at the phone in surprise. 'Oh how rude, he's hung up on me.'

'Heavy breather?' Tasha asked.

'Don't know what he was really,' I replied, genuinely confused. 'Why waste time calling now, if you can only manage 'annual sex', I mused. 'Imagine only doing it once a year? Sounds like me! He hung up, so today obviously wasn't the day.' I shrugged and smiled.

Then I became aware of Victoria's patronising frozen stare, the pink penis still held aloft like a flag.

'What?' I said, feeling foolish and defensive with no idea why.

'You really are incredibly stupid,' Victoria said indignantly packing her toys back into her bag of tricks. 'In fact I think you lot should just give up now. You've got no chance of surviving in this business; you're like a bunch of useless infants, utter imbeciles the lot of you.'

'W...Why? What?' I stuttered.

'He wanted anal sex, not annual sex you fool. A. N. A. L...'

She was right, we were idiots. Of course that's what he meant. Embarrassed, I could feel the giggles of humiliation bubbling up inside me as I pictured the poor man staring at the receiver wondering what kind of nutter was at the other end. But Victoria didn't see the funny side. She was getting visibly more irate by the second.

'Anal is a speciality service. If a man wants to put his cock up my back passage, I'd charge him an extra seventy for the privilege, on top of the booking fee. You've just lost me two hundred quid Becky.' She picked up her bag and gave us all a scathing, sweeping glare. 'Sod it, that's enough for me. I'm leaving. This agency is unprofessional and ridiculous.'

Looking at Tasha's crestfallen face I started to snigger. When you try to hold it in the forbidden laughs come down your nose as squeaky grunts making everything appear funnier. Victoria was one of the most anal people I'd ever met, and the more scathing she became the more hilarious I found it. By the time she'd marched out, slamming the door behind her, all three of us were helpless with laughter. From then on anyone who wanted any sort of bum fun was booked in for a special 'Madam Beckys' annual' seeing to and charged extra accordingly.

We were glad to see the back of Victoria and her passage. I hoped she was slightly jollier with her clients than she'd been with us, but I doubted it. Although I'd now grasped the concept that there were a lot of men out there who'd pay handsomely to be shouted at by a stern lady in her forties. One thing Victoria did make me realise was that just because you have a fanny, it doesn't make you a good prostitute. Just like just being able to count didn't make you a good bank manager.

There was a lot more to this shagging for money than met the eye. If we were going to stay in business I needed to take a much closer look at it.

I certainly didn't want any of us to be Victoria clones but it was time to get serious and time to grow up.

CHAPTER TEN

As the client base increased, I was determined to recruit more girls. An interesting selection of ladies is essential for an agency to be a success. You can hear the disappointment in men's voices when they phone up and ask…

'Who's available to see me today Becks?'

I would have to say it was Debs and Tasha as usual, and they'd say, 'ok thanks, I'll leave it for now.'

It felt as if I was letting them down somehow, and I knew they'd be taking their business elsewhere if I couldn't fulfil their needs. It wasn't that the gents didn't like Debs and Tasha. But most clients don't like to see the same lady again and again. Variety is the spice of life and all that. If they'd wanted monotony, they'd get married and stay home.

Over my many years as a madam I've met men who only ever saw the same escort. They'd loyally wait for a booking with their special lady forsaking all others, but that devotion was the exception rather than the rule. To make money you need a constant supply of fresh faces, women of all shapes, sizes and colours, to keep everyone coming.

Yasmin was an experienced escort, having worked for several years with different out call firms like mine, and a couple of parlours. She'd responded to my advert and, so far, her only job with Treacle's had been John from Northampton. She didn't specialise in wives and strap-ons, but she was stunning and foreign looking, so John had been happy to see her for a straightforward shag when his wife was working away. For my part I was delighted to be able to offer him a girl I knew he'd fancy. It felt like a great achievement, a bit of a coming of age for me in my new profession.

Yasmin was wonderfully sultry and exotic, a glorious mixture of various southern hemisphere nationalities. I was glad we'd found John someone nice, but as it turned out, his tastes were too adventurous even for Yasmin, despite her being far more worldly and open minded than we were. So John from Northampton was still a challenge for me.

In her early thirties, tall, curvy and elegant, with luxurious jet black hair that she flicked and fondled with immaculately manicured, long, slender fingers, Yasmin was a real lady. Obsessive and meticulous about the way she looked, she was my first introduction to fake nails and correctly fitting lingerie. Everything she wore, did or said oozed a seductive classiness. Grooming herself continuously throughout the day, she would sit with us in my house waiting for bookings, and I would watch her filing, tweezering and preening herself with utter fascination, as she told us of her escorting adventures.

It soon became obvious that Yasmin was happily and quite openly operating a somewhat unique bartering system that involved exchanging sexual favours for a full range of goods and services.

'My hanging basket man's dropping off my autumn displays, so I'll need to rush off home now,' she said, packing her make-up accoutrements and matching magnifying mirror back into her handbag.

'I'll have a spare one if you'd like it Becky.'

It was a slow day and we were in the kitchen, the kettle was boiling and I was nibbling the smashing orangey bit from a Jaffa cake. I must admit I was only half listening to what she was saying.

'I do hate a straggly floral display. Don't you? I've had the devil's own job this summer with earwigs, so I'm replacing all the old plants.'

I realised she was looking at me expectantly. 'Earwigs?' I asked confused.

Yasmin glanced out at my tatty garden. I'd focused all my recent attention on fulfilling the rampant urges of Milton Keynes males so, despite my green fingers, I'd not spent much time trimming my own bush as it were, and my undergrowth was looking decidedly neglected.

'Mmm… it's a bit grim,' I agreed.

'I've been trying to calculate how many times I'd have to have sex with my gardener to get him to dig out the rockery and build me a water feature.' I looked at her with wide eyed surprise. She had my full attention.

'Yasmin, are you telling me that you're paying for landscaping services and busy lizzies with sex?'

'Yes, of course Becky! Why not? He's very sweet, and in exchange for an hour's full personal, I always get five flowering baskets. But with sucking his dick as well as a shag, he'll owe me six baskets.'

'Bugger me,' I said, 'that brings a whole new meaning to the term 'summer bedding'.'

Yasmin grinned, picked up her car keys and opened my front door. She paused, pointing out to her smart black saloon. 'That wretched BMW, I had to bonk the man in the garage four times last month for new tyres, and the MOT's due next week, so I'll be busy on my knees in the oil again.' She smiled saucily. 'Don't know what his wife thinks when she suddenly gets a week off from her conjugal duties. I wonder if she thinks, ah... that Yasmin and her car are getting serviced again,' and with that she straightened her handbag on her shoulder and headed up the garden path.

I had to phone Yasmin later that evening, at around 9.30pm with the number of a rather unusual client who wanted to make a booking. 'Any luck with that pond?' I asked.

'Yep' she said, not as happy as I'd expected. 'Plants and carp included.'

I heard her tut down the phone.

'I've just had the bloody TV licence man at the door,' she grumbled. 'I'd forgotten to pay the wretched thing.'

'Oh no, that's court and a big fine Yaz.'

'It's sorted Becky, no worries, he's let me off. It was just a real pain in the arse.'

'Ha! You've not bonked him as well have you, you crazy bint?'

'I sure did Becks. Nice and quick. Like I said, it was a pain in the arse!'

'No! You didn't do annual with the telly man?'

'Well, he's promised that would be enough to keep me off the data base until next year, so he'd better keep his word, or I'll be calling his bosses.'

Briefly speechless, her behaviour astounded me. Although unpleasant it had sounded far quicker than setting up a direct debit. After she'd spent a few minutes talking me through her process of seducing and corrupting a civil servant, I butted in and explained about a client I wanted her to visit.

I called him Wiggy. I'm sure he had a name, but he was always Wiggy to us, and he didn't seem to mind.

Wiggy was a tall, gaunt, retired businessman in his late sixties with an impressive property portfolio. He was also a closet transvestite with surprisingly ladylike legs, and a perpetual hang-dog jowly scowl. He hired escorts not for sex but for friendship and shopping.

I think he needed someone to talk to and validate his love for cross dressing. In the early nineties the internet was not yet the focal point for fetishes and fantasies, but Wiggy was lucky enough to be able to afford to buy company and friendship by the hour. When he first enquired, I wasn't quite sure what he wanted, and until I'd checked him out I wasn't happy sending any of the girls.

Wiggy met me at the front door, still dressed as a miserable old man, at an unassuming secret house he had bought for cash, in the middle of a housing estate - a private place where he could be whoever he wanted to be, whenever he wanted to be it. It was bitterly cold and empty, containing a sad, dusty old sofa and a wonderful collection of the most fabulous wigs. Literally hundreds of unopened packets of silk stockings were stored in piles in the large two person bath tub, and expensive make-up littered every surface. Wiggy's covert semi resembled a strange middleclass squat. Top of the range kitchen units, gleaming granite and integrated appliances stood in odd contrast to the stained, second hand, scratchy blankets nailed up at the windows to prevent prying eyes.

He'd refused to have the gas connected to fuel the boiler, so I huddled in front of a small electric fire, one side of my body red and overheated, the other blue from cold, whilst I applied foundation to his slack, tired skin. The room was illuminated only by a wobbly desk lamp which feebly shone its light on the long daunting process of turning Wiggy into the woman he – sometimes - wanted to be.

Hiding out in the darkened rooms, Wiggy, ever fearful of exposure, was taught about cosmetics, deportment and being a lady. We'd read the tarot cards, natter about endless rubbish and divine his future. Happily playing girls together, we'd try out new lipsticks whilst delicately eating fried chicken from a box.

After several hours of painting and polishing, my elderly companion would be transformed into what can loosely be called female. I'd then drive a colourful, giggling and girlish Wiggy to a local nightclub where we'd park outside, and sit for hours in the safety of my car.

Listening to the radio and chatting about men as ladies do, we'd smile and wave through the windscreen to the drunk lads falling out of the disco in the early hours of the morning. Convinced all the boys would see him in all his finery, slightly distorted through the glass, and think him a stunning diva, Wiggy loved his outings. I'm not sure what the drunken revellers thought they saw, but we certainly attracted attention from male passers-by, and once or twice from patrolling police, which took some explaining.

Wiggy would feel elated, desired and fabulous; buzzing with the sexual power attained by winding up daft pissed men. Knackered and getting bored, by 6.00am I would be desperate to go home. I would leave him to relieve his excitement, have a sneaky wank and like all good girls take his make-up off and get to bed.

Entertaining as he was, Treacle Tarts was getting busier and I needed to be at home, manning the phones, so all-nighters outside dance halls were no longer possible for me. It was time to pass Wiggy on. I thought he'd adore Yasmin, who was far more ladylike and glamorous than I. So after a bit of coaxing from me, off she went. They had a great time as I knew they would, and over the years, Wiggy became not only a client but a dear friend, business advisor and personal shopper to us all.

My relationship with Wiggy and my new recruits was providing lots of laughs, but the bigger the business got, the trickier it was to control the staff.

Trying to organise working girls is akin to trying to herd cats through a field... exhausting, and almost impossible. Late for bookings, phones off, or just totally AWOL. I've heard all the excuses. The truth is that sex workers can earn a fortune, but it's hard work. When I'd finally catch up with them, the blame for their unprofessional disappearance was placed on sick, plague-riddled children, a plethora of dead grannies and so many bouts of food poisoning, you'd think these girls were feeding their families out of skips.

If a girl earned seven hundred pounds the evening before and not got home until 4.00am, she'd often not bother to go to her lunchtime booking the next day. She'd just stay in bed. Later, she'd be spotted out shopping, not having bothered to inform either me or the client that she was taking the day off.

Some of these guys saved for weeks to see a lady. The poor chap would be sitting there in his dressing gown, showered and scented, ready and waiting, having spent the previous few days in a heightened state of expectation, checking his watch every few seconds.

He'd call me, I'd make excuses for the girl and apologise. I'd heard nothing, she must be on her way, she's known about this booking for over a week. I'd call her and her phone would be switched off. He'd call back, getting more irritated. I'd make more excuses until the poor sod had to go back to work, disappointed, sexually frustrated and angry. I look like a prat and the girl's fired.

This scenario played itself again and again. It drove me utterly bonkers.

A very poor show, but that's how it was, and no amount of cajoling could make them change their ways. Mr Pip always said, 'if you can't change the people, change the people.' Wise words indeed and it wasn't long before I got a reputation for sacking girls who repeatedly let me down. The more reliable ladies became part of the team, some staying with me for many years, through thick and thin

It's normal for those who work as escorts to drift between employers, and if they're unreliable, no agency will keep them for long. Some days the girls' erratic behaviour would have me in tears of frustration, and I would complain bitterly to Wiggy. He suggested I should pen them all up together like sheep, or hobble them by their slender ankles like gypsy horses to the side of the road, so they couldn't wander off to Debenhams for hours on end.

Of course, tying girls up so they can't escape is not far from the sad truth in some areas of the sex industry, but my treacle tarts were all free agents. If they let me or the clients down more than twice then they were out, perfectly free to go and be irritating elsewhere.

Wiggy's confidence was increasing and he believed the constant chorus from the girls which told him what a divine creature he was. Sometimes Wiggy and I would enjoy shopping trips to London. His strange obsessions often saw him buying literally hundreds of pairs of stockings and dozens of wigs at a time for fear that the world's fake hair and hosiery supply would run dry, and he would be left as a balding, hairy-legged chap. He knew his idiosyncrasies were as daft as we all thought they were, so we laughed at them together, but he'd carry on bulk buying anyway, just in case.

The girls and I were fast learning the sex industry terminology, deciphering our OWOs from our CIMs. Debs was becoming ever braver and was considering a two girl lesbian booking and was trying to talk Tasha into it. But she charged too much, and priced them both out of the market. A fact for which Tasha, who was still not very comfortable with the job was very grateful, but I know Debs had enjoyed thinking about it, blossoming as she was in her new career.

You would have thought the arrival of free tickets to Ladies Day at Royal Ascot would have been cause for celebration. They were a gift from Wiggy, and god knows I needed some relief from the organisational nightmare that running my business was becoming. I was thrilled, but Yasmin wasn't looking happy.

'Here...' she said, 'Wiggy has just given me these,' she handed them to me with a worried look on her face. 'One each for us and one of them is for him.'

'Wow.' Wonderful! I was so excited, a VIP day at the races. All expenses paid. But the frown on her face said something was amiss.

'What's up?' I asked, not really wanting to hear anything that would dampen my excitement. 'Bless him, that's so sweet. It'll be fun. You look as if he's asked to go to the races for the day as a woman in a hat and a frock,' I joked laughing.

But Yasmin didn't laugh back.

'Becky, he does want to go to Ladies Day as a lady. In fact, he's determined to go out for the day in a hat and a frock.'

'No,' I said smiling. 'You're winding me up!'

'Nope. Sadly I'm not. He's been shopping already, and he wants to choose our outfits for us, so they're not prettier than his.'

'No!' I repeated. The full horror of the situation hit me. 'But he's nearly seventy and six foot four!' I shrieked. 'He'll be like the bride of Frankenstein at a village fete. He's so rude. He'll get pissed and start a fight. We'll never get away with it!'

I looked at Yasmin hoping that she would suddenly yell 'April fool' at me.

'He'll get us all killed,' I said. 'There's no way on God's earth Wiggy can go to Royal Ascot dressed as a woman.'

But he did, it actually happened.

He wore us down with his begging, bribing and pleading. He absolutely had his heart set on it and promised to be on his best behaviour. Foolishly we gave in, and all looking swanky in our new co-ordinated hats and dresses, we escorted Wiggy to the races.

The day started well enough. Yasmin had bonked a caterer twice in a golf club kitchen in exchange for a splendid picnic hamper of smoked salmon, wine, a summer fruit Pavlova and finger food. She must have put her back into it, and used all her extensive skills, because it was an amazing spread, fit for a queen, well drag queen, but I could still hear the portents of doom over the thudding of galloping hooves.

Before lunch, both the other racegoers and Wiggy were discreet, polite and sober. I noticed we were getting some hostile stares, but Wiggy kept his floral bonnet pulled well down over his eyes, and his mouth shut. I've always been teetotal, and I watched with sober dismay as a nervous Yasmin knocked back as much bubbly as Wiggy.

By 3.00pm Wiggy was staggering with his hat slipping further back off his head revealing his face, from which his eyelashes were slipping and his make-up was melting. The wolf whistles soon started. Shouts of 'Fuck me lads! Look, it's a geezer!' and 'Oi Mrs! Show us ya tackle.'

We needed to leave; I was really quite scared. The crowd had become louder and more aggressive. Wiggy and Yasmin, arm in arm, stumbled through the champagne tent, bumping into revellers, oblivious to the imminent danger, and seemed to be having the time of their lives.

Attendance on Ladies Day is staggering. Eighty thousand elated, or disappointed people, were getting increasingly more drunk and frisky. To me, it felt as if at least forty thousand over-heated, over-emotional and overly excited, pissed Essex lads had just noticed an elderly tranny in their midst - a tranny that was getting mouthier and more outrageously offensive by the minute.

The first bowl of strawberries was thrown at us shortly after Wiggy saucily pinched the muscular bottom of a stocky rugby playing Tarquin type. This was followed swiftly by several further punnets and a ham and melon starter. Wiggy was furious at getting fruit stains on his new outfit. Roaring loudly, his hat flying off into the onlookers, wig tilting dangerously, Wiggy lunged at the perpetrator of the crime. Too tipsy and aggressive to coordinate his own movements, he fell headlong over a table, upending himself and showing his tatty, old man's scrotum to the crowd as it popped out from the side of his frilly panties.

One of his mauve, size twelve sling backs spun off, sailed gracefully through the air and hit a lady hard across the bridge of the nose. In pain, furious, her eyes watering, she screamed into the faces of the group of alcohol-fuelled men she was drinking with to defend her honour, which they gallantly did, and all hell broke loose.

Eventually, and not a moment too soon, the racecourse's security separated everyone. With a burly man in a black padded jacket on either side we were marched, humiliated, dresses shredded, towards the exit. The sanctuary of the car park and the journey home was so close, but as we passed the last block of toilets Wiggy demanded that he needed to powder his nose.

As fast as a racing ferret, before anyone could stop him, Wiggy ignored the sign for the gents, and ducked into the ladies toilets to empty his bladder and straighten his dislodged hair piece. A shocked scream rang out loudly from the convenience interior. Some poor woman, horrified at the terrible sight of an inebriated pensioner in drag re-adjusting himself at the basins had sounded the alarm. The handbag holding husband, waiting outside, heard her cry and rushed in to her aid. Bracing himself, and using all of his considerable body weight, the furious spouse punched dear old Wiggy straight in the face.

The poor crumpled cross dresser was out cold on the rancid lavy floor. Blood mixed with strawberry juice and clotted cream on his frock. His eye shadow blended badly with the imprint of the irate fellow's gold sovereign ring as Wiggy lay broken and twisted, like a massacred pantomime dame.

Security had seen enough and called the police, and we were carted off to the cop shop.

When we finally left the Ascot area, Wiggy had a caution for indecency, a black eye, headache and a missing shoe. I drove us all swiftly home to Milton Keynes, listening to his drunken snoring, and temporarily hating his guts.

Two days later Yasmin and I sat and stared at Wiggy, utterly incredulous. It wasn't his florid bruising or the nasty gash on his cheek that had our mouths dropping open in utter shock; it was what he was saying.

'...yes, I can safely say Royal Ascot was the best day of my life...'

Yasmin and I looked at each other. Surely he wasn't serious?

'I'm inspired by it,' he said as he touched his face and winced at the pain. 'I want to meet more people like me, to have others to share my hobby with and I want to go out as much as I can dressed as a beautiful lady. It was thrilling.'

'Thrilling?' I suppose it was one word for the experience but it wasn't quite the one I would choose.

'I just can't stop thinking about it,' he continued. He was more animated and excited than I had ever seen him. 'I've told you Becky about these dressing services for men like me?'

I nodded my head. He had told me many times.

'There's a big one in London and one in Birmingham. Somewhere a man can be transformed into a woman.'

'You want me to take you?' I asked. 'Maybe I should leave you there? See if they can control you.'

He shook his head. 'No,' he said. 'You should open one here in Milton Keynes, half way between the two. You'd make a fortune.' He glanced at me and grinned. 'They organise outings as well you know. I'm sure they took a big group to Ascot the day we went.'

'What?' I emitted a noise that was half laugh and half scream, and Yasmin groaned, putting her hands over her face, shaking her head.

'Taking a large group of Wiggys on an outing to Ascot?' I shuddered at the thought. He had to be winding me up. But Wiggy took my horrified response as encouragement.

'Think about it Becky. You could rent a flat, and have one room as a dressing service, and use the other rooms for the girls to see their punters in. I can give you wigs and stockings, but you'll need to buy clothes in different sizes.' He was so animated and excited, barely pausing for breath. 'Oh and you must have several wedding dresses...'

'What?' I appreciated my life was slightly bizarre but even I was struggling with this random madness.

'Oh yes, wedding dresses are essential. Most transvestites have a bridal fantasy that they want to act out. And of course we all love lots of lace.'

'Lots of lace? Of course you do.'

'Oh, and lots of PVC, that's another favourite. The tart fantasy.'

I couldn't hear any more. I held my hand up to stop him. 'Wiggy, as God is my judge, there is no way I am ever taking men in dresses to a public gathering ever again.' I continued emphatically. 'You can't make me. In fact even the good Lord Himself couldn't make me. Where's all this come from?'

'You won't?' he whimpered, genuinely surprised.

I felt awful, like I'd just stood on a puppy. 'I'm sorry but I can't.'

'She really can't,' Yasmin added helpfully.

'But I'm just trying to help us both,' he shrugged, looking deflated. 'How many clients do you lose everyday because you've got nowhere for them to see a girl?'

He was right. Half of the calls we received everyday were from men who wanted to be able to visit a girl as they had nowhere discreet for a girl to visit them. But I thought we were talking about a tranny dressing service?

'You must lose fifty percent of them,' he continued. 'It makes business sense to open somewhere so clients can come to you. And imagine it Becky, all the girls can be in the house, you'll know where they are, it'll be easier to manage.'

'Yeah, it's called a brothel Wiggy,' I said. 'I've narrowly avoided prison once; I'd rather not go there for running a knocking shop.'

'You run an escort agency already, that's illegal.'

Another valid point, but the police didn't tend to pursue escort agencies, as we stipulated clients were just paying for a girl's time. Pre-organised sexual services were difficult to prove in the privacy of a client's own home. It was easy to say that a lady was booked for an hour or so of company. If they happen to get on so well that after a glass of wine, all their clothes fell off and in the heat of the moment they had sex – well what can you do? That's life. Generally the police had better things to do than get into that argument.

'Well,' Wiggy continued, 'I think it's a good idea. You could run a transvestite dressing service while you answer the phones for the escorts, and the girls could still see their regular punters in hotels as well if they wanted. I could counsel and entertain the cross dressers and run a support group.'

Support group? It was getting more ridiculous by the minute.

'It's me that needs support, having to deal with you,' I said, meaning every word.

'A dressing service isn't illegal.' He looked at me seriously.

'True. But a brothel is.'

'Think about it Becky. I really want to do it.'

'I think having somewhere we can accommodate clients is a great idea,' Yasmin said joining in. 'We all lose so much money just doing out-calls. I think we should give it a try.'

It was all very well them being keen, but it would be my head on the block. Being a prostitute isn't illegal, and neither is being a client, or a tranny, as long as you don't go into the ladies loos. If prostitutes work individually from their homes they're not breaking any laws. But being a madam and running a brothel is very illegal. If the clients know where to find you, then the constabulary also know where to find you and you're a sitting duck.

But Wiggy and Yasmin had started me thinking. More money, and less organisational stress, it might just be worth the risk, but it was a big risk.

CHAPTER ELEVEN

My brothel opening dilemma was confused further by the fact that I'd had another daughter in 1995 after an unsatisfactory liaison with a Libran. I had two young children to worry about and I really didn't want them both to end up in care if I got sent to prison for running a disorderly house.

I discussed my thoughts with Mr Pip, who tried to talk me out of escort agencies altogether, and into a proper job. He was still seeing my potential as a bona fide business person, and I was still avoiding gainful employment at all costs.

My mum had moved to Milton Keynes when I had Emilia, my second daughter. She wanted to help out with her grandkids, and maybe keep an eye on what I was up to, now there were two little ones involved.

As a mum myself, I was realising that parenting was often a thankless, exhausting job and that we all made mistakes and just got by the best we could. I don't think I was a particularly good mum. But seeing the truth about how hard it is to bring up kids, had given me an understanding of my own childhood and difficult relationship with my mother.

I could have done better as a parent and I would watch Debs, her organisational skills, immaculate children and Sunday lunches with gravy and puddings in awe.

I think I did ok with what I consider the important job of helping my offspring become decent members of society. But I could never really get the hang of what I thought were the dull bits like cooking, cleaning and putting hair into bunches tied with pretty ribbons. The problem with housework was that you made the beds, washed the floors, then a short time later you had to do it all again. It seemed pointless.

I was hopeless at packing Abi's school lunch box, or doing a weekly shop. In fact I have an irrational terror of Tupperware. I would often just throw the entire thing away at the end of a school day rather than open it and be faced with a blackened, stinking banana coated in rancid warm yoghurt.

Luckily we lived opposite a local convenience store in West Bletchley so a morning dash to buy provisions for lunch was the norm, followed later by an evening dash to buy something for tea, which I'd also forgotten all about.

I taught my kids that they had choices in life. Every moment of everyday presented them with a new decision to make. In any situation they needed to decide to do the right thing. They knew what the right thing was by then, and if they didn't they could ask.

If they decided to do the wrong thing, that was up to them, but consequences would follow swiftly and there would be no escaping them. I had no concerns about smacking my children, or anyone else's for that matter if they were rude, disrespectful or unkind to people, property or creatures. It would have been a hanging offence if my kids were cheeky, noisy or generally pesky and irritating to others, and most of the time they weren't.

I learned the 'Mr Pip patronising eyebrow raise' which I would deploy, and that alone would quell most uprisings. If I said NO, it was NO, and remained NO, and we would all have died from old age before I ever changed my mind.

I didn't inherit my mother's need to obsessively control my children's every move either. I felt my job as a parent was to help them develop an understanding of consequence, good and bad, physical, emotional or spiritual. Every action has a reaction. Every pebble thrown into the water will create ripples that will flow where they will. If you don't want the ripples, don't throw the pebble.

Misdemeanours such as forgetting to do homework, incorrect uniform or pretending to be ill if you had maths were overlooked by me as the less important things in life to be stressing about.

By the time Abi was eight or nine she was having a lot of time off school. She had been born with severe hearing problems, which had been corrected with several operations, but as she got older I noticed that there seemed to be a problem with her eyesight. Abi was a very serious but gentle and unassuming child, who never made a fuss, or complained about anything. From when she could walk, she'd always seemed more grown up and sensible than I was ever going to be. She never bothered to mention that she couldn't see, she just got on with it and did the best she could, and would often scold me for being disorganised in the home. She was eventually diagnosed as having a rare bi-lateral squint, which caused her constant double vision, and by the time she was ten she'd lost her peripheral vision completely. Very unpleasant and painful surgery at Milton Keynes hospital was deemed unsuccessful. I was informed that there was nothing more that could be done and that she would gradually go completely blind.

I totally fell to pieces; I got shingles and took to my bed in a fit of the vapours. My mum was brilliant. She did what she does best and took charge, and this time I was so grateful. Applying a firm hand, she re-organised my family, shopped for us, fed us, looked after everyone including me, and refused to accept MK hospital's conclusions. She paid for a Harley Street consultant, and took Abi to Moorfield's as a private patient to get her 'sorted out'.

Life was complicated enough, and I wasn't sure that opening a brothel would make it any easier. Emilia, my youngest daughter, was bouncy, healthy and the comedy turn of the family, with her huge blue eyes and strawberry blonde, corkscrew ringlets. But I was having problems with her dad who I'd separated from, and who thought my connection to the sex industry was the work of the devil. Strange really, how a person falls in love with you because they admire who you are and what you do, then when they've got you, they spend the rest of the relationship hating you for the same things they fell in love with you for. Life's a funny thing. I knew my ex would be horrified by my deeper immersion into debauchery, and to me, it seemed as good a reason as any to do it.

Two things happened that finally made up my mind to open a 'working' flat. Firstly Abi had to do a project in school. 'My mum's job.' That was never going to go well. I knew nothing about it until the school phoned me, slightly concerned and looking for clarity on what Abi had told them.

She'd stood up and explained to her class of friends and her teacher that her mum talked on the phone all day and always said the same thing - that a lady costs one hundred and fifty pounds for one hour, and there were different ladies, and sir could choose who he wanted to buy. She went on to explain that

Grandma didn't have much money because she didn't have any ladies. That meant that the police wouldn't chase Grandma, which was why Grandma did the shopping and took her to hospital for her eye appointments.

Clearly it was time to get the phones and the gossip out of my house, away from the kids, before they got me hung, and I just hoped my fake explanation to the headmistress about arranging Anne Summers parties for a living was enough to pacify the school and prevent them from despatching social services forthwith.

Secondly, Abi discovered that she shared my love of all things equine, and desperately wanted to learn to ride. Her eyesight made this quite risky, but she was determined. I paid for her to have several lessons, and she was hooked. Standing, leaning on the rail, I watched two young girls supposedly teach my daughter the art of horsemanship. They chatted to each other, stuffed sweets and paid very little attention to their partially- sighted student while Abi struggled to stay in control of a hairy, barrel- shaped pony that hurtled around the arena and made headlong dashes for the gate, leaving the skin from my daughter's little knees on the fence as it went.

The pony was undoubtedly running this show. In its mind it was tolerating thirty minutes of child wearing before it could get back to eating hay, rather than the instructive half hour of pony riding I'd paid quite a lot of money for.

I stood, hands over my eyes, afraid to look and becoming angrier with each dangerous swerve into the splintering wood. I had British Horse Society and Riding for the Disabled qualifications, and was more capable of teaching Abi than both these girls put together. If I opened a flat, I could have set opening times and therefore more time off; then I would be able to get Abi her own little pony and help her myself. What was I waiting for?

I don't know what I was waiting for, but something was still holding me back. The financial outlay was a concern, but for once in my life I was scared of the legal consequences.

It's one thing breaking the law when you can run away and hide, try to dodge the bullet, but it's different if you're advertising your whereabouts, and sitting there answering the phone until they come to arrest you. It didn't seem like very good odds to me. I was also concerned about the business itself. What if we didn't have enough clients to pay the rent? If we didn't get any new clients, we wouldn't be able to afford the monthly outgoings and all the bills as well as the existing newspaper adverts.

I'd always worked through situations in my head, and looked at all the worst case scenarios. If I'm prepared to accept the consequences of my actions I go ahead. If I'm not, I don't do it. I had little interest in lumbering myself with regrets or guilt, so I make sure I'm happy to take whatever shit might hit the fan, before I turn the fan on, or throw the shit into the air.

The worst case scenarios of opening a brothel were arrest, prison, confiscation of earnings, and my kids being taken into care. Or just failing to attract clients and putting myself in debt, and getting stuck with a six month tenancy on a property for no reason. I needed to consider this decision logically, looking at all the pros and cons.

Mr Pip said, 'no one in their right mind would do it, but I'm sure you will.'

The girls were all desperate for me to open a flat. They all loved the idea of having somewhere to work from and avoid driving around the Home Counties day and night. Un-beknown to me, they had devised their own helpful plan that nearly got us all killed.

I finally heard about it from a punter who was worried. He was one of Tasha's regulars, a sweet guy, who I think had a bit of a thing for her.

I confronted her in the kitchen between bookings. 'I've heard a whisper that you're playing away,' I said, standing in the doorway so she couldn't avoid me. She hated confrontation.

'It's not what you think Becks,' she pleaded guiltily. 'We knew you were worried that we wouldn't find enough customers to pay for a flat...'

'So you joined a rival agency...'

'Only to nick their clients,' she said.

'It was a very sweet thought,' I replied, 'but don't you think it might be a bit risky?'

'It seemed a good way to get more work; we thought you'd be pleased.'

I knew that Tasha and the girls meant well but I had a bad feeling about this. 'If someone did this to me, I'd be proper pissed off.'

'Yeah, but how would they find out?' Tasha said.

I walked into the kitchen and put the kettle on; I needed a cup of tea.

'I'll work with them tonight,' she said, 'and then I'll tell them I won't be in anymore.'

'Phone and tell them you quit now. Don't go in tonight. Please Tash, stop this before someone gets hurt.'

'Ok,' she said sulkily as she headed out of the room.

I didn't care if she was a bit miffed with me. I knew I was right. Messing with other agencies was not a sensible game.

What we didn't know then but soon learned the hard way, is that punters tell tales. Most of them used most of the local agencies. They picked up gossip from the girls and passed it on to other girls, who then passed it on to their bosses. Often punters and pimps had a close relationship, and it's very difficult to keep your business cards close to your chest. We were new to the game, naive and daft, and hadn't yet learnt about the darker side of this life, or the lengths the competition would go to protect their interests.

In later years, nothing could happen in the sex industry within a hundred mile radius that I didn't know about first. But that type of influence and network takes years to develop, and Treacle's was still very much in its infancy and we were right at the bottom of the food chain.

It had been a quiet evening for Treacle Tarts, and by 2.00am, curled in bed, I was dropping off to sleep when I heard the phone ring. Sighing, I threw back the duvet and sleepily stumbled downstairs to find it and turn it off for the night when I saw that I'd missed a call from Tasha. She'd had the night off, so I thought she'd called me by mistake. Not wanting to call back and get into a conversation at this late hour, I sent her a text... *U ok? U called.*

I headed back upstairs and crawled into my still warm bed, tucking the duvet between my legs. The phone beeped a response. I opened the message and froze in horror; the reply from Tasha just read...

Help.

Wide awake and gripped by fear, I rang Tasha's mobile. 'Pick up, pick up...'

But she didn't. It rang out again and again.

Heart racing, hands trembling, I called Debs.

'Where's Tasha?' I urgently demanded. 'Do you know what's happening?'

I could almost hear Debs' dozing brain struggling to surface and understand what I was asking. If she was asleep, she wouldn't know Tasha was in trouble. 'Becks?' she mumbled sleepily.

'It's Tasha. Something's happened to her. Deb listen! Do you know where she is?'

'What's going on with Tash? She's not here. Her kids are staying over,' Debs muttered sleepily.

'I know she's not there!' I shouted with frustration and fear. 'She must be out somewhere. She tried to ring me.'

'Probably by mistake,' Debs said, clearly not taking my panic seriously.

'She sent me a text. It just said 'help'.'

Debs was silent at the other end of the phone.

'Just help?' she said.

'Yes. I've tried to call her about a million times, but she's not picking up. Where did she go?'

'She had a job with 'Honey's', I don't know where,' Debs said her voice thick with worry.

Dear God, I closed my eyes, trying to make my brain think. Could I ring the police? But what could I tell them? I had no idea where she was or who she was with.

'Honey's?' I said, thinking aloud. 'I don't know who they are. Do you have a number for them?'

'You can't call them. They'll go mental!'

'Debs, I don't care what they think, I need to know where Tasha is, and that she's ok. Just find me the number.'

Honey's Escorts knew it was me phoning looking for Tasha. I could tell because the man who answered the phone told me so. He swore and shouted and called me names before warning me that he knew where I lived, and that they were coming to get me when they'd finished with her.

I slammed the phone down onto the table. Great. I'd have to worry about myself later, but for now I had to find Tasha.

I thought about the police again. Maybe they would go and force the information out of that shit from Honey's. Make him tell them where Tasha was. But I didn't even know where Honey's was so how could I send the police to them? And even if I did, they would deny everything.

I rang Tasha's phone over and over and suddenly it clicked through. 'Oh my god Tash...' I cried.

But she didn't answer me.

'Tasha!'

'Becks help me,' she screamed.

'Tasha!'

I heard a voice, a male voice. 'You sly bitch...' and then the line hissed and crackled and died.

I strained to listen, praying that she would call me back and say something that would let me know where she was. But she didn't. I tried calling again and again. But it didn't even ring. It just clicked straight to answer phone.

I called Debs back.

'I'm coming over now,' she said. 'These kids are ok without me for an hour.'

I paced the floor watching and waiting for Debs' arrival. I just wanted to jump in the car and drive. But where did I drive to? I had no idea where she was.

I nearly had a heart attack when the phone rang again. I grabbed it and glanced at the display. It was a land line number that I didn't recognise.

'Yep?' I snapped, anxiety making me abrupt.

'Becks?'

'TASHA! Where the hell are you? Are you ok?'

Tasha was sobbing, so I could hardly understand her. 'Come and get me...'

She was in Luton. I told her to ring back in ten minutes to give Debs the address, when she could speak and knew where she was. I figured that I just needed to get going, to get to her as fast as I could. I began hunting for my car keys, throwing things off the kitchen work surfaces and running up and down the stairs. They'd gone; I just couldn't find them anywhere.

'Damn it!' I shouted in frustration, forgetting the car, and grabbing the keys to my old Scrubbers van, that had sat rotting outside my house for years with no tax or MOT. I'd take that. I prayed it would start. I didn't have time for anymore searching for lost car keys. I was still in my nightdress - well an oversized man's shirt and a pair of my ex's boxers, which I'd got custody of when he left. I shoved my feet into trainers and pulled on a long coat, then I dashed outside to make my way to Luton to rescue my friend.

The smoky old diesel engine coughed into life, and I threw thanks up to heaven. Reversing out onto the road, thoughts racing through my head, I considered what I would do if the police tried to pull me over for no tax. Would I stop and make Tasha wait, where ever she was? No, I decided, I'd speed off, and let them chase me. I'd deal with them once I knew she was safe. Besides a few Old Bill with blue lights behind me might be useful in this situation.

Once on the motorway, I pushed the knackered van to its screeching, belching limits. I juggled with the gear stick and the phone to call Debs. I'd left the front door key under the flower pot for her to get in. I knew she'd only be a few minutes away.

'Has she rung?' I demanded, the moment Debs picked up.

'Yeah. She's ok I think.'

'Got an address?'

Debs told me where to go and gave me some basic directions. 'Becks...' she said, sounding worried. 'Be careful. It might be a trap.'

The same thought had been sneaking up on me. Honey's shit of a spokesman had told me they were after me. Was this a trap? Lure me to Luton to save Tasha and then... well I didn't have a clue what the 'then' might be. Nor did I want to dwell on its possibilities.

'Did she say something?' I asked, remembering how in the early days we used to have a code for danger, usually something stupid and random like 'my knickers are too tight'.

'Well it's more like she didn't say anything,' Debs replied. 'She was cagey. I kept asking what had happened but she kept putting me off.'

'I'll ring you when I get there,' I said and hung up.

The motorway was pretty empty and it didn't take long to reach the exit. But then panic stopped me thinking straight, and I got lost several times. Eventually I arrived at the address. It looked like a nice house, huddled against a bush-covered embankment, with a barrier at the top that looked like it may be the dual carriageway I'd just come down.

Having no idea what to expect, I parked up and called Debs. I gave her the registration number for the car that was parked in the drive, and the different registration of a newish looking caravan that was tucked under a carport. We agreed that if I didn't ring her back to say we were both safe in five minutes then she was to ring the police. I looked at the immaculate caravan suspiciously, and it's proudly displayed tourist stickers. I didn't think girls got kidnapped by people who had membership of the World Wildlife Fund and the National Trust but you never knew.

I squared my shoulders and braced myself for a fight with whoever had Tasha. I knocked on the door. Despite my shaking hands I made sure the knock was firm and loud and determined. I didn't want to show any weakness.

The door opened the length of the security chain and a small, wrinkled, old lady dressed in a housecoat peered out. Looking me up and down, observing my naked legs sticking out from under my nightshirt, and general dishevelled look, she turned around and called, 'your friend's here now dear.'

Opening the door she apologised for being in her housecoat and explained, 'I'm not used to being up at this hour,' in a voice that was much firmer and stronger than her frail frame suggested. 'Not unless I'm going on holiday, and trying to get to Hunstanton before the Bank Holiday rush. Then my Albert hitches up and makes us leave at the crack of a sparrow fart.'

For once in my life I was speechless.

Tasha half ran towards me from the kitchen, bare-foot, bare-legged, holding her coat tightly round her.

'You make a good pair you two,' the lady laughed, nodding towards our bare legs. 'You look like you're off to the swimming baths.'

I hugged Tasha. 'You ok?'

She nodded.

'Just make sure you stay away from that lad young missy. Once they know they can push you around, they'll always do it,' the old lady said firmly but kindly. 'He's a wrong 'un that one, to do that to you. He'll do it again, you mark my words.'

'I will,' Tasha replied, as we headed for the door.

'Thank you for looking after her,' I said, my voice thick with emotion and confusion.

'We've all had our share of useless men,' the lady said with a smile. 'Good luck love, enough excitement for me for one night, I'm back off to me bed.'

The door shut behind us. I looked at Tasha quizzically and she shrugged. As Tasha slowly climbed into the van, I got a glimpse of her bare bum.

'Tasha! You're naked!'

She started to cry again.

I rang Debs to tell her we were both safe and then started the engine. When the tears finally stopped, Tasha recounted the story. I drove in silence, the fury mounting now that the fear had subsided.

Tasha had tried to cancel the booking and resign as I'd asked. But Honey's persuaded her to go. They said the customer had requested for her personally as she'd seen him the week before and he thought she was wonderful.

'He was nice,' Tasha added, 'and I was pretty sure I could nick him for us.'

I managed to keep my mouth shut. No point in 'told you so'.

The man, who not surprisingly called himself John, seemed a bit tense. But other than that it was a normal visit. As Tasha was about to leave, John suddenly got tetchy and started hurling abuse at her. He called her names and told her it was her own fault. Tasha left in a hurry.

They were waiting for her. Two of them. They grabbed her and bundled her into the back of the car. She was shoved down onto the floor. One man drove, the other sat in the back, his feet pressing painfully into her back.

Terrified and screaming, with her face pushed into the dirty carpet, Tasha somehow manoeuvred her phone from her pocket. She tried to ring me and when she got no answer she'd started to text. She only got as far as HELP, and then she didn't know what else to say. She had no idea where she was or where they were going.

The man in the back seat, with his heels grinding into her spine, had seen her texting and, cursing at her, had kicked the phone out of her hand, under the seat. At the memory, she held up her hand and tried to wiggle her bruised fingers. It was on silent; she could see it flashing from my constant calls, and so could her captor, so she didn't dare reach it to answer me.

The car finally stopped and Tasha managed to grab her mobile before she was dragged by her hair onto the tarmac. They pulled up in a lay-by on a fast road. She had no idea where they were. Terrified for her life she tried talking to them. But they swore and shouted. It seemed that 'John' had told them about her attempts to lure his business away. The whole evening had been a set up to teach her and me a lesson.

They searched her for the money he'd paid her. They pocketed that along with every penny in her purse. Then they tipped her bag upside down and she watched through her tears as the wind carried everything away. Luckily she didn't carry cards or ID when she was on a job.

She tightly clutched her phone that was still hidden in her coat pocket. She could feel it vibrating, as I rang her yet again. While they were distracted with the handbag she took her chance and made a run for it. That's when she answered my call.

They caught her in seconds. One grabbed her coat from behind. She shrugged it off and kept running. But they were faster and she was quickly caught. The other man grabbed the mobile and stamped it into the road.

Utterly alone with the two monsters and terrified for her life, she begged them, even offering them sex, anything they wanted. They just laughed at her and ordered her to remove everything she was wearing. Then they watched as she stripped down to her underwear. But even the undies had to go.

'They took all my clothes, threw them into the car. Then they told me in detail what they would do to me if I ever went near one of their punters again.'

Poor Tasha. She was fighting the tears and the shock and fear to tell me everything. 'Then they drove off.'

'Left you butt naked at the side of the road?' I said angrily.

'Yeah. Luckily they'd forgotten the coat. It was a few feet away where it dropped when I ran. I climbed up the bank away from the road, but there was nothing the other side but fields. I could see lights in the distance the opposite way but that meant I had to run across both sides of the road.'

I glanced sideways at her. She must have been absolutely terrified. I indicated left and took the exit off the motorway. 'Nearly home,' I said.

'I made a run for it across the duel carriageway. The buttons were ripped off my coat and I struggled to hold it together and run at the same time. Drivers kept hooting. I got stuck climbing over the fence thing in the middle. It was higher than I thought. I've taken all the skin off my Minnie. When I finally got across the road I climbed up the bank and slid down the other side to the houses...'

'And ended up with the housecoat lady,' I added for her.

'I told her I'd had a fight with my boyfriend. I asked if I could phone you.'

We were nearly home. Tasha needed a hot bath and sweet tea. She was bruised and traumatised. She wasn't going to shake this off very easily.

'I've cut my legs to bits,' she said as she bent forward to rub her shins.

I saw the deep rips from the bushes, and the gravel rash on her knees from where they had pushed her out of the car.

'Oh Becky, I thought they were going to kill me.'

Racked with sobs now, she couldn't explain anymore. I reached over and squeezed her arm, to comfort her, but she flinched away in pain.

'It's over now, you're safe.'

But it wasn't over. As I pulled up outside my house, Debs was standing at the front door looking worried.

Deb put her arms around Tasha and looked at me. 'I heard a noise, so I peeped out the window.' She shook her head. 'So sorry Becky, but I was too late.' She pointed to my car, and in the soft dawn light I could see a strange wet pattern on my car windscreen.

Looking more closely, the pattern became bubbles that flowed down from the roof, over the driver's door and across the bonnet. Scraping at it, my finger stung, and I watched my acrylic nail melt away along with my metallic paintwork, under several litres of acid that was eating its way through my car.

I looked from the car to my friends. There was nothing more to say.

We'd glimpsed the dark side of the sex trade and survived. I was swamped by that familiar childhood feeling of the furious victim - helpless, being pushed around and threatened by people bigger than me. Taking a deep breath, I looked at my slowly eroding Shogun and then back at Tasha.

The helplessness subsided, replaced quickly and coldly by a steely gut-felt determination to find a flat and expand my business, and to hell with all of them.

CHAPTER TWELVE

The threats and vandalism carried on sporadically for a few months. Tyres slashed, more acid thrown, but my irksome enemies stopped short of attacking people again which was a relief. I think they felt kidnapping Tasha had made enough of a statement. Plus it must have been obvious to them that I wasn't going away. Eventually they gave up.

Tasha was really upset and had barely worked since her dual carriageway ordeal but Honey's Escorts' declaration of war had made me even more determined to make my business a success.

I talked it over with Mr Pip, who had become even richer and more successful. He tutted and disapproved and suggested maybe I should take the hint and get a proper job.

Yasmin had seen all this before over the years and warned me with terrifying tales of how people who make a living from prostitution get rival brothels shut down shortly after they opened. There were several tried and tested disruption tactics deployed by pimps and gangsters with grudges, which included informing the police and the neighbours of a competitor's whereabouts, or fly posting large photos of the girls in the communal areas of flats, with big headings like *'I'M A PROSTITUTE AND I PLY MY FILTHY TRADE FROM FLAT FIVE.'* Or one of the favourites, and most embarrassing, was to stick large sheets of paper saying 'I'VE JUST VISITED A PROSTITUTE' onto visiting clients' windscreens with wallpaper paste. If the aggrieved neighbour dashed out and stuck it on the glass as soon as the client went in for his booking, then by the time he'd left, having done the deed, the paste would have dried solid, making it impossible to remove. It would also have been read by a large number of residents who would give him hell when he returned to his vehicle, named and shamed.

Sometimes it was more serious. One local place had been set on fire during a feud, and totally gutted in a bid to get the occupants to close up and to move on. I was very aware that we still had a lot to learn, and I wasn't going to put anyone deliberately at risk. After a lot of thinking I came up with a plan.

'Ok ladies,' I announced to them all as we sat in Debs' kitchen drinking tea. 'Let's not open a brothel....'

They all groaned and I put my hand up to stop them.

'How about I open a massage parlour?' I added quickly.

'Massage?' Debs said, screwing her face up and looking like a kid who had just been handed a plateful of brussel sprouts.

'Yes. We'll just do massage. Well, massage with a happy ending. A wank, you know...'

Tasha nodded her head, 'no sex?'

'No. It'll need to be a topless or naturist massage, but on proper massage couches with the paper on a roll like they have at the Doctors. We can have fancy candles, and whales singing from the stereo - classy and relaxing, and not quite so illegal.' I looked around the table, they didn't seem convinced.

'Would the punters go for that?' Debs wondered. 'No one else does it around here.'

'That may just be the beauty of it, the reason it will work,' I ventured. 'We'd be the only ones at it. We could create more of a pampering service for guys who couldn't be bothered to have sex.'

They looked even less convinced.

'Oh come on. Not all men want to have sex all the time.'

That lost them completely.

'Yeah right!' Debs said laughing.

'Trust me,' I smiled. 'I've got a good feeling in my psychic handbag about this.'

Debs, Tasha and I settled ourselves with tea and cake around the dining table of destiny and shuffled the cards. The Eight of Swords, card of interference from others was making a regular appearance, but so were the Pentacles, the money cards. I interpreted the cards in front of me in a way that suited my plan and decided they were telling me to go ahead.

In Milton Keynes at the time there were several brothels, but no 'massage only' parlours. In theory, the police would be more lenient with an operation that wasn't providing full sex, and the other agencies would have no axe to grind if we weren't in direct competition. It seemed like a good compromise all round.

I didn't know how the 'massage only' places worked, or what they charged, so I enlisted Wiggy to do some market research.

'You want me to go to a massage parlour and let someone cover me in oil and tug my old todger?'

'Yes please,' I said. 'You've got to take one for the team Wiggy. And I need you to pay close attention to all the details, what the rooms look like, how they do the massage, technique, prices and that kinda stuff.'

'While a young lady is tugging my todger?'

'Yes please.'

'And who's paying for this? Are you?'

'No,' I said, 'you'll enjoy it, you know you will and if we set up the massage place, you can have a room for your dressing service, so it's in your interest to help me out, and get me started.'

'Well,' he said thoughtfully, 'if I'm paying, then I'm making the most of it and wearing my stockings and bra.'

'Can you get massaged properly if you're wearing stockings and a bra?' Tasha asked. 'Won't the lady get herself all knotted up in your straps?'

'I'm not planning to get massaged properly,' Wiggy replied giving her a lecherous wink.

'Eeeww... Too much information!' Tasha laughed and threw a jammy dodger at him. 'That's like imagining my Grampy on the job!'

Wiggy let out a theatrical sigh. 'I honestly think eventually you girls will cure me of my cross dressing, or just put me off women and sex completely.'

'Come on old man,' I teased him, thrusting a local newspaper at him, 'get phoning these numbers and get yourself booked in for a good time.'

The biggest difference, apart from not providing intercourse, officially referred to in the trade as a 'full personal service', was that massage parlours charged less. A lot less. Forty five pounds for an appointment rather than a basic starting price of one hundred and twenty. The girls would be taking a big cut in their money. I hadn't realised how cheap it was to get a massage and a hand job. I knew it would be a problem.

'It's a shorter booking,' I said, doing my best to put a positive spin on it. 'Just over half an hour as opposed to an hour with the out-calls, and no wasted travelling time, so you can squeeze more in... Well, squeeze more out if you know what I mean!' I laughed, trying to convince Debs that massage was the way forward, but she didn't look pleased.

'And you don't have to have it off with anyone,' I added, smiling encouragingly.

'But I don't mind having it off with them,' she countered. 'I look forward to it sometimes! Can't I just shag them all and be done with it? This seems like much harder work.'

I tried not to sigh. I had to be patient. Nobody ever likes change, especially when it's going to cost them money.

'That won't work as a system Debs; if the police find out someone is offering a full personal then we're for it, all of us. Doing the wanking bit is bad enough. We have to stick to the plan, so everybody knows the rules. I really don't want to open a brothel and get myself locked up or chopped up. I'm trying to stay out of trouble.'

She reluctantly agreed to give the massage service a go. But as she and Yasmin enjoyed being escorts and earning the big bucks, we agreed that they should carry on visiting their regular clients from the existing out-calls as well if they wanted to.

Whittards of Chelsea, the fancy tea leaf and coffee bean shop, gave us the idea for the name of the new massage emporium. They were selling their old shop displays - five foot tall, papier-mâché characters out of Disney's Aristocats cartoon in their Milton Keynes store. Passing by, I saw Duchess, the sassy white cat. She was for sale, complete with a red feather boa, bold as brass in the shop window like an Amsterdam whore. You could have her for ten quid, so I rescued her and struggled home - sexy paper pulp ears sticking out of the sunroof, and red feathers coming loose and flying around inside the car.

Opening my massage parlour, in a totally unsuitable and indiscreet little residential terraced house, I placed Duchess, larger than life, in the front window for all to see, like a feline lighthouse guiding the rudderless, randy men folk of Milton Keynes into a safe harbour of naughtiness.

The legendary 'Becky's Kittens' had begun.

'Becky's Kittens' was advertised as a massage and pampering service, not a brothel. With the picture of Duchess, the saucy cat, looking seductive with her feathers in the corner of the advert. Mr Pip, the marketing magus, had not produced this art work either. He just tutted, disapproved, and suggested I stopped mucking about and got a proper job before I got thrown in the slammer for the rest of my life.

There were no beds in the new place, just professional treatment couches, and all the girls were forbidden to indulge in any sort of sex in case any coppers were lurking. We wouldn't even admit to hand relief over the phone, saying a 'relaxing all over massage sir, with full tension release.'

The forty-five minute booking started with tea and biscuits. Then the gent undressed and prepared himself for an assisted bubble bath and a game of hunt the soap. An assisted bath meant that the lady of his choice dangled over the edge of the tub, scrubbed his back and washed all his bits and bobs, making sure everything was nice and clean for manhandling later in the appointment.

Clients would relax in the hot soapy water, with a tray of tea and a plate of quality biscuits resting on the loo seat, by way of a table. I always provided my gentlemen with a nice pot, with milk jug and sugar on the side. I find drinking from mugs distasteful. But a cup and saucer would be almost impossible to handle in a steaming bubble bath as a nubile young lady washed your willy. So, in the interests of health and safety in the work place, I provided those nice bone china vessels that are more than a cup, but not quite a mug, but had a feeling of quality about them. I lovingly prepared the trays myself, and was proud in the knowledge that I was one of the only people left in the UK, apart from Italian grandmothers, who still liked to lay out a nice spread on a hand-crafted doily.

Gingernuts tended to be the preferred accompaniment at 'Becky's Kittens' to a nice tray of Darjeeling, and caused less trouble than chocolate coated confections. It was my job as the receptionist to clean the bath after every client. On one occasion as I swilled away the remaining bubbles, my finger slid right into the middle of what looked to be a large lump of human poo, hidden in the shallow water. Horrified, with a customer's soft turd under my long nail, I turned and vomited violently into the loo. Embarrassed, but unable to deal with the lumpy intrusion, I interrupted the client's massage and asked him to clear up his own mess. My shame gained epic proportions when, using toilet tissue to lift the offending stool from the tub, he informed me that it was actually a quarter of a chocolate biscuit that had dropped off his side plate during bathing – a distressing experience for us all which I never wanted repeated.

After a chocolate free bath and refreshments, the gent was towelled dry by his masseuse, and whisked off into a softly lit treatment room for a full body massage and hand relief. HR to abbreviate it correctly.

The piece de résistance of a 'Becky's Kittens' massage were the hot steam towels. An idea plagiarised by Wiggy, during his market research, from a massage parlour on the Luton and Dunstable border.

Similar to the small heated serviettes you get given in an Indian restaurant at the end of your curry, I'd developed the idea further and adapted it for inappropriate, X rated usage. Now hidden in each massage room was a microwave oven that zapped large dampened terry nappies, reincarnated as hot steam towels, for thirty seconds at the end of each session.

Gloriously refreshing, the nappies were whipped out of the oven and laid over the naked customer. As they cooled, the girl used them to remove the massage oil, and any other resulting stickiness from the gentleman, leaving his smile as the only evidence of his visit to 'Kittens'.

The clients loved them, and I believe it was these little touches and attention to detail that made us different from the others - made us stand out from the crowd, in a trying not to be noticed type of a way.

Wiggy always used to say, 'I adore the hot steam towels, but I couldn't eat a whole one!'

He thought this was hilariously funny, and would say it every time they came up in conversation. Silly old devil.

Whilst the 'Becky's Kittens' onus ideally was on relaxation and pampering, it quickly became obvious that high jinks and naughtiness were more the norm. Debs and Yasmin, bored with making the effort required for providing a bona-fide massage, messed about and entertained clients in ways I tried to ignore. I was sure they were charging the clients extra and engaging in forbidden fornication. I would sit in the kitchen folding clean laundry, and listen to the rickety squeaking of the massage couch coming from above, which had altogether the wrong rhythm for a relaxing back rub. They of course denied everything, but secret smirks shared with their flushed victims gave the game away.

Not many people I knew were aware that I worked in the sex industry.

People are so quick to judge, but what with looking after two kids, dogs, horses and a massage parlour, I didn't have too much time for chatting with casual acquaintances. I passed the time with the ladies at the stables when I attended to Abi's little pony, and some of the other mums I saw at school. But as a single working mother I was always supposed to be somewhere else ten minutes ago, so I kept myself to myself and got on with it.

It is surprising how adaptable humans are, and how quickly the strangest situations become the norm. When you're surrounded by sex and its machinations all day, it's not long before you become desensitized to it. Soon conversations about spunky towels, ejaculations and men with suspenders under their suits are as normal and casual as discussing the irritating quirks of an office vending machine.

I was becoming quite immune and non-judgemental to all the comings and goings. Even I was shocked however, when a client rang the doorbell one Saturday morning. Just as I went to answer it, through the glass panel I saw that it was Abi's best friend's dad, standing outside shuffling his feet, waiting to be let in.

This chap's wife was a friend of mine. They had no idea how I earned my money, but their daughter was often at my house, and I'd shared many a coffee and a chat with both parents when we waited for our girls to gather belongings at the end of a sleep over. Debs sat at the kitchen table and watched as I sprinted away from the door.

'Bugger, bugger, bugger,' I hissed under my breath as I ran down the hallway, and then back to the door several times, flapping my hands and squeaking at Debs. 'It's Abi's friend's dad...It's Abi's friend's dad!'

The glass panels of the door meant my bizarre sprinting would have been clearly visible from his side as well. He rang the bell again.

'Open the sodding door,' said Debs, 'he may just want to ask you something about the kids. Maybe he thinks this is your office. I'm sure it's perfectly innocent.'

I paused, she could be right.

'Stop with the running, he's going to think you're mental,' she added.

He knocked again.

'Oh damn and bugger.' I said taking a deep breath and letting him in.

An awkward silence followed as we looked at each other.

'I've come for a massage with Yasmin,' he eventually said, grinning. 'Can I see her?' Normal as you like.

Stepping aside I called up to Yasmin who was tidying the massage room after her last visitor, and she came down and took him away.

Lowering myself into the chair opposite Debs, my eyes wide with shock, I said, 'Oh my God I know his wife! This is so wrong.'

'Why?' asked Debs. 'Why's it so wrong? Lots of them have wives. What's the difference?'

'I suppose you're right, I don't know what their marriage is like. I can't judge him if he feels he needs to come in for a massage.' I still wasn't comfortable. 'He's a builder, so maybe he's got a stiff back, and a massage will help loosen it up,' I added, trying to make myself feel better. 'I can't help feeling embarrassed for him and bad for his wife.'

'He's got a stiff something,' said Debs looking upwards as the couch started a rhythmic squeaking. I slumped across the table and groaned.

Twenty minutes later Yasmin dashed into the kitchen to collect some hot steam towels that she'd forgotten at the start of the appointment.

'That poor man,' I said anxiously to her. 'He's my daughter's friend's dad. He must be so embarrassed, and I feel so bad for him, coming here and me opening the door.' I shook my head. 'Poor, poor man.'

'Poor man my arse!' she retorted with an angry snort. 'He's just shagged me twice. Then tried to force me to do annual, and then asked me to come and get you, to see if you want to join in.'

I was mortified.

'Don't feel sorry for him,' she added. 'He's awful. I'll not see him again. What a twat.'

I was strangely upset at my friend's husband's disloyalty to her, and by my own hypocritical double standards, but I was never going to tell tales. As a result of his visit, I now knew for sure that these girls were breaking the bonking ban, and I was going to have to speak to them about it.

I noticed that both Yasmin and Debs seemed to be rushing their clients as well as shagging them. I kept mentioning it, but they always had an excuse why the customer needed to get done and on his way quickly. If the man wanted to go, how could they stop him? But I was seeing a pattern forming and it was worrying me. These guys paid for a forty-five minute service, with an assisted bath, hot towels, cup of tea and a gingernut, and I thought they should get what they paid for.

I wasn't having a problem with Tasha. She had never been very comfortable with the sexual services. She much preferred just providing a massage in the safety of an organised, friendly environment, and was happily just coming in for a few shifts a week. 'Becky's Kittens' was only open from 11.00am until 5.00pm Monday to Saturday, giving us all some time off. Tasha felt she could earn a decent enough living and not feel she was compromising herself. The other two were different, focusing on the money, and their quality of service was getting worse.

The matter came to a head when a punter called back to complain about Debs just five minutes after leaving us.

'I'm not quite sure what just happened to me,' he said. 'I remember sitting on the massage table and taking my shoes and socks off, and the next thing I know I'm back in my car! I wasn't offered a bath, or the steamy towel things or anything. I'm not even sure I've had a massage, it was all so quick.'

He was half joking, but customer satisfaction was one of the reasons I'd opened in the first place, and this was really getting to me.

Debs had another client, and I sat at my reception table in the kitchen and fretted about how I was going to tell my friend that if she couldn't work the way I needed her to then she would have to leave. I was so engrossed in my thinking that I barely heard Debs' booking leave a short while after he arrived. Pulling on her coat she informed me she was going to the shop to buy fags and followed him out.

I flicked the kettle on and shook loose some gingernuts from the packet to nibble. I thought I got the whiff of smoke. Not fag smoke, but a dirty burning smell. We never used the kitchen for cooking, so I assumed it was coming from outside. Not concerned, I proceeded to dunk my gingernuts and contemplate my staffing issues. Suddenly the smell was back, much stronger, and glancing up I saw tendrils of smoke curling around the bottom of the stairs. I leapt from my chair and, spilling tea everywhere, I ran upstairs.

Debs' massage room was on fire. Flames reached up from the microwave consuming the curtains. Running towards the oven, I realised that its turntable was still going round and an over-cooked steam towel was blazing away inside. I yanked the plug out of the wall. Foolishly, in panic, I opened the microwave door and snatched up the unlit corner of the terry nappy. I ran through the house with it and flung it, still aflame, out into the front garden before running back upstairs to soak the room with left over bath water.

The house was now full of smoke and fumes and there was no way we could stay open for the rest of the day. The burning towel on the lawn was attracting the unwanted attention of the neighbours who'd called the fire brigade and Debs wandered back into the chaos unperturbed.

'Ops, sorry,' she said casually. 'I must have put the microwave on for thirty minutes instead of thirty seconds. I've done it a few times before.'

She shrugged her shoulders and lit a fag. 'That man didn't want a hot towel as he had to get back to work quickly and couldn't wait for a full massage, so I must have forgotten it was in there.'

The lies tripped so easily off her tongue.

That was it, I'd had enough. Debs had to go.

CHAPTER THIRTEEN

Life is full of difficult decisions and the one I now faced kept me tossing and turning at night. I either had to let my friend down, asking her to leave 'Becky's Kittens', or go against my businesses ethos and continue allowing her to provide an inferior service. Satisfaction really needs to be guaranteed if you're selling sex of one sort or another. Pissed off patrons wouldn't feel the need to come again if they'd not been helped to cum nicely in the first place. I felt that I'd come so far, I really didn't want all my hard work spunked away to nothing just because Debs would rather copulate than titillate.

Debs had been the catalyst, the reason I'd started an escort agency in the first place. It was helping her that had put me on this bumpy but interesting life path. But because she wasn't competent at massaging hairy backs and rubbing oily willies to orgasm, I was considering sacking her. I felt so disloyal, and it was tearing me apart.

It felt even more disloyal discussing my worries with Tasha. But it had become obvious that she was getting frustrated with our friend's lack of professionalism during the rub and tug sessions. Tash was in the direct firing line of complaining men lying on her treatment couch, and the continuous apologising had upset her enormously. I was less concerned about the grumblers than the ones who were so hacked off by the shoddy service that they never came back at all.

In desperation, I put the kettle on, opened a packet of malted milk biscuits and broached the dreaded subject of Debs' disappointing manhandling with Tasha. I confessed that I thought it may be time to ask our friend to leave.

She listened thoughtfully and then she said. 'Have you considered that Debs might be feeling the same way as you?'

No. I hadn't thought of that.

'It's possible that she'd like stop working here and go off and do her own thing, but is worried about letting you down. You've done so much for us. Maybe she thinks leaving and dropping you in it would be a really shitty thing to do.'

I dunked a biscuit into my tea and let her words sink in.

'Has she talked to you about wanting to go?' I asked, suddenly realising that she must have. 'What does 'doing her own thing' mean?'

'I'm not sure really,' Tasha said.

But I could tell by the way she looked down at her hands, picking at the cow shape on the small square biscuit, that she knew full well. I hated putting her in this position, but we were here now, and I needed to deal with it before we all went mad with frustration.

'She must have said something,' I pressed. 'She's not happy, that's obvious. I know she hates doing the massage and can't really be arsed to stand there for forty-five minutes doing it properly... Debs and Yaz would rather just shag them all and have done with it. Just 10 minutes in and out.' I paused and looked directly across the table at my ally. 'But what's she thinking Tash, I really need to know.'

'I think she may have been talking to Yasmin about setting up a flat on their own,' Tasha finally said, fidgeting uncomfortably. 'You know, doing their own thing.'

I felt like I had been slapped hard.

I couldn't have masked the overwhelming feeling of betrayal very well, because Tasha, clearly embarrassed, stood up abruptly and flapped around re-filling the kettle and wiping down the worktops, keeping her back to the conversation.

'A flat?' I'd wanted her to leave if she wasn't prepared to work properly, but the thought that she and Yasmin had been making plans behind my back and plotting against me was devastating.

'Not opening here.' Tasha said quickly, 'not in Bletchley or Milton Keynes.' She tried desperately to make the situation less distressing. 'They've been offered a flat in Bedford by one of Yaz's regular regulars; they're going to put an ad in the paper and go back to doing full personals, no massage, so not competing with you at all really.'

I was dumbfounded. This didn't sound like a passing thought. This sounded like a plan that had been set in motion, a plan about which I was the last to know - a plan that had been discussed secretly behind my back by my so-called friends. Since when had we been competing with each other?

I needed time to think, to be on my own. I gave up trying to appear nonchalant. Handing the phones to Tasha I ran out of the house and drove away. I drove for a long time in a total daze, and eventually on auto pilot I found myself at the stables.

Caressing Abi's pony's little fluffy ears I started to feel better. Smudge, the little grey fella was so like the pony I had in Devon when I was growing up. Animals are damn good listeners. Smudge had been told plenty of secrets since he'd been brought, half dead and full of worms, from the sales in the New Forest. But today I had a more human confidant. Brian, the owner of the stables, leant on the stable door and listened to my woes. I'd arrived, piggy-eyed, lemon lipped and obviously upset. He'd asked me what was wrong, and after a few moments trying to lie to him I gave up and the truth poured out.

Interested, but not judgemental, he talked to me about the basics of running a business. The way he saw it, running a massage parlour was the same as running a shop, or a livery stables, it had to be about profit.

'No friends in business,' he offered clichés wisely.

I looked glum.

He shrugged his wide shoulders; he was a big man with the worn look that comes from working outdoors year after year, and dealing with hundreds of horsy women.

'I'd like to think we worked as a team Brian, together, like a cooperative.'

'But you're not are you?' he pointed out. 'That lass is planning to leave you, and just bugger off, and it sounds like she may or mayn't been going to tell you.' Giving me a conspiratorial grin he continued, 'You don't want her there, she wants to go, and she's useless, but you've not got the balls to deal with her in case you lose your friend. As soon as feelings get in the way you've got problems - especially with a load of bloody women!' He chuckled, his blue eyes twinkling with humour.

Maybe he was talking sense.

'It's like this place,' he pointed with his thumb across the stretch of fields. 'I like you, but if you don't pay the bills for that little 'osse, I can't keep it here. It's nowt personal, but I have a farm to run. I can't do that by worrying about me friends.'

He paused and looked expectantly at me.

'You're right I suppose,' I grudgingly replied.

'Work has to be work, so you'll need to decide. You doing a job, or just helping out some lady friends? If you're in business then you'll need to toughen up a bit love.' He smiled. 'I'm sure running a bawdy house is much worse than running a farm. I'm glad it's you not me! Bloody lasses, nowt but bother.'

My talk with farmer Brian made me see things more clearly. I knew it was time for me to make a change in my attitude towards 'Becky's Kittens', and to commit myself to running it properly, or give it all up and walk away. In some ways I was guiltily relieved that Debs and Yasmin had decided to move on, as I was becoming more paranoid daily about a police raid. The girls providing full sex on the premises was making getting nicked all the more likely, but driving back, I knew one hundred per cent that I didn't want to give it up.

In hindsight, not just the staff, but the location was totally unsuitable and very indiscreet. Still a bordello novice I had a lot to learn about what makes an ideal working establishment. Up until then we'd just grown organically; things were going well, but we were still incredibly naive. Gentleman callers commented about feeling exposed by my massage parlour location, and I could see their point and that added to my paranoia.

Operating from an overlooked terraced house, half way down a cul de sac in a very close knit residential area was ridiculous. When a prospective client drove by slowly to check the house numbers, then turned around and drove slowly past again, I'd watch out of the window and cringe. Often the curb crawl was repeated several times before the chap decided to park up and walk the walk of shame up the long path and knock on the highly visible front door. An active neighbourhood watch scheme just made everything even more precarious.

With farmer Brian's lecturing still ringing in my ears, I made a sign for the door which read, 'PERFECT PEOPLE RECRUITMENT AGENCY'. I hoped that it would explain to prying eyes the steady stream of male visitors during office hours. Now all I had to do was confront Yasmin and Debs.

It felt like a new beginning for 'Becky's Kittens'. My mind was clear about how I wanted things done so I made it as easy as I could for Debs and Yaz to go their own way. It was awkward, and threatened to damage our friendship for a while, but we got through. People say that life is too short to hold grudges, but I disagree; for most of us lucky ones life is too long. If you could rely on being dead within the next few weeks, it would be worth being pissed off with people who may or may not have let you down. But most of us live for almost a century, and I wasn't planning to spend the next seven decades fretting about what my ex-Kittens were up to. People always have their own agenda, which may or may not fit in with yours. It's our own expectations of people that upsets and disappoints us. I'd learnt to expect the unexpected. Debs, Yasmin and I kissed, hugged and parted as friends.

Short staffed again, my main focus was on recruiting masseuses. Ideally, I needed a different type of person than Debs, someone who thought earning a hundred pounds a day was a lot of money. As an experienced escort, Debs wouldn't get into bed for so little. I needed students, beauticians, or even dare I say it, girls trained in massage. Whilst I was advertising, I considered employing a receptionist so I could have a whole day off now and again. I was feeling very managerial and grand. Mr Pip would be proud of me.

I placed a situation vacant advert, which read 'Help required for Becky's Kittens.' I realised something was very wrong almost as soon as the papers were pushed through the letterboxes. I took a call on the parlour hotline from a very small child, who said she could help me with my kittens after school, what colour where they, and were they fluffy ones?

Totally confused and perturbed by this phone call I felt like a pervert having answered the phone to a minor in my most seductively slutty 'get the punters in' voice. On checking the paper I realised that the *Personal Services* columns are set next to the *Pets* column, and my advert '*Help required for Becky's Kittens*' was appearing adjacent to '*5 beautiful baby hamsters for sale*' and '*8 year old pug seeks new home through no fault of his own*'. When a shaky-voiced senior citizen called for a chat, and kindly offered me the services of her lactating cat, I hurriedly switched on the answer machine and went home to hide.

What I did get the next day was a call from a young girl I named Belinda and her stunning friend Jamie. These new recruits became internet legends, still reminisced about many years later on the Punter forums. Over the next few years these two pesky critters gave me some of the most trouble and the biggest laughs I've ever had.

They were the sauciest, loudest and most outrageous nineteen year olds imaginable. And they were destined to put 'Becky's Kittens' on the massage parlour map.

CHAPTER FOURTEEN

It was Tasha's job to instruct Belinda and Jamie, the dastardly duo, in the finer points of sensual massage. Training involved each girl undressing, lying on the treatment table and pretending to be a punter. Tasha showed them how to stroke, rub and titillate a chap until his tensions were released into a hot steam towel. This tuition wasn't deemed as a success from an educational point of view. Tasha wasn't impressed. However their first victim on whom they were let loose (as a double act for moral support) exited the room grinning from ear to ear and dangerously flushed. I made him a cup of tea, and fed him gingernuts to re-balance his blood sugar whilst I wheedled the story out of him.

Apparently after a brief back rub, which he likened to being pecked half to death by over-sexed ducks, they'd turned him over, and then forgetting him entirely, commenced squirting oil over each other's naked bodies. A Benny Hill style chase around the couch, on which he was lying, marooned, but keenly interested, then degenerated into a hot towel flicking contest. The rules to this game seemed to include shrieking loudly in a girlie way whilst aiming the corner of a flannel at the opponent's bare buttock or nipple to score a win. Since neither of them was overly keen on strenuous exercise, it soon ended with them both collapsed in a giggling heap across the recumbent punter and snogging each other. Not what could be described as a traditional massage appointment, but deemed hugely enjoyable by the viewer.

Belinda and Jamie had been glamour modelling for at least a year before they became Kittens, and were totally relaxed about being naked and adored by the male of the species. Physically polar opposites, they both possessed a natural but naughty sexuality that many men found unforgettable.

Belinda had thick wavy auburn hair, pale skin, and the huge gentle brown eyes of a dairy cow. She was naturally very pretty, only five foot two and a tiny dress size six but she had the most colossally enormous natural bust. So big, that she would teeter around on her impossibly small size three feet, with gravity threatening to tip her forwards, tits first, at any moment. Dressed in clothing tight enough to see her heart beat and killer heels, she managed to never look cheap, just traffic stopping top heavy. Belinda's greatest assets though were her personality and sense of humour. Riotously funny, but warm, kind and considerate, you couldn't help but love her instantly. I adored her, so did the punters.

Jamie was equally stunning, but totally different. She was one of those girls that everyone looked at. Almost sub-consciously there was something about her, a raw knowing sexuality that would draw your eye. Women hated her; men were terrified of her, but couldn't stop themselves becoming transfixed. You could tell just by glancing at her that she'd give you the ride of your life straight to hell. The way she moved, her relaxed arrogance, the husky laugh of contempt that held promises of forbidden adventures and secret lust - tall and willowy, sometimes blonde, sometimes brunette, but always perfect. Her hypnotising azure blue eyes held your gaze and challenged you, dared you to get involved, to take a chance, to make your move. Those who did quickly regretted it. With the mouth of a sailor, and an acidic wit, sharp enough to strip paint from doors, upsetting her would prove emotionally fatal, and she was easily upset. Highly strung and aggressive, Jamie was ready to take offence at everything. She switched from sweet and submissive to a cuttingly sarcastic she-devil in an instant. The sexual pied piper, she led men a merry dance. As Belinda's beautiful accomplice she was perfect and just what I needed.

Shutting the front door behind the girls first over-heated consumer, I walked into the kitchen for a de-brief with Tasha.

'Well,' I said with a wide smile, 'I'd say that was a resounding success. He'll be back. Bet he thought all his birthdays had come at once.'

'I'm surprised they've not killed him off,' she replied slightly tersely as she folded and bagged hot towels.

'You don't like them?' I asked surprised.

'We've gone from one extreme to another,' she snapped. 'Dreary Debs, to Laurel and bloody Hardy. I don't know which is worse.'

'Well I think they're great; maybe just a bit loud. We'll have next door round complaining soon.' Grimacing, I pleaded up the stairs to Belinda who was in the process of submerging the next client in his assisted bath to keep the noise down. Jamie was in her element and ignoring my requests for less volume had thrown the relaxing whale music CD onto the massage room floor and replaced it with clubbing tunes. Whooping excitedly she demonstrated her stripper moves on the landing to her delighted aquatic audience.

Tasha made a tutting sound and continued with the towels. I suddenly realised that maybe she was threatened by the new girls. She'd lost Debs and Yasmin and was probably feeling a bit lost. Belinda and Jamie had only just arrived but already their noise, chaos and personalities dominated the house.

'Hey,' I said smiling at her, 'come on Tash, I need you to help me keep them in order.'

'Damn right you do,' she said, glancing up the stairs, a small smile hovering at the side of her mouth.

She would get used to them. We both would.

Wiggy fell in love with Belinda as soon as he met her, and the feeling was mutual. She spent hours with him, brushing his hair pieces, and putting on his makeup. Belinda had no misgivings about Wiggy flouncing around in Marks and Sparks wearing a dress and fawning over lingerie. He'd spoil her rotten and she'd come back with bags full of goodies and a big smile. Then the pair of them would be out for the evening at Pink Punters, a well-known transgender and gay club, which as luck would have it was just around the corner. Belinda treated Wiggy like one of the girls, which was all he'd ever wanted.

He was more reserved with Jamie. When a situation called for it she was perfectly polite and gracious, but Jamie's main interest was Jamie. Transvestites are also generally slightly self-obsessed and like to be the centre of attention. Wiggy was never going to get what he wanted from Jamie, so Belinda and the new dressing service received his entire focus.

In all fairness to Wiggy, the dressing service was a good idea. He'd gleefully recruited my mum into endless trips around charity shops hunting for wedding dresses in a size twenty and tulle extravaganzas for those who preferred to be 'mother of the bride'. 'Narnia' I'd christened the new tranny arm of 'Becky's

Kittens'. I thought it sounded quaint with a magic wardrobe connotation. Very quickly the bookings started coming in, and it gave me a way to earn a bit more money while I did the phones for the girls. I never seemed to be earning enough money somehow, and there always seemed to be so much to pay out for. Wanting to provide a comfortable environment and complimentary refreshments meant a surprising amount was spent on loo roll, laundry, tea and biscuits.

'Maybe you should just stop eating them all,' Wiggy joked when I complained about the cost of everything. 'I prefer the hot steam towels, but I can't eat a whole one!'

I groaned and threw a spunky flannel at him.

Dressing appointments were generally a few hours in duration, and a lot cheaper than 'the other'. The result was a full transformation of what was previously a gentleman into a glamorous lady. Wiggy had donated his rattiest old nylon weaves, so in the female form, the newly created lovelies could be blonde and bobbed, or slutty and shaggy, with long wild tendrils that needed to be firmly fixed if tantalising hair tossing was to occur.

There's nothing more demoralising to a trainee transvestite, than to see your crowning glory fly off, and into the lap of whom so ever you are performing an erotic dance for. He was also right about the popularity of the wedding fantasy. But try as hard as we could, Belinda and I struggled to get our tattooed and bearded truckers, postmen and civil servants to ever look more than just the brides of Dracula or in most cases, overly-egged dinner ladies.

It was a funny old life. Amidst washing and folding towels, making tea, calming staff and watching for the police, I'd added the joys of stroking the egos of fashion-challenged, gender-confused men and applying make-up to firemen and bricklayers in nuptial attire.

Killing off your cross-dressed customers isn't always ideal, but we came close with Ronnie. A new 'Narnia' prospect, well into his seventies, Ronnie was a very camp, gay, butterball tranny. Wiggy took an instant dislike to him. A social fairy for many years, Ronnie had seen and done it all, so greeted Wiggy's bitchy comments with a snort of distain, and turned his wide back on him, which heightened the tension.

Ignoring a spiteful Wiggy, Ronnie talked us through his fantasy du jour and his wish to be dressed as a baby bird. He wanted to sit in a nest whilst

Belinda, mother hen, was to feed him small sections of curly whirly in the guise of worms from her brightly painted lips. In all my years of watching the discovery channel, I had yet to see a fledgling of any breed sporting a sequined bra and panties with turquoise eye shadow and short ginger syrup. He looked like a badly groomed, startled guinea pig. But what did I know? So with Jamie's fallen angel wings strapped to his back, and a cardboard beak on a bit of elastic, Ronnie proceeded to get himself settled into a rather comfy looking nest of old bedding and feather boas.

Maybe it was his first time as a baby bird, so the problem hadn't previously arisen. Or maybe with all the excitement of being fed chocolate worms it had slipped his mind. But I know for an absolute fact that Ronnie had not, prior to his collapse, informed me of his serious feather allergy. The choking, swelling and asphyxiation was the first I knew about it, and just a little too late to prevent his airways closing up.

Ambulances and paramedics with lights flashing tend to draw attention on small housing estates. The removal on a stretcher of a fifteen stone chick in a disco bikini had them out in their front gardens, arms folded watching the show. As I drove out of the street behind the ambulance, with all eyes following, I had the feeling we had cooked our goose, and our days there were numbered. Luckily for me Ronnie was alive and kicking after some treatment for anaphylactic shock and a large dose of ridicule from Wiggy.

The Dastardly Duo's two girl massage had become the talk of the web and the randy Romeos were forming a queue. The term 'massage' is used here loosely. With Belinda and Jamie it was more akin to watching a cabaret from a treatment couch, and with the selection of items for them to dress up in from the tranny 'Narnia' wardrobe, a booking at 'Becky's Kittens' became more like a lewd adult panto. All we needed was Bobby Davro, and a cow to swap for magic beans and we could have sold tickets. Luckily, we were just about to meet Mr North, who would fill that bovine vacancy perfectly.

Mr North didn't want a relaxingly sensual oily rub, but he did want to get up on the treatment table on all fours. His was a vet in practice fantasy, with him playing the part of the animal, me the vet, and Belinda the nurse. A fur throw was commandeered from my sofa at home; cut and pinned until it covered him snugly like a fluffy hide. I remembered the ears that John from Northampton's lovely wife had created. With coloured cardboard triangles glued on a headband, we made Mr North some splendid cow ears and some matching cardboard horns, stuck to Abi's long hair clips, and we were ready for action. Attaching everything to his person, I stood in front of him, squinting and concentrating, straightening his ears. He knelt patiently like a good bullock, naked under his furry gilet on his hands and knees up on the table.

Belinda and I were totally helpless, howling with laughter, clutching each other and leaning against the walls to prevent us rolling on the floor in hysterics. The humiliation at being laughed at was all part of the thrill for him; he wanted to be 'medically examined' and Belinda would stick an imaginary thermometer up his bum and count to twenty loudly.

Feeling frisky, I carefully made myself a goatee beard from cotton wool, and dug out a white doctor's coat from our dressing up box. A pair of thick rimmed spectacles completed my transformation.

On the day Mr North re-assembled himself onto the table, this time as a sick cat, I waltzed in dressed as Rolf Harris from his Animal Hospital series, a fantasy our client had secretly held for a long time.

'G'day,' I said in my best Aussie accent, 'this little fella crook?'

Holding Mr North's imaginary little feline front paws tight to prevent him jumping down from the examination table and fleeing, Belinda proceeded to rectally take his temperature with a blunt pencil and give him a thorough if slightly rough inspection.

Sadly, Mr North, the fantasy cat didn't make it that time, despite my best resuscitation attempts and Rolf Harris renditions of Tie me Kangaroo down and Jake the Peg to cheer him up, with Belinda on the virtual didgeridoo.

'Poor little critter, dint stand a chance,' Belinda snivelled through mock tears, then laughed so much she peed herself and had to go home for a change of clothes.

I loved being Rolf Harris, although the beard itched. Love the Auzzie artist as I did, it took a gigantic leap of imagination to see him as a middle-aged man's sexual fantasy. I did my best to play the part, but uncontrollable fits of the giggles turned my accent more Indian than Australian. Belinda, the incarnation of Rolf Harris and I alternatively killed or cured Mr North's fantasy critters on a weekly basis until he progressed into puppets and poor old Rolf was usurped by Sooty in this interesting man's affections.

As well as producing cardboard ears and antipodean facial hair, I'd been working jolly hard building a website to deliver 'Becky's Kittens' into the internet age.

At various lulls between punters, I produced sets of images of Belinda exercising, but in her own special way for our new fancy site. Belinda's only regular exercise was the walk between shoe shops, or up to the bar for more Sambuka, and her idea of healthy eating was to sit upright on the sofa to eat her pot noodle rather than lying flat and poking it down her throat with a fork. With no co-ordination or natural athletic ability and her massive mummeries pulling her off the vertical, how I managed to stop laughing long enough to take the photos I'll never know.

The naked star jumps, kickboxing and nude yoga photographs were equally successful on line. None of us had any idea how to correctly perform yoga, but we put an instructional video on the telly and got the camera out ready to capture the hilarity of Belinda's clueless karmic influx and meditative posturing.

Our internet following was growing rapidly, but I had no idea there were websites run by punters for punters. That these sites specifically existed to discuss the merits of various establishments, girls and prices was news to me. We became overrun with enquiries from 'Punternet', the biggest and best of such forums, which seemed to have been discussing us at length.

Call after call would come through saying 'I've read a report on Punternet about your two-girl massage...' I needed to check out this Punternet.

Working life became a maelstrom of excitement as the Gruesome Twosome ricocheted from one bout of emotional boyfriend crisis to another via alcohol poisoning and shoe shopping. They'd forget to turn up for bookings, lose their work keys, cook pot noodles in the hot steam towel ovens whilst performing massages, and upset girls by snogging their boyfriends. They trod make-up into the carpets and provided a constant wall of noise, music and movement. I loved them dearly. They almost drove me to an early grave, but never in my life have I laughed so much or enjoyed each working day, all be it with such trepidation.

Not only did we seem to be building a reputation for role play scenarios, but we started getting phone calls from men who wanted to be maids or slaves. I saw these frequent offers of assistance as the sex industry's version of double glazing tele-marketing. Annoying and pointless, if I wanted a slave, I'd get one for myself.

I always said, 'no thank you, I'm not interested' before I politely hung up.

Wiggy thought I should consider it. He said most houses of ill repute had a slave to do the chores, and he thought one may come in handy for cleaning the trail of crisp packets and fag ends discarded by the frisky kittens. So the next time a potential serf called I asked them to come and see me for a chat and see how we could be of mutual benefit.

A tall, slim, wan-looking chap called Andy arrived, rattling like the ghost of Christmas Past due to a carrier bag of chains he was clutching.

'I'll do all the jobs you don't want to do,' he said happily. 'I don't mind what. I'll lick the toilet clean if you want, or eat from the ashtrays.'

'I don't think that'll be necessary,' I replied, remembering why I'd resisted for so long. 'You can start straight away,' I conceded grudgingly. 'I'm sure we'll find you something to keep you busy.'

I left him for a moment whilst I answered the door to a client. When I walked back into the kitchen Andy had stripped naked, decorated with a leather harness, with his balls tied up behind him with garden string.

As if that wasn't awkward enough he requested that after he'd finished his duties, he was to be restrained for an hour or so with the chains he had in his bag.

I knew I could do with the help that morning as Belinda was off shopping with her mum, so with some reservations I agreed. 'Make sure you keep out of sight,' I warned him. The massage clients found bumping into Wiggy and other men in dresses disturbing enough, so a Gollum looky likey in a cock and ball harness would have them running back to their cars.

The day progressed well enough, although I found trying to keep him hidden a pain in the arse, but after the bathroom was cleaned the conventional way and the tea pots rinsed, I kept my side of the bargain and chained him up tight behind the door in the little room we used for storing the exercise equipment for the photo shoots.

Before I dashed off for the school run, I gave the girls their instructions and asked Belinda who'd now returned from buying shoes to lock up for me.

I phoned Belle later that evening to see how many clients they'd had since I'd left at three pm.

'What time did that slave leave?' I enquired.

'What slave?'

'That lanky lad that Wiggy talked me into having. It was more trouble that it was worth to be honest,' I said. 'I don't think I'll bother again.'

'What lanky lad?'

'The lad that I chained behind the door in the back room, silly arse,' I laughed at her, but I had a really nasty feeling I knew where this was going.

'Eh?'

'Belinda, after lunch today, I chained a man up behind the door in the back room, and you and Jamie were meant to let him go at about half four before you locked up. Don't do this to me.'

'Oh shit,' she said. 'Really? I think Jamie forgot, he must be still there.'

Looking at my watch it was nearly 10.00pm, pitch dark and really cold.

'You're joking?'

'No Becky, seriously. Jamie never reminded me.'

'How the hell can you forget a naked man chained to the back of a door Belinda?'

'Sorry Becks, he never made a sound.'

'He's been gagged with his underpants for Christ's sake, of course he can't shout for help.' The image of a bollock-naked dead man dangling from my massage parlour architrave flashed before my eyes.

'The kids are in bed now Belle, I can't leave them. You'll have to get a cab and go and release him, you've still got the keys?'

'Yes,' she said dubiously. 'But why me?'

'Take Jamie then, but you two left him there; I'm buggered if I'm taking the flack for forgetting him.'

On returning to the dark, silent house they did indeed find poor Andy where I'd left him, suspended and silent. The little star she was, Belinda told him this abandonment was his punishment for such poor quality toilet cleaning, and made him bend over her knee whilst she spanked his bony bottom. The girls then demanded he masturbate himself, then spanked him again for being so filthy and sent him home happy and eagerly looking forward to his next visit.

CHAPTER FIFTEEN

Like young people the world over, Belinda and Jamie were in a constant battle with their parents, a war that I was only too familiar with. Both sets of parents knew that the girls made money from glamour modelling, and that they worked for me as masseuses. Not delighted I dare say, but I'm sure these mums and dads, like mine years ago, had realised that there was no reasoning with their strong willed kids. I'd just turned thirty, and my mum and good friend Mr Pip were still worried sick about me and mithering me to get a proper job. I was still ignoring their advice and treading my own rocky path, so some things never really changed.

This pesky pair were going to do exactly what suited them, and to hell with everyone else. I'd met their families, and at least they knew the girls were safe with me. Legally they were adults, but mentally they were still teens, and as such, would do the opposite of what grown ups told them was good for them. At thirty I was still doing the same, but I'm not sure what my excuse was.

They earned a lot of money in comparison to other kids of nineteen; in fact they earned a lot of money in comparison to most adults of any age. They'd pocket at least five or six hundred quid a week, with the money from each massage, and their tips. I nagged them endlessly to save a percentage into premium bonds, buy a little flat or even poke it in a biscuit tin under the bed. All advice was enthusiastically ignored. I suggested they took driving lessons as they usually spent over a third of their winnings on taxis. But it all fell on deaf ears. Leaving work at five everyday when the 'recruitment consultancy' closed, they jumped into a cab and headed to the pub to fill up with food and alcohol.

The girls always seemed to be surrounded by lots of friends, who had no money, but were happy to be fed and get pissed on the proceeds of the Kittens' hours at work. Out clubbing four or five nights a week with all their hangers on, they'd often arrive for the following shift penniless. Unable to scrape together three quid between them, I'd have to go out and pay the driver.

Jamie did in fact eventually pass her test, bought a car and rented a flat, but Belinda's money just funded several bouts of alcohol poisoning and a million pairs of tiny colourful shoes.

Desperate sex workers trapped in a cycle of abuse and violence is an argument endlessly discussed by those who wish to end the flesh trade. But actually it's money not violence that traps most ladies who work in the adult industries. The cycle of fast bucks for fast fucks, day after day.

But there isn't always more money tomorrow, and that's the problem. Life has a nasty habit of throwing a curve ball when you least expect it. What happens if you get caught, or raided and shut down? What do you do if you meet someone that evening, and fall hopelessly in love?

The Dynamic Duo, like teenagers everywhere, were at the age where they still knew everything, and didn't appreciate my lecturing. I did my best, but in the end I had to let them get on with it. The money in, money out cycle continued. At least they were part of the universal flow of commerce and they kept cabbies, breweries and the makers of pot noodle in business.

After another argument with her mother, Jamie phoned me in angry tears. Her mum had kicked her out of the house with all her belongings, and she had nowhere to stay. Exasperated but not willing to see her out on the streets, I told her to collect the work keys from Belinda, and make herself comfortable on the waiting room sofa for the night if she could.

The following morning, I collected up the fresh laundry, and headed in to work to open up for the day. As I walked down the path towards the house, I noticed something stuck to the front door. Getting nearer, I saw it was a large piece of paper, attached with sellotape, the words 'WE HAVE CALLED THE POLICE' in large, angry, black capital letters.

Oh dear, that wasn't good.

I opened the unlocked door, irritated that the girls had left the place open and noticed more correspondence on the mat. A letter from the neighbour informed me that the previous night's mayhem of countless taxis, shouting, laughing and loud music until 5.00am had been the last straw. They'd notified the authorities. The neighbourhood watch had drawn up a petition, and they were not stopping the crusade until the young ladies and I had left.

Oh dear, that wasn't good either.

All was deathly silent now though. I stood on the door mat listening for signs of life with anger steadily building up inside me. Where the hell were they and what had they done?

Pissed off, I threw the bag of clean washing under the table and marched upstairs to the room we used as a reception for clients, to see if anyone was there, and was going to tell me what on earth was going on.

As I reached the top of the stairs, the stink of booze, fags and stale bodies assailed my nostrils, the 'swish, swish, swish' of a CD stuck endlessly between words was the only sound. All else was perfectly still. Following the smell of sweat, with what was possibly an undertone of aftershave, I opened the waiting room door. In the dim, curtained light it looked like the aftermath of a shipwreck. Countless naked bodies washed up onto the shore. The floor was covered in people. A tangle of arms and legs, it was almost impossible to see where one stopped, and another one started. I could see though, even in my state of shocked fury, that most of them were men - very well built, lithe and lovely young men.

'Oi! What the hell are you lot doing!' I yelled. 'UP! NOW! All of you!'

Very little movement, but I could make out the word 'Shit, shit shit shit...' being repeated very fast from somewhere under the muscle mountain. A crow's nest of blonde matted hair slowly disentangled itself from biceps and bare buttocks. A slightly abashed and totally naked Jamie emerged, attached to the explosion of tresses. She staggered to her feet, whilst trying not to stand on any of her guests. As she stood upright, I gasped in horror. She'd been completely tattooed from head to toe.

'What the hell have you done to yourself?' I squeaked. Fear made my words small and tight.

She looked down at her exposed inked skin, a wry smile forming on her lips, as the memories of last night's adventure were reforming in her hung over mind.

'Oh, the Dream Boys...' swaying slightly, she gestured limply to the troop of recumbent male strippers who slept on peacefully. 'They autographed us... Everywhere.'

'Us?' I looked around knowing full well who 'us' was. 'Where's Belinda?'

Turning slowly, raising one hand to her alcohol-addled head, presumably to stop it rolling off and getting lost on the floor amongst the bronzed body parts, she pointed downwards. 'In there somewhere,' she slurred before she lurched towards the bathroom to throw up.

'Belinda!' I shouted, my anger re-surfacing rapidly, disturbing the Dream Boys from their dreams and into my nightmare. Her head popped up like a meerkat at the sound of her name, and she blinked at me. The boy laying over her rolled off, and she pointed to his early morning erection and giggled.

'Don't worry Becky; I took photos for the website. You'll love them. They're really funny.'

'Funny!' I yelled at her. My sense of humour had been left on the mat where I'd found the note from next door.

'You won't be laughing when the Old Bill get here,' I fumed. 'Get dressed now you stupid arse.' Her pretty face crumpled and she looked like she was about to cry. Yelling at Belinda was a bit like pulling the wings off a butterfly, it didn't make me feel good but I was so angry.

I stormed out of the room and down to the kitchen to put the kettle on. I needed caffeine and lots of it.

The locals must have been keeping watch because they waited until the eight touring 'artistes' had located their g-strings and marker pens and left before they banged on the door mob-handed, followed a moment later by a pasty faced man from the council who had the power to shut us down, and two constables who had the power to throw us in the cells.

'We've received a large number of complaints about noise nuisance at this residence,' the elder of the two officers said, 'and the council have received allegations that you have been running an illegal business from a residential property...'

'A property that does not have commercial planning consent,' the lemon lipped chap butted in.

I stared at the two stern men in uniform, and then at the washed out town hall official who clutched his clip board nervously to his pigeon chest.

'We'd like to come in,' the policeman demanded, and stepped forward through the doorway without waiting to be asked.

I stood back and let them file in past me, and then slammed the door on the smug victorious faces of the locals. I lent heavily against the wall, trying to think of a cunning plan, fast.

In the kitchen, the three representatives of the establishment were staring speechless at the two girls who calmly stood at the kettle, boiling water for pot noodles. They were topless, like native tribes people, in nothing but knickers, with almost every inch of their bare skin covered in words and hieroglyphs. Their nipples were coloured in with eyeliner, and made into the centres of badly drawn, primary school flowers and hearts.

'Good lord!' exclaimed the man from Planning. 'What sort of wicked madness is going on here?'

'They had a sleep-over,' I said defensively. 'No law against that as far as I know.'

'There are laws about running brothels,' the older policeman said, 'and that's what we want to talk to you about.'

The younger of the PC's eyes followed the girls interestedly as they picked up their chicken and mushroom re-hydrated string and went back upstairs.

'Get dressed please; we'll need to speak to you both shortly,' he called after their departing backs.

I wished it had been a couple of rookie Bobbies. Between Belinda and I we would have had them smiling and conciliatory. But the old policeman had seen it all before and was immune to Belle's ample charms.

They looked around the house, went through all the rooms, and checked the girls ID's.

I showed them the couches, and forgetting to mention hand relief or Rolf Harris fetishes, I explained that we just provided a massage service, and no-one offered anything illegal. We didn't even have any mattresses, but they didn't believe me.

'That pair seem to get up to plenty of mischief without a bed, so what does that prove?' the older copper nodded towards the girls. 'From the council surveillance reports, we believe you to be contravening the Immoral Earnings Act, and running an establishment that provides sexual services.'

I could see the girls were getting annoyed at being accused of prostitution. I could see an altercation building in Jamie's eyes. The man from the council kept interrupting my explanations, and wittering on about having the correct planning consent, and paying the right council tax for a business run from a residential address, and that I'd not submitted the relevant paperwork.

Tensions were rising, and I really wanted to punch him, and shove his jobs worth clipboard up his arse. As he railed at me for my blatant disregard for the due processes of local government, I wondered if he made notes and drew pie charts whilst he got a good rogering from behind. I could always spot a punter from a hundred paces. Images came unbidden, of this officious official enjoying the delights of annual with Victoria and her strap-on, and played themselves across the backs of my retina, leading me to let out an involuntary giggle.

That did it. All three stood up to leave, but not in a good, 'we are letting you off with it', sort of a way.

'You have half an hour to pack up and get out,' the officer in charge announced in a tone that broached no argument. 'Or we'll arrest you all under the Immoral Earnings and Indecency Act.'

'But we only do massage,' I protested, even though I knew it was futile. 'How can that be immoral?'

Ignoring me he walked to the door. Glancing back he repeated, 'half an hour.'

The council rogerer followed him out with a smug, satisfied smirk on his face. Jamie saw it too and raised her fist, prepared to wipe it from his lips. I just managed to grab her arm firmly and prevent assault of the mirthless being added to our crimes.

Last out was the young policeman who paused briefly beside us. He shrugged his shoulders and smiled apologetically.

I shut the door on them all and turned to the girls.

What could we pack? We had nowhere to go, and nothing but my car to carry it in, but we had no choice. Gathering together our personal bits and pieces, I phoned Wiggy and asked him to rush to my home for a crisis meeting. Leaving a message on the answering machine, explaining to clients we were closed due to staff holidays, we got ready to walk out. We'd have to just take what we could quickly, and risk coming back under cover of darkness to pack up the rest.

Through the window I could see the group of neighbours still standing in the front garden, and I wondered if we should wait for the police to come back and arrest us, then at least we'd get out safely.

'This is bloody ridiculous,' I said to Belinda. 'It's not as if you've even done anything wrong. What's the harm in giving blokes a backrub? Just because we do it from here rather than a salon in town, everyone thinks you're hookers. Thinks we're all hookers. I bet the beautician woman that owns 'Butterflies' doesn't have to put up with this shit.'

The three of us stood, squashed in the hallway with what we could carry, not wanting to run the gauntlet to the car. My ingrained defiance took over.

'Right, that's it,' I said, gripping my bag tightly. 'Come on girls, let's do it. Heads up. Boobs out.'

Belinda took me at my word and removed her top, freeing her enormous chest.

'Not literally you arse,' I said laughing. Trust Belinda to ease the tension and raise a smile. 'Let's just get out there, and show them we don't care.'

But we did care, of course we cared.

I'd tried so hard to create a respectable if somewhat illegal business. Somewhere fun and safe for the girls and guys, and I'd tried to be discreet and respect my neighbours. I'd never wanted to upset anyone, and in many ways I understood why they didn't want us there - the 'not in my back yard' cliché. I would probably have been the same before I'd started 'Treacle's' and 'Kittens'. My experience had shown me that prostitutes are ordinary ladies like Debs and Tasha who were doing their best to get by and feed their kids. Punters aren't filthy raincoat-wearing perverts who molest children and old ladies; they are normal men. Some widowed, some single, some disabled. Men who found a simple alliance with sex workers helped them through certain stages of their lives.

The people who stood outside and shouted and heckled, shaking their fists like the witch finders of Salem, would believe the media stereo types of prostitution. It was all they had to go on. They'd imagine lurking paedophiles waiting to snatch their babies; the lowering of property prices, and a finger-pointing scandal in the press; drugs and violence; pimps in fur coats and infected needles thrown into front gardens. In reality, Belinda's pot noodle was the most life threatening chemical substance that had ever been on the property. But I wasn't going to stand out there on the path and try to explain that to them. Thanks to the press our entire industry was tarred with the same seedy brush.

I opened the door and stared out at the waiting crowd.

'Thanks for this you two,' I sighed. 'I hope last night with the dancing boys was worth it.'

I stepped out the front door, head held high, to face the music.

CHAPTER SIXTEEN

We'd only moved a little way up the road, the third floor of a very smart block of nearly new flats. We'd fibbed to the letting agency, not mentioning massage parlours at all. I hadn't been quite sure how to broach the subject, and the right moment to tell them I wanted to operate a criminal enterprise from their flat just never seemed to come up.

We settled in quickly, and I was surprised that the clients took the disruption in their stride. They just followed along, not at all bothered by the relocation. It was quite normal in this line of work it seemed; we'd get used to it they said. Lucky the regulars knew more about it than I did. Sadly Tasha didn't make the move with us. She'd decided that the forced eviction was a sign from the ethers that it was time for her to find a new career path.

The gents thought the new flat was far more discreet and luxurious and they much preferred it. The only downside was that sound did seem to travel dreadfully, funnelled and amplified down the central staircase. Entering the front hall four floors down, Belinda's shrill voice could be heard, word for word, teasing Wiggy. You could hear the noise of girls as they laughed and shrieked at something or nothing and thumping music and party anthems reverberated around the walls. If I'd lived below, I'd be out on the landing and banging on our door.

'I can hear you two silly arses from out on the bloody pavement,' was often my first utterance on arrival at the flat after running errands. They didn't take any notice; they probably couldn't hear me anyway over the racket.

On a slow afternoon, when the girls' incessant chatter had given me a migraine, we received a bizarre call from ITV.

'Good afternoon, 'Becky's Kittens'. Can I help?'

'I hope so,' a bright perky voice replied. 'I'm a researcher for ITV and we're making a six week series about prostitutes and wondered if you'd be interested in taking part?'

Just like that.

Apparently, they had spent two years looking for sex workers who were willing to share their personal and working lives in a week by week documentary. It was an almost impossible task. Prostitutes had learned the hard way that it's best to keep a low profile. Despite the media and public interest in them, working girls preferred to remain private and hidden away. It was always wise to avoid the scathing judgements, condemnation and double standards of the general public.

As my Kittens were only providing a massage service we were not quite what the producers wanted. But after an afternoon visit to our new flat, which included tea, cake and transvestites, the director general of ITV decided that our comedy carrying on was too good to miss.

Allowing the cameras into my parlour was a risk. I knew it would potentially upset our gentlemen callers, plus it would flash my name in neon lights in front of the authorities. I was, after all, barely clinging to legality. Ok, I was officially illegal, so I discussed the idea with Jamie and Belinda as ITV was keen for them to feature on the program. We all agreed that it was time to show the world the truth of how we earned a living - that they were just girls doing a job, like everyone else. We would champion the cause, dispel a few myths and misconceptions, and it might just help their modelling careers as well.

My first meeting with the production team was when they visited us to film some test footage to see if my Kittens had the right image for the camera. They came into the flat with all their boxes and tripods and started to set up quietly so as not to disturb the several clients who were enjoying their happy endings.

One of our visitors was a very prominent Member of Parliament who had a thing for Jamie. He seemed to like the saucy younger girls and would insist she attended to him in a school girl outfit. This made her uncomfortable as did his pawing and letching. Once he asked her to call him 'daddy', whilst she masturbated him. Jamie refused, horrified, and walked out of the booking.

On the day ITV arrived he was hiding in one of the rooms fearing for his reputation. I tried to re-assure Mr MP that to be filmed he'd need to have signed all types of permissions and no-one would to try to take sneaky shots of him being wanked with a frisky kitten. But he refused to leave the room at the end of his session, fearing recognition and political ruin. So, bored with trying to pacify him, Jamie left him on the couch and came out to say hello to the TV crew.

The program researchers phoned for a pizza as it was getting late and they'd been with us for hours listening to stories and drinking Earl Grey. After paying the delivery driver, a sound technician came back into the living room.

'You got someone still working?' he said, with a slightly embarrassed grin. 'Only, there's moaning and shouting coming from down the hall. They're either having lots of fun or they're a bit distressed.'

Jamie and I looked at each other. Laughing loudly she jumped up and rushed from the room. I followed her, and realised that a very annoyed Home Counties Minister had been forgotten, and left shut in a tiny room for five hours. Unwilling to call a massage parlour number from his personal mobile, and demand someone walk five steps down the hall to sneak him out, he'd angrily sat on the massage table for the entire afternoon, listening to everyone enjoying themselves. We weren't the only establishment to be graced with his favours, and after that experience he kept a separate unregistered mobile, no doubt subsidised by the taxpayer via his expenses, for the sole purpose of contacting the youngest looking prostitutes he could find for his unhealthy schoolgirl infatuation.

The ITV docu-soap, 'Personal Services', was first aired in 2003 on Wednesday evenings after the big film.

We'd been given some editorial rights - a concession to the others in the programme who were working full time as prostitutes and had to take their families into account. As I'd sat with my kittens months earlier at the ITV studios being fed complimentary sandwiches watching the final edit, it had all looked rather tasteful and wonderful. Sitting on my own at home, watching episode one, I was in a different head space. I was having second thoughts, sadly much too late.

The truth was out. I'd let the cat, well kittens, out of the bag.

I sat, rigid with worry on my sofa, kids asleep in bed, and considered the reactions of my elderly neighbours who were blissfully unaware of my working life. I watched myself on the screen and realised how mental a day at Beckys' Kittens must look to ordinary folk. There I was, on mainstream TV, sniffing spunky towels, and helping a young girl dressed as a saucy waitress, search through a wardrobe for a Rolf Harris beard and a wooden spoon to spank an old man's bottom.

During the ad break the phone rang. Mr Pip was full of criticism. 'Abi is having enough trouble at school with her eye surgery. This isn't going to help is it? Her old dear outed on the telly for running a knocking shop.'

'We just do massage, you know that.' I was defensive but I saw his point.

'I know you just do massage, her school friends won't give a shit. They'll call you a hooker. You know what twelve year old girls are like.'

I hated to admit it but I knew that Mr Pip was right.

After a stressful night full of regrets, the stupidity of confessing on national television to owning a massage parlour was weighing heavily on me as I approached Emilia's school the next morning. I was hoping Emilia's six year old friends would be kinder than Abi's.

I'd considered how appearing on the program might affect my children, but I'd not really appreciated how day to day life may change. Looking at all these mums I wished I had rejected ITV's advances and remained anonymous. In the cold light of day, facing real people, I was scared and feeling like a perverted freak.

I'd been exposed. Well technically I'd exposed myself. What the hell had I been thinking when I'd agreed to do it? Everyone knew about me now.

I'd parked outside the school in the only free space I could find and pulled the cap down over my face, hoping to hide. What was the worst that could happen? It wasn't really me I was worried for. It was Emilia and Abi. I didn't want them to be subjected to a whispering campaign. I knew that if mothers gossiped to their children then their schooldays would be miserable. Now Abi had gone up into secondary school, the bullies were targeting her failing vision and were making her life tough enough already. They would have loved more ammunition. I didn't mind upsetting the police and the men from the council, but other mums, and my daughter's friends - that would be tough.

'Mummy, I don't feel well,' Emilia said looking tense and distressed.

I knew she was picking up my fear and didn't understand what was wrong. 'Mummy's telly program was on last night. You know the one with Belinda in it? I watched it when you were asleep. It was really good, but some of these mummies may have seen me on the telly, and may not have liked it much. I'll come with you into school today.'

She nodded at me reassured, with a six year old's sense of cosmic order. 'I love you Mummy, to the moon and back.'

'I love you too Stinky, come on, let's do it. Don't forget your lunch.'

I opened the car door, and swung my legs out. Then I wished I hadn't. How had I forgotten the pyjamas? Why hadn't I, just this once, bothered to get dressed before the bloody school run? Normally it wasn't a problem as I dropped off my small curly child and watched from the car as she skipped into school. Abi was walking to her school these days, so that was easy; besides if ever I did have to get out, who'd care? I wasn't part of the yummy mummy gang. In fact I didn't know the name of a single school gate parent or guardian and I don't suppose any of them knew me.

Until now...

Resplendent in blue and yellow brushed cotton nightwear, a fluffy pink jacket and unlaced trainers, I clutched a small precious hand in mine and commenced the walk of shame.

It had been a long night and my lumpy kohl eyes were focused hard on the safety and sanctuary of the school gates. I needed to get my daughter into school and then get home to review last night's recording. Maybe watching it again would make me feel better. Maybe it hadn't looked like me, or Milton Keynes. I'd phone Mr Pip again and see what he thought now he'd slept on it. He'd tell me the truth.

A few more steps and Emilia would be in school and safe.

I looked up and realised someone was walking towards me; I tightened my grip around Emilia's fingers and stepped off the pavement. I was tensed and primed, ready for the impending attack. I didn't want my little one to hear the insults that any minute now would be showered down on me.

The woman approached, I tried to keep my eyes averted and my child close to me for her protection. If only I could get her into school first, then I'd come out fighting.

I was already thinking ahead about new schools if the worst came to the worst.

Abi wanted to be home schooled, and that was looking like a bloody good idea. Emilia was happy here, but I wouldn't let her suffer bullying and abuse because of me.

'Hey!' the woman shouted; well-groomed, she wouldn't be seen dead in her jimjams at her front door let alone on the school run. The type of mum who ran a perfect home, baked her own cakes, and kept jars of tadpoles alive until they became frogs, or even newts.

I kept walking.

Reinforcements arrived, two more women, eyes wide with curiosity as they examined me and my sherbet bed wear. I could almost hear their thoughts – 'she doesn't look like a prostitute.'

True. But as the school run didn't inspire me to even get dressed, it was hardly going to inspire me into a full fantasy outfit and thigh boots.

The gate was in sight, but the woman was persistent.

'Hold on,' she shouted louder, 'I just want you to sign this...'

I paused, confused, as a copy of the TV Times was thrust towards me. I looked at her. She nodded, still smiling and wafted Wednesday's viewing guide at me. A photo of me in a skin-tight black cat-suit, bright red lippy and a jaunty smile took up a quarter of the page. Robert Carlyle, British actor, and hero of the working class, was next to me in bright Technicolor promising to show us 'The Full Monty,' in the Wednesday film - just before I started doing my own slightly fuller massage parlour Monty at 10.00pm on ITV.

My busty, glossy image smiled out provocatively at me from an inset box, below a bold headline, 'Viewers' choice - A behind the scenes look at running a British Brothel.'

I guess if you're going to go public, then you might as well do it in style.

'Ah,' I said warily, 'so you watched that then?'

She nodded her head. 'You did make us laugh. We loved that thing with the dildo and that fifty year old lady. Well who'd have thought she'd make money! Hope for me yet I reckon.'

She held the magazine towards me again. 'For my husband, he does love his rubber.'

She was smiling at me, a rueful grin. 'You know what these men are like. Well, you would, wouldn't you?' She passed me a pen, glanced at the pyjamas and then at the picture she was asking me to sign. 'It is you? You were on the TV last night weren't you? You do wear that rubber all in one thing?'

Bemused, I nodded. 'Just not for the school run, it squeaks when I walk.'

The gathering mums laughed and circled around me. I knew I looked dreadful and I was feeling ridiculous.

'My 'ol man told me to ask you for a job!' another lady joked. She was early thirties and pretty in a shell suit sort of way. I was confident I could get her some custom. Her lips smiled, suggesting it was all in jest, but her eyes were shrewd and assessing and I had a feeling I might be getting a call from her later. I began to relax.

In all my panicked expectations for that morning, being asked for a job had not featured at all.

'We've all been talking about it,' someone piped up from the back. I looked over at the other mums and saw them smiling encouragingly at me.

'It was really good. Don't know why people make such a fuss,' someone else added. 'It's the oldest profession. I bet it stops loads of rapes and stuff. Who knows how many more women would get attacked if it wasn't for places like yours.'

I was so surprised by this positive welcome that I didn't bother to point out that rape is widely acknowledged as a power crime, and generally has little to do with sex. The provincial, middle class massage rooms of the Home Counties were not generally the domain of axe murderers and serial rapists.

My daughter ran, half skipping into school, enjoying the attention. Returning to the car I breathed out heavily. I let myself relax, and watched my new friend proudly show her autographed paper like a trophy to the other mums. Was that it? Had I really got away with it so lightly?

I self-consciously reversed my four by four through the gathered throng, and quickly headed home.

I had survived the school run. Surely that was the worst over.

I kicked off my trainers and hung up my pink jacket then caught sight of myself in the mirror over the fireplace. Dear God, I looked shocking. I've always felt if you need to have a tricky confrontation, it's always best to do so in full make-up. Bad enough to have strangers judge you, shout at you for being a prostitute or an abuser of women, but you should at least have the protection of knowing you look good. I would have to be more careful before I left the house in future. No more pyjama runs for me.

It seemed as if the school mums had accepted me but would my appearance on TV have scared off the punters?

Wiggy thought it would be good for business, but I wasn't sure. He'd really wanted to be part of it, but he hadn't dared. We all pretended to him that when he put on a nice skirt and blouse, he was totally transformed into a stunningly attractive twenty year old film starlet. I think truthfully he knew that he just looked like a silly old bloke in a charity shop frock, who'd be instantly recognisable to any of his friends and colleagues from two hundred paces. He had politely but sadly declined the glamorous allure of an on screen appearance.

To be honest, I really hadn't known what to expect when the program aired. Which I suppose was a bit naive. I'd never openly discussed the fact that I owned a massage parlour, or that my staff provided Rolf Harris fantasies and sexual services, however limited, to gents during their lunch hours. I didn't know if the retired couple with the beautiful roses, who lived next door to me, realised that the girls and I dispensed hand jobs and baby wipes from a nice residential block of flats in Bletchley.

I made myself a cup of tea and opened some chocolate digestives and watched the programme again. I'd felt reassured that it really didn't seem that bad. I'd turned off the TV and got dressed in my smelly horse clothes to go and muck out Abi's pony. ITV had also filmed me at the stables; that was in episode four, and would be hard to avoid. I wasn't looking forward to the fallout from that one.

On the way to the farm I stopped for petrol and paid the cashier. When I paused to allow an elderly lady through the automatic doors to the forecourt, I spotted someone I thought I recognised on the cover of Closer magazine on the newspaper racks. Doing a double take I was horrified to see it was me, smiling happily with a huge headline - 'I'm a middle class mum and I sell sex.'

'Oh bloody hells teeth!'

Grabbing a copy I went back to the cashier, who took my payment, and looked at me with an expression of awe. Had he actually winked at me as I turned to leave?

I trembled as I drove away and pulled into the nearest lay-by to read what they'd written about me. *How did this former public school girl end up working in the sex industry?'* There was a bit of waffle about my privileged background, and expensive education, but no mention of tormenting my mother, credit card fraud or crime co-ordination luckily.

I sat in the lay-by and re-read the article. It was written as if I was telling my story, and I sounded a bit daft, but pleasant enough, and not at all sordid. I didn't think my life was sordid or seedy, we all had great fun, and most of my motivation for taking part in the TV series had been to show the viewers just how normal and ordinary being a sex worker can be. Whilst well intentioned, maybe I hadn't thought carefully enough about the consequences of the viewers not agreeing with me. The school run had gone better than I could imagine, but I now had to face the posh horsey gals at the stables. Maybe they would be blissfully unaware. After all I hadn't (yet) appeared in Horse and Hound magazine. It was a flimsy hope, but one I held on to.

As I finished reading, my phone rang. It was a researcher for BBC's, This Morning, and Philip Schofield was inviting me to join him and Fern Britain on the sofa to discuss being a Madam. A chatty lady nattered on about paying expenses and how much fun it would be, and how much she'd enjoyed the programme...

This was all going a bit too fast; I was starting to feel a bit peculiar. I thought I might throw up. Flustered, I agreed to appear, and as she hung up I had another call waiting from Jamie.

'My frigging dad's gone mad,' she shrieked.

Oh bugger. Jamie having a tantrum and bursting into fairy lights was all I needed.

'We were all sat there having breakfast; my dad was reading the paper. Next thing I know, he's spat his cornflakes across the table, and he's chasing me up the frigging stairs.'

'What did he see?' I asked a bit puzzled. The girls had both been confident that their families wouldn't watch the programme.

'In the Mail, there's a photo of you, me and Belle, the one from the TV studio, with the black cat-suit. It says we're prostitutes, you as well, not just us...'

'Oh shit,' I said. I hadn't considered the National's response. 'Jamie...' I wanted to calm her down but she cut me off.

'He knew it was me straight away. He keeps calling me a whore, and won't believe we just do massage. There's no way I'm coming into work with all this going on.'

I lent my head back against the seat, rubbed my eyes and groaned.

'I'll come and speak to him,' I suggested. 'I can try to make him understand you've not done anything wrong, and that you thought being on the programme would help your modelling. Have you heard from Belinda, is she ok?'

'Come round if you wanna wake up dead!' she said dramatically. 'I wish I'd never done it now, it's all gone to shit. Now my dad's bloody shouting again. I bet they kick me out.'

She hung up on me. Great.

I scrolled through my recent calls list and dialled Belinda. As it rang, I leant my arms against the steering wheel, sighed heavily and nervously made patterns with my finger in the dust on the dashboard. It just rang and rang. Twice I tried and twice it clicked through to her giggly voice mail message. The clock blinked 09.50. Not even a media shit storm was going to upset Belinda's sleep before 11.00am. Belinda would be fine if Jamie left her alone.

I'd deliberately outed myself. There was no one else to blame. But like getting married or having a tattoo, it had really seemed like a good idea at the time. Now, not only were Jamie and her dad on the war-path, I had to face the Barbour-clad mummies who would be popping in to feed and groom their fancy horses. Would they look at me and know that I was the same woman who, just the night before, was strapped up in leather bondage gear, brandishing a dildo like a sword. The woman, to whom they smiled or nodded a, 'Good morning,' had been plastered across their TV screens talking about spunky towels and happy endings.

Before I drove to the stables, I pulled back into the garage for a second time in ten minutes to buy a copy of the offending paper that had upset Jamie's dad. I needed to know what I was dealing with. I carefully checked the news rack to see if I was gracing anymore front pages, and then grabbed a Daily Mail. The cashier raised a questioning eyebrow and I just shrugged.

The paper slated us in very descriptive language, and recommended everyone turned off their sets to avoid stupid, banal twittering girls (Jamie and Belinda) and prostitute grannies boring the viewer into a painfully dull death.

I liked it. It was very rude about us but funny and well written. I could see why Jamie's dad had hit the roof. What had I done? Maybe this hadn't been such a good idea after all.

I was not surprised to find myself alone when I first arrived tentatively at the stables. My children spent all their free time with their ponies and their friends; it would be a disaster for them to have to move to somewhere new because everyone was being unpleasant. I pulled my cap down over my eyes for the second time that day; I hoped to pass into the feed store un-noticed.

No such luck.

One after another, horsey, middle-class, ladies swarmed around me. I felt like I was being ambushed. I took the same approach as I had at school and tried to avoid eye contact.

From the edge of my line of vision I saw a lady being nudged forward. Her name was Pam and she was the queen bee of the pony club. I often heard her chatting and caught snippets of gossip. Her husband worked in the city and they lived in the large thatched cottage on the edge of the village. I knew that Pam was not a lady to make an enemy of.

She was tall, a couple of inches above me and I'm no short arse. She had that look that seems to accompany money and breeding. My family had had the money when I was growing up, but I was seriously lacking the breeding. With my mum's tough Welsh background I was more pit pony than racehorse like Pam.

I stood up straight and waited for the abuse to begin.

'That was a damn good show last night,' Pam announced.

I was speechless, still expecting outrage; any second now they would collectively expel me from the stables. I looked around at their faces; they weren't scornful or condescending, but rather curious and friendly.

'Do you charge by the hour? Not that I've ever met a man who could last for an hour,' Pam added, making me wonder if this humorous woman was really the same prude I'd always been cautiously wary of.

I hadn't been ostracised; I'd become the centre of attention and polite interest.

Who'd have thought it?

Chatting all day at the stables had made me late for the afternoon school run, so feeling fabulous, buoyant, and as famous as Victoria Beckham, I speed dialled my mum to ask her to collect Emilia for me. She answered my call immediately, and before I could speak she hissed.

'What the bloody hell have you done? You stupid fool.'

What had I done?

It could have been anything really. No way would my Mum have seen my TV debut. It would have been a library book and bed for her. It had to be something else. Although we had to some degree put the past behind us, I knew I was still a constant source of disappointment to my mother.

'My friends have called me,' she shouted at me down the phone, her voice dripping with disapproval. 'You are, apparently, displayed across the front page of 'Wales Today,' in that hideous black plastic suit thing you insist on wearing, with a headline 'Confessions of a Welsh Sex Queen.''

Mother's scorn poured down the phone. Normally immune after so many years, so cutting was her attack, I thought my poor ears would start to bleed.

'Those poor nuns at the convent; you'll have the Pope and all the Catholics after you next. They've named Brecon Convent in the paper, so I can't even pretend it's not you.'

I hadn't exactly forgotten about my mum and her Welsh Salvationist upbringing, but I hadn't thought it would be an issue. If I considered her at all, I'd decided that she and all her family and friends wouldn't watch the series. So therefore they would have remained in blissful ignorance of how I earned a living. Once again I had failed to anticipate the media's reaction.

I let her rattle on, it was a familiar tirade. When she finally paused for breath, I hung up and sighed again. I seemed to be doing a lot of sighing today.

I knew my mum was fond of Wiggy and Belinda, and I was sure that she'd remember the people, not the tabloid scandal, and forgive me eventually. She normally did.

'Personal Services,' ran for six weeks and the viewers loved it. It quickly became hugely popular, boasting the highest ratings of any late night ITV show to that date. I was labelled a 'female twenty-first century Benny Hill,' by the producers, and headed off to appear on the daytime TV chat shows and be lied about in the tabloids.

The anticipated backlash never really happened. My fears were unfounded. My mum got over it and so did Jamie's dad, and much to my relief she wasn't kicked out of home again. People were mostly amazed and fascinated by the Kittens' antics. Abi was taken out of school and home tutored but not directly because of the program. She'd been struggling for a long time, and I didn't think the quality of education she was getting warranted her being so unhappy. Wiggy offered to help with her lessons if he could teach in a dress, and it seemed the best result all round. Emilia was Emilia, and bounced on regardless.

I joined 'Toastmasters International' and told my tales on the after dinner speaking circuit.

There'd always be the awkward moment, when I pushed my cold, half-eaten dinner away, and stood up from the top table to start my speech. I'd scan the diners, looking for anyone I recognised. Invariably, a gent or two would be studying their napkin avidly ignoring me. At one luncheon engagement I locked eyes with a member of the audience. In a moment of panic I recognised him as a client. He realised their guest was Madam Becky in the same heart stopping second and the colour drained from his face.

A consultant at a nearby hospital, this charming man was very much at the top of his game. He was a very frequent visitor to Kittens, and the girls would pester him about their various aliments. He would patiently put them on the massage couch, prod them, and make reassuring noises suggesting, politely, they went to see their G.P.

I stood clutching my notes, momentarily speechless. He saved the day by removing his beeper from his pocket and waving it apologetically at the other diners, then hastened from the room to deal with his phoney emergency.

Despite the embarrassment he continued to visit us, following us, as so many clients did, as we got moved from one flat to another by the neighbours and the police.

Several years later, he was caressing the breasts of one of his favourite ladies, Laura, when he felt a lump. I'd read the tarot for this girl recently, and huge health issues were foreseen, but she felt fine and laughed it off. But lumps were this man's speciality, and he helped her to arrange a professional visit to him for an urgent diagnosis.

It was bad news. Laura had breast cancer. She had access to the best treatment possible, thanks to our kindly client. But sadly she lost both her breasts, and then finally her life in 2006. She had been a great friend to many of us, clients and girls alike.

None of us were able to attend her funeral as she had kept her working life a secret from her family. But we needed to grieve and say our goodbyes. So we held a small memorial service for her, all the Kittens and several punters shed a few tears together.

The media interest in me continued, and I was booked to appear on the Trisha show. Trisha Goddard was a charming and diplomatic lady. She came into my dressing room before the show to check I was alright.

'Might be a bit rough out there,' she said. 'You could get a fair bit of abuse.'

'I'll be fine,' I said, knowing I would be. I was well past the point of fear or embarrassment. I was happy with who I was and what I did. I wanted to change the public perception of prostitution and welcomed the opportunity to speak out in defence of my girls.

She was right, there was abuse. But it wasn't anything that I couldn't handle. There was some shouting and finger pointing as I sat on the stage and justified selling sex, but I was actually amazed and delighted by the interest shown in the program by other women. I've been surprised over the years by the relative normality of the sex industry and the women who work in it. Despite the public perception, it's not all about heroin, coercion and organised crime.

Trisha looked into the studio audience. 'There are at least forty two thousand visits per day made to sex workers in the UK,' she said. 'All you men in the audience put your hand up if you have ever visited a prostitute.'

No movement.

'Okay,' she said sceptically, 'so what about the ladies. Any of you ever worked as one of the hundred thousand escorts known to be active in the UK?'

Once again, no show of hands.

Trisha looked into the camera in that earnest way she has. 'Well you know it's strange, over four billion pounds are spent by British men on sexual services and pornography every year. That's a lot of men spending a lot of money, and a lot of ladies earning it,' she paused to look around the audience...

'yet no one seems to participate.'

She had a point.

CHAPTER SEVENTEEN

I enjoyed my high profile fifteen minutes of fame, but the down side meant that now I was being recognised a lot locally. When I arrived at the flat at 9.30 every morning, carrying bundles of clean towels, and left at 5.00pm with a pile of dirty towels, people started to get suspicious.

It wasn't easy to keep a low profile in a residential apartment block, especially not with laughing, squealing girls, a full camera crew and various men in frocks wandering around the place. Not to mention up to a dozen gents a day, who irritatingly left their vehicles in resident's parking bays, buzzed up to the wrong flats, and knocked on the wrong doors.

I had a real unease creeping through me, like luck was about to turn its capricious back on me. Everyone else on the staff seemed to be oblivious to my constant paranoia. They carried on noisily as if living off immoral earnings didn't carry a long prison sentence. You'd have thought that having upset the previous neighbours with their heady mixture of disco music, dancing boys and general disrespect, Jamie and Belle would have turned down the volume, but it seemed not. I spent half my time looking over my shoulder for the first sign of more trouble. I could feel it crawling up behind me. My role as a Madam was to keep everyone safe and out of jail, ideally that included me too.

We heard on the grapevine of other flats and parlours being raided, and the threat that we could be next was a constant worry. But the immoral earnings laws are antiquated and confusing. Just giving a chap a cup of sweet tea, a quality biscuit and a massage with no pants on could result in all of us being sent to prison for ages. So I was being extra careful.

When a caller enquired about services, it was mostly me who answered the phone. I would have to stipulate that we didn't provide sex, just a massage with 'tension relief'.

The police were known to be cunning, and would call our number advertised in the personal columns and pretend to be enquiring clients, trying to catch us out with a lewd sexy confession. Bearing in mind that they had just spent six weeks watching exactly what went on behind our closed doors on the telly, it seemed a bit daft for them to keep asking if we provided sex, when everyone else in the UK knew we didn't.

But the constabulary had dirty minds, and I just couldn't convince them. In the end, I'd hang up on them, as I did with all the other time wasters and nuisance callers.

'Old Bill again,' I'd say to the girls and they would roll their eyes and turn back to watching their Donnie Darko DVD.

Clients who asked too many questions in the room, or wouldn't pay up-front were refused our services and asked to leave for fear they may be police or the press. We really did do our best to stay away from the law and out of trouble.

But when a man from Bedford started robbing girls at knife point before beating them senseless, the authorities, local papers, brothels and parlours called a truce, and all worked together to help and support each other and stop him before he killed someone.

It was a strange and scary time. The girls were afraid and the police for once were on our side.

They circulated an emergency contact number to call if we saw him. CID even encouraged working girls to break the existing laws about running brothels, and work together in groups, as this guy was targeting independent girls who worked alone.

Strangely, it is not illegal for a lady to work as a prostitute if she does it alone from her own house. It's a crazy law which puts women and their families at terrible risk, but great for this guy who was attacking several vulnerable women a day.

Fear was fuelling increasingly wild stories and rumours throughout the escort community.

'It's because he can't get it up,' Belinda stated in a knowing manner, 'that's what I heard. My friend Gemma said...'

'Oh yeah like she'd know.' Jamie pulled a face that made it clear what she thought of Gemma. 'I heard he stabbed someone, left them to bleed to death on the carpet.'

'Enough,' I said, shooing them out of the kitchen. 'It's just hearsay; you two of all people know you can't believe anything the police or the newspapers say.'

I shared their worries though. I'd heard my own stories and I knew it must be bad because the police were being so nice and helpful to us all.

But despite the panic and the drama, I don't think any of us really faced the reality that we could be next.

Until he attacked my friend Sharon.

Sharon had worked for me briefly, but she was used to working on her own providing a full service with lots of extras. So she soon got bored with the massage, left me and started seeing her gents in her spare room while her kids were at school.

I went to visit her in hospital a couple of days after she'd been viciously beaten and slashed. She was as comfortable as you can be with eighty stitches in your face and arms. The swelling and bruising made her almost unrecognisable. I was horrified.

'Jesus Shaz,' I put a box of her favourite chocolates down beside her. I wanted to take her hand, but was afraid to hurt her.

'I thought he was a genuine bloke,' she whimpered. 'He was so nice. The first time he came round, he even thanked me.' Tears were streaming down her puffy cheeks.

I handed her a tissue.

'But then he came back. Just a few hours later. I didn't mind...' she wiped her face and winced. She closed her eyes for a few seconds. 'Oh Becky, I liked him, he was attractive and really kind. I can normally tell if they're dodgy. I didn't sense a thing.'

I sat quietly; I gently took her hand and held it while she composed herself. I wanted to know every detail about the bastard, but I would have to be patient, and let her take her time.

'He waited until after...you know...' she kept her eyes closed and spoke in a whisper. 'He asked for the bathroom while I was getting dressed. Then suddenly he charged back into the room and laid into me. Punching and yelling at me to get the money.'

I had to lean in close to hear her as her broken ribs made it a struggle to catch her breath between words. But she wanted to tell me, to tell someone who wouldn't judge her.

'But how could I get the money when he kept hitting me? I was on the floor. I curled up to protect my face, but the bastard just kept hitting.' She paused and took a long, deep breath. 'Then he stopped and I thought 'is it over? Please God let it be over.' But it wasn't. He pulled a knife from his pocket and pushed it in my face.'

'The money, bitch, he kept saying while he was kicking me.'

'Oh honey,' I said, stroking the back of her hand.

'He got my work bin from my room; he tipped it upside down and pulled out all the used condoms. 'Business is good,' he kept saying 'where's the money?'

Sharon opened her eyes and looked at me. I nodded; I knew where the money was. Sharon had been robbed before, several times, so she'd taken to hiding her takings from jobs tucked into the lampshade of the living room's central light fitting hanging from the ceiling.

'I was getting it for him.'

I could picture her standing, terrified on a footstool, as she reached up to get her day's takings from within the folds of the paper shade - struggling to gather the notes with shaking hands, trying not to leave any behind for fear of angering her attacker further.

Sharon tried to lift her arms up to show me the damage, 'but he did this anyway, with his knife, he slashed at me as I was reaching up. Ah Becky, the pain, and blood everywhere. He grabbed the money and took my handbag and my phone.'

'Bastard,' I hissed under my breath. I was struggling to contain my revulsion. What kind of animal was he?

'He even took my car.'

'What?'

'Yeah, he took my keys then left, covered in blood. Just drove off in my Fiesta.'

I learnt a lot about him that day. When I left Sharon I rang the number I'd been given by CID and they filled in a few more details for me. At least then I had facts. Although I think I preferred the rumours. I got the clear impression from the detectives that given his level of violence it would escalate further. Sharon had very nearly been his first murder.

The dressings stained with blood and antiseptic fluids protected the raw gashes and spidery black stitches that ran in a line across both underarms and cheeks where, in two powerful swipes of a blade, as Sharon had lifted her arms to get him her money, he had narrowly missed cutting her throat and ending her life.

Apparently he was tall and muscular with a soft Jamaican accent. And he was smart using an initial visit to check out security and then counting the used condoms in the girl's bins to calculate how much cash should be on the premises.

He'd threaten his victim after he'd beaten her. He told her he had her ID; that he knew where she lived and who she was. If she went to the police, he'd be back in the night to torch her house and kill her and her kids. He'd laughed in Sharon's face and said 'you're just a filthy whore, the cops don't care about you, you're nothing.'

After the attacker had left, with no phone to call for help and terrified she'd bleed to death, Sharon staggered next door to her neighbour who thankfully dialled 999.

My friend would be scarred for her life; even if the physical wounds healed I wasn't sure the emotional ones would.

When Sharon was well enough to be released from hospital we helped her pack up her home and move her family into a rented house. While she was in hospital, the neighbourhood watch, of which she had been a member, started a petition against her. The residents refused to live in the same street as a prostitute, they wanted her gone.

It was a dreadful time, and not surprisingly Belinda and Jamie were terrified just to be at work. I put security procedures in place and told them that they were never to work in the flat alone. I'd recently met Keith, a friend of one of my good mates, and Keith was, to be honest, a lunatic. Not to everyone. I loved him, but Keith had a very over exaggerated and dangerously dysfunctional sense of paranoia and loyalty. You were with him or against him. It was that simple, and Keith adopted me. I keyed his contact numbers into the girls' phones and instructed them to call him immediately if they needed him. Unfortunately I needed to leave them alone for an hour to attend Emilia's school sports day, a promise to her I just wouldn't break.

I'd barely reached the playing fields before I received a hysterical phone call from Belinda.

'He's here. It's him,' she screeched down the phone at me. 'Becky, tell us what to do? Oh my God, oh my God, oh my God! Becky help! Where's Keith? We need Keith.'

'Leave the flat,' I instructed urgently, trying to keep my voice calm and authoritative. 'Get out, and lock the door behind you. I'm on my way. Five minutes. I'll call Keith, he won't be far away.'

I ran frantically through the bemused parents, back to my car. I called Keith to check he'd spoken to the girls, and told him to meet me there. Speeding back to the flat, I rang the mobile number for the officer leading the investigation that Bedford police had given me.

'Come on, come on,' I begged, willing it to answer. 'For pity sake pick up the phone.' I had an image in my head of the crazed attacker smashing his way out of the flat and attacking my girls. I could see them lying in the hallway in their skimpy undies and sexy shoes, oozing blood onto the communal floor.

'Can I help you?' a pleasant sounding lady finally answered the phone.

Her husband, the detective in charge of the case, was walking the dog and left his phone behind. Shit. Bugger. Bloody typical. Never a policeman around when you need one.

'I'll have him ring you the minute he returns,' she promised helpfully.

Thanks, but not helpful enough. It seemed that saving my girls and apprehending the attacker had to be down to me and the ever ready Keith. Luckily he just happened to have a larger friend and there were a couple of baseball bats in his boot.

The three of us dashed into the building and up the stairs, driven by panic and adrenaline, memories of my visit to see Sharon feeding my fear and anger. I was so relieved when I saw my Kittens - they were half naked and shivering in the hallway, but they were safe.

The man had been locked in the flat for nearly fifteen minutes and was extremely aggressive. We could hear him shouting and kicking the front door. The corridor was vibrating from the force of his blows, and the resident from the next door flat was peering out, visibly distressed by the disturbance.

I unlocked the door and ready to rumble, my two terrifyingly large and pissed off lads exploded into the flat to deal with the problem. I followed behind them cursing and shouting to see Keith face smash a large, furious African guy back into the massage room. Screaming death threats and slamming him against the wall, they searched for his knife.

They found nothing. The boys knocked him to the floor face down. Struggling to get up, the man lashed out hard catching Keith on the knee with his fist. Suddenly, there was a massive white flash, a loud crack and what seemed like an explosion. I shrieked and fell backwards against the wall, knocking over the small corner table and sending candles, CD player and baby oil tumbling to the floor. Everything was very eerily still and silent.

'What the hell?'

'Cattle prod!' announced Keith leaping up almost joyfully, beaming with a huge, cheerful Cheshire cat smile and proudly holding up above his head like the Olympic torch what looked like a black baton with two metal prongs.

'Shit! Is he dead?' I was horrified.

'Naw. He'll wake up in a bit, and not know what's hit him. He'll think he's been bitten by a vampire, with two swollen holes in his arse from these little beauties.' He pointed at the metal ends that conducted the electricity.

'He's waking up. Becky, chuck us those stockings and I'll tie the fucker up.

I left them to do the knot tying while I went back outside. I was shaking, and almost as stunned as the man on the floor. I reassured the crying girls then my phone rang; it was Bedford CID finally returning my call.

'Thank God you called,' I panted, still short of breath from the shock. 'It's that bloke that's been attacking girls...'

'It's ok, it's ok. Becky breathe,' he said, interrupting me. 'You ladies can all calm down.'

'But...' I tried to tell him we had the bastard but he just kept talking over me.

'Calm down Becky. The suspect was apprehended this morning in Luton. He tried to rob another flat. We got him. He's safely locked away in one of our cells.' He sounded very pleased with himself.

My blood and my stomach contents flooded towards the floor. I didn't know which I'd do first, pass out or throw up. Slurred shouting could now be heard coming from our hostage, followed by bangs and thuds, the origin of which I had no wish to consider. Now whilst some clients would pay handsomely for what could be sold as a Silence of the Lamb's torture and kidnap experience, the person Keith was still merrily abusing didn't seem to be one of them.

We lost that client, he never did forgive us. I suppose we were lucky he didn't sue for unlawful imprisonment and assault.

We all breathed a collective sigh of relief that it was over and the temporary truce with the authorities ended. It was back to police raids and harassment. Business as usual.

Top left: Piano lessons, ballet and The Pony Club. The Brecon Convent days.

Top right: About 5 years old when I ran away for the first time.

Bottom: Aged 2 and tormenting Matthew.

Matthew aged 17. Looking more ladylike than me in his New Romantic days.

Copyright: Matthew Glamorre by Paul Morgan 1985

Matthew and Gill his friend from his early London adventures. Adam and Eve.

Copyright: Matthew Glamorre and Gill Beckett by Paul Morgan 1987

The Sun: Scrubbers Topless carwash caused a hoo ha in Milton Keynes

The Scrubbers give
the Milton Keynes
concrete cows a
good going over

Copyright Derek
Wales Photography
1992

Scrubbers taking it
easy as usual.

Copyright Derek
Wales Photography

Wales On Sunday: TO THE MADAM BORN
The Newspaper paper article that let my Welsh friends and family
know about my chosen career

Copyright Wales On Sunday

£1.00 6 – 12 September 2003

Closer
to the people making news

ONLY

'I'm a posh mum who sells sex!'

AMAZING REAL LIFE STORY!

BEFORE   AFTER

SH

'I was a middle-class mum – and a madam too'

How did this former public-school girl end up working in the sex industry?

TOSSING HER BLONDE HAIR over her shoulders, Becky Adams called out a cheery hello to her neighbour and strolled up the path to her home.

To the residents of Becky's road in Milton Keynes, she was known as a devoted mother. Her smart clothes and confident walk hinted at a privileged background.

But as she closed the front door behind her, the phone rang – and Becky answered in a seductive drawl very different from the jolly tone she'd used just seconds earlier.

The seemingly respectable mum was now in work mode – and if her neighbours could have seen how she made her living, they would have been stunned.

For Becky was running not one but two prostitution businesses from her home.

And although she handled the punters who rang and asked her to put them in touch with girls with ease, nothing in her upbringing would have prepared her for a career in the sex industry.

Becky, now 36, was brought up in the lap of luxury by her wealthy parents. They lived in a manor house on a sprawling country estate in Wales and pony-mad Becky had wanted for nothing in her childhood.

Becky explains: "Dad was an interior designer and Mum was a business manager. They sent

me to a private school to get a good education. I was always taught the importance of hard work and success."

After she left school, Becky took a job in sales, but found it incredibly dull. She yearned for adventure. Her brother ran nightclubs in London and Becky found herself increasingly drawn to the colourful characters he introduced her to.

Some of the girls talked openly about working as strippers and escorts and Becky was intrigued.

"One afternoon, I was moaning to friends about my boring sales job when one of them joked about me starting my own business in the sex industry," she says.

"They thought nothing of selling their bodies. As the conversation progressed, someone suggested topless car washing. It wouldn't involve actually selling sex, just showing off my body. I thought it sounded like a good idea and decided to give it a go."

Becky approached her new business venture seriously, taking an advanced car valeting course before setting up Scrubbers in 1990.

"I worked with a dozen girls and the idea really caught on," she says. "We charged £80 and received bookings for stag nights and birthdays, often

turning up to offices to clean cars in the car park."

It was while washing cars that one of the girls suggested setting up an escort agency. Becky realised that there was even more money to be made from the idea and decided to give it a go.

'I wound up penniless and in a homeless shelter'

Closer Magazine

The front page image and editorial that gave me a nasty shock in the garage after the ITV Personal Services first episode was shown

Copyright closer magazine

relationship and Robert grew increasingly upset at the way Becky would have to speak to clients on the phone.

She decided to give up work so they could spend more time together, and with Robert's job as an HGV driver, they had just

Becky's first business was a topless car washing company

enough money to live on.

Becky already had a little girl from a previous relationship. Then, in August 1995, she gave birth to a baby daughter. Ironically, it was to signal the start of bad times.

Becky says: "I thought a baby would bring us even closer, but Robert became edgy about commitment and we split up.

"Things went from bad to worse. I wound up penniless. I was on benefits and in homeless accommodation. My comfortable upbringing seemed a lifetime away."

In 1999, though, Robert got back in touch and they started seeing each other again.

"We'd been through so much and still had feelings for each other," Becky says.

"Robert told me he wanted to make a go of it again and that he needed me."

Back on her feet, Becky decided to begin working again. When friends asked her to help with a massage parlour, she leapt at the chance.

So in 2001, Becky found herself answering calls and making bookings for two girls working out of a rented flat in Milton Keynes.

Next came a website, Becky's Kittens, featuring glamour models.

Becky says: "Robert hated the idea of me going on shoots and of other men ogling me. I reassured him it was harmless and took him along one day, which put his mind at rest. He even keeps one of the pictures on his desk at work and proudly shows off to his colleagues."

Two years on, Becky has now given up the massage parlour, although she still contributes to the website.

"I worry about my daughters being tarred with the same brush but I'm careful to shield them," she says. "I've explained my job to my eldest girl, now 15, but the youngest one, eight, doesn't really understand."

At 36 and a mother of two, Becky accepts that she's not exactly typical of the sort of person you would imagine to be working in the sex industry.

She adds: "I'm now edging towards a quieter life and thinking of returning to my roots by becoming a horse-riding tutor. Whatever I do next, though, I can at least say that I've lived my life to the full." ■

By Christine Smith and Felicia Bromfield

● Becky will appear in **Personal Services**, Wednesday, ITV1

Becky with her partner Robert

Becky now works for a glamour models website

By 1993, Becky was running two agencies – one exclusive and one offering a much cheaper service – and business was booming.

Her own love life was also on the up after meeting her boyfriend Robert at a club.

"From the start, I was open about what I did for a living," says Becky. "I didn't feel I had anything to be ashamed of.

"He told me that his previous girlfriends had been staid and sensible, and he was attracted to me because I was so different."

However, it wasn't long before jealousy crept into the

Top Left: Mk News Front page scoop about the charity calendar. 200 papers
were delivered with the image mysteriously cut out.
Copyright MK News

Bottom left: The Sun joining in on the calendar action
Copyright The Sun

Right: The original 'Miss April' Brickhill Playgirls Calendar image
Copyright: Ivan Mears 2004

Outside the Red Lion in Great Brickhill. The Calendar signing dinner from which I'd been banned

Copyright Becky Adams 2004

Cardboard sheriff stars made by Mr Pip and I to preserve my dignity at the calendar signing bun fight.

Copyright Becky Adams 2004

Top left: All in a days work dear… messing about on the furry throw that would become Mr North's little cat costume for his Rolf Harris fantasy.
Copyright Becky Adams 2003

Bottom left: Repairing paintwork at 'Madam Becky's' Bletchley after a police raid.
Copyright Becky Adams 2007

Top Rright: A balloon bikini made for me by Luke. Playing silly buggers in the pole dancing room
Copyright Becky Adams 2006

CHAPTER EIGHTEEN

Skipping forward a few years to the chilly wintery end of 2004, I was heading enthusiastically towards my late thirties. I'd worked hard over the last fifteen years, enlarging my circle of trust, meeting the people I needed to meet, and building a network of associates in high, but mainly low places. Making friends and influencing people is vitally important when you're living at the dangerously shitty end of the stick.

We'd been closed down and moved on countless more times. I could remember at least fifteen different locations up to the early 2000s, but there may well have been many more. Occasionally we were bodily removed from a flat by the police after just a few days, whilst still unpacking the baby oil and gingernuts. These brief property encounters have slipped from my mind, but somehow, in a magical act of furniture moving and strumpet organising we never lost a day's trading, even if we always lost our rental deposits.

Jamie had left us several years before, having got herself engaged, and was now the proud mum of a beautiful little girl. Wiggy was still coming in to dress up, as well as helping me with Abi's education and the dressing service. I'd fallen in and out of love a few times and was enjoying a platonic relationship with my self-defence teacher - a sportingly decent chap called Darren, who'd recently separated from his wife.

Generally, we were a happy and supportive team. Belinda was still numero uno in my affections, but she'd been joined by some great new ladies and things were looking up. Thanks to a property developer friend, I'd taken over the entire top floor of a converted bank in Bletchley which I saw as a very auspicious location. Safe, smart and discreet, with plenty of parking, my new flats were a short thirty second dash from the shops, so Belinda need never be without a Pot Noodle or baby wipes. Smashing.

Under pressure from the new girls who'd joined us, we were now bonking everyone who asked. Offering a full personal service - oral sex, kinky sex, group sex and the good old Madam Becky's annual sex. If you wanted it, someone would generally do it for you for an extra fifty. We still had the original massage couches that had travelled with us to all our various locations but we'd added beds, rubber sheets and strap-ons for the services that required them. I was now fully flouting the law, and totally illegal, but as we kept getting raided and closed down anyway, I thought bugger it, if you can't beat 'em you may as well shag 'em and threw caution and abstinence to the wind.

With so much more now available on the menu, the business required re-branding again. Mr Pip finally gave in to a decade of pressure, and put together a smart, classy new marketing campaign. I dropped the cute, massage only Kitten's image and became the slick looking magenta and black *Madam Becky's Gentlemen's Club*.

He'd given up trying to get me to see the error of my ways, and had now conceded that if I was determined to tread a rocky path to my own damnation, that at least I should do it with a spankingly good corporate image and some of his snazzy advertising.

Mr North, our Rolf Harris fancier, had loyally followed us from pillar to post like so many of our other clients. He'd progressed nicely with his fetishes, thanks to the internet - the devils window, which provided fast and easy access to any bizarre sexual support system that took your fancy. If girls weeing their knickers turned you on, sharing a bowl of vomit, or being sat on by a thirty stone lady, you could find a Yahoo chat room to discuss it in.

When Mr North shared his stories of his Animal Hospital sex scenarios on line with like-minded folk, he discovered that he was in fact into Plushism, the sexual love of plush and soft toys. It was being covered in fur when Belinda and I dressed him as a little creature that turned him on, making him officially a 'Zootaphile' - a person who got a sexual thrill from wearing a furry suit. I tried not to think about leagues of football mascots tossing themselves off inside their unwieldy outfits as they flapped, waddled and lolloped up and down the touchlines watched by unsuspecting crowds. Mr North it seemed was both a pulshophile and a zootaphile - a fact confirmed when he'd put to the test a recommendation from some of his new web chums that he shagged his teddy. Well, to be technically correct in plushist terms, he 'yiffed' his teddy. It went well by all accounts, and Mr North was a yiffing convert.

We found lots of plushists lurking in the on line communities and they were a great source of information to us all, as humping a teddy isn't as easy as you'd think. Mr North was a stout chap, and in an adult relationship with a medium sized bear that kept getting thrust off the side of the bed in the throws of passion. Frustrated at constantly having to reposition Paddington, he asked his new associates for advice and someone suggested he purchased a glove puppet and gave that a good yiff. Eventually, after a few auditions, Mr North employed Sooty and his friends to work with Belinda in his sessions at the all new Madam Becky's.

Belinda kindly did him a weekly episode of Sooty and Sweep complete with squeaker. Luckily Mr North had his own puppet supplies, but we had to get back on line for research, as Belinda was too young to be overly knowledgeable about 1970s children's telly characters. Belinda felt it her professional duty, and hilariously funny, to study Sooty and Sweeps' idiosyncrasies to make sure her client was given a quality servicing.

Mr North occasionally paid an extra fifty for me to join in, as second puppeteer. I would stick my hand up the sour-faced, grumpy Sue Bear's arse, and sit next to them animating a patronising female puppet and saying, 'ooh Mr North, do you call that a penis? That's not a proper penis is it, Sooty?' Ah well, all in a day's work I suppose. I have to admit to being a bit of a furvert myself. I was often to be found stroking my way through the soft toy shelves in shops but was able to use market research for Mr North as my way too convenient excuse.

My work life was wonderfully good fun and the new flats were a resounding success. Home life was trundling along nicely. I'd bought Emilia a tiny pony called Squeak and we'd added Dogbaby, a Bichon cross Jack Russell to the family, and all my spare time was spent at the stables in Great Brickhill.

Inspired by the recent Calendar Girls' film, a colourful gay chap from the village where I kept the kids' ponies, decided to create a similar nude calendar for 2005 using the local horsey ladies to raise money for Cancer Research. Having lost Laura, one of my Kittens, to breast cancer, and another good friend to ovarian cancer a few years before, I was delighted to be involved, and keen to do my bit.

As Miss April I sat artistically naked on a chair and had my photo taken. But when the press discovered I was a Madam and purveyor of prostitutes, the local scandal and outcry resulted in more TV and tabloid hysteria. The Milton Keynes paper which first broke the story had printed the tastefully nude photo of me on the front page of the paper. They received a record number of complaints to the editor, and several hundred papers had been delivered with my photo carefully cut out from the cover, leaving just the story, and a gaping hole.

The paparazzi had been annoying the other liveries, and I'd been drummed out of the village, forcing me to move my horses. Everywhere I looked there seemed to be some scandal about me in the papers.

I'd pack the children into the car and as we drove around Bletchley, builders would wave and toot their horns, people would shout my name, and the kids would say 'what have you done now Mum?'

Often I wouldn't know until someone arrived in work with The Sun or The News of the World and I'd discover that I'd been supposedly spanking the royal family again, or having sex with a spaniel for an extra fifty.

Everyone was gossiping about me and all the fuss and the red tops buying the infamous nuddy chair photo to shock their readers, raised a huge amount of money for cancer research. But it was a bit strange and slightly worrying when I was approached in shops, usually by men, who knew more about me than I did. Worried for my personal safety, not at work, but in my day to day life, I was spending more time with Darren, my self-defence teacher and sometime minder, and it looked like a romance was on the cards.

The charity calendar, 'Miss April's a Madam' hoo ha rumbled on. I was hearing all sorts of fanciful rumours about myself, which seemed to have their roots in the Brickhills. Apparently I had stolen ten thousand pounds from the charity fund, and was spending it on crotchless knickers, wild parties and cocaine. Next I heard that I'd personally beaten someone half to death on their doorstep with their kids watching, but I never found out who or why. The newspapers didn't help with their crazy headlines about my imaginary lurid behaviour.

There's nothing wrong with a bit of scandal or some malicious lies if they sell charity calendars, and it all sounded far more exciting than the truth. The reality was I went to bed at 10.00pm to listen to Today in Parliament on the wireless with a nice cup of tea and a shortbread petticoat tail. That dull morsel wasn't going to raise funds for anything, so I let the gossip mongers peddle their lies, and the money kept coming in.

December was the official calendar launch. A thank you dinner, photo opportunity and group signing was organised at the pub in the heart of Great Brickhill village, the centre of the furore. Twelve months in a year. Twelve ladies on the calendar, but only eleven invitations were sent out. I'd been banned.

Both the local paper and I had been overwhelmed by requests and donations for signed photos and calendars from all across the globe. My photo had raised a fortune to help save the lives of cancer victims but I wasn't allowed to go to the official signing because of the way I made a living - because of people's fear and prejudice towards sex work. The chap who'd worked so hard and produced the calendar was upset and embarrassed about the way the villagers were treating me. As an openly gay man he was used to the locals pointing their hypocritical fingers at him.

'They hate you Becky. They say if you come to the signing then they won't. They'll boycott the evening. It will be all about you they're saying. The press are only interested in Becky bloody Adams...Miss April.'

He was in a really difficult position. 'I want you to come,' he explained. 'That photo of you has boosted the cancer appeal by thousands. I've posted copies of the thing all around the world because of you. It's really not fair. They're all such miserable conservative shits.'

'Maybe I should just come anyway?' I said, the mischief maker inside me willing to rise to the challenge. 'Just turn up and make a nuisance of myself. They can't hate me anymore than they do surely?'

'Maybe you should,' he winked.

I don't think he really thought I would. But never one to back down, that's exactly what I did.

Several hours before the advertised start of the 'Brickhill Playgirls' calendar signing dinner, from which I was still banned, I was at Mr Pip's house carefully cutting out large cardboard stars and covering them with tin foil.

'Do you think they'll stick?' I wondered. 'It's bloody freezing out there.'

Mr Pip was sitting in his expensive, well-appointed home giggling like a fool. The pair of us sticking and gluing like primary school kids and getting very excited about our forth- coming daring do.

'How's that?' Arts and crafts completed, I strode into his kitchen, and flung out my arms, turning slowly in a circle so he could inspect my outfit.

'Bloody marvellous Major!'

'Will it have the desired effect Mr Pip?'

'Yes Major. I do believe it will.'

He always called me Major Banger these days after some long forgotten private joke. He stood up and smiled, delighted at my apparel. 'Come on Major! Let's take some photos, and then we'd better get going.'

He went to find his camera, and I checked myself out in his hall mirror.

It was mid-December, and I was heading out into the freezing night topless apart from a John Wayne hat and the two silver foil Sheriff stars that Mr Pip and I had made earlier, stuck to my 'soon to be' frostbitten nipples. My bottom half was only slightly more obscured by tiny knickers, full length leather riding chaps and cowboy boots. I fluttered my fake eyelashes dramatically at my reflection and prepared to gate crash the charity knees up I'd been banned from.

Photos taken for the album, Mr Pip said, 'right then Major Banger, let's go and find you something big and sturdy to ride!' and off we went into the pitch dark, winter night to commandeer a horse and arrive uninvited, but in style, to the calendar signing dinner.

It was a horrendously foggy, bitterly cold evening just before Christmas, with almost zero visibility. I rode a borrowed two-coloured pony down the steep narrow road towards the pub. It was a surprise attack. A stealth mission so neither I, Mr Pip, or the two photographers from the Sunday Sport who now followed behind on foot had any way to see where we were going.

A car climbed slowly towards us up the hill, its driver carefully navigating his way through the murky gloom. A few feet in front of us, the headlights caught the unexpected shape of a brown and white horse, coming towards the car through the night, then the glint of the silver modesty Sheriff stars on my very obvious bare chest.

I sat my horse, proud and erect. Mr Pip, walking next to me, laughed at the driver's disbelieving face as the emerging hallucination of Wyatt Earp's least dressed deputy came towards him out of the mist.

The car swerved sharply, its front wheel hitting the curb hard.

'Honestly,' tutted Mr Pip. 'You'd think they'd never seen naked cowgirls before in this village.'

'I should change my name to Buffalo Bill. Doc Holliday maybe.'

'I suppose you'll have to be 'Nurse Holliday', being a lady. Well, female.'

'Oooh Matron!' I countered, and we started giggling again as Mr Pip did his best Sid James laugh.

We plodded our way carefully down the road to the bun fight at the OK Corral.

My un-requested calendar signing appearance went like I thought it would. It ended up in fisticuffs. My stars got knocked off leaving me exposed to the elements. When I was eventually chased back outside the pub astride my trusty stead, the landlord turned off all the interior and exterior lights in a bid to prevent the accompanying paps taking more photos of me for their publications. They'd come equipped with camera flashes, so plunging me into darkness didn't stop them. But the thick fog and the blind bend on which the pub was situated was putting the horse in danger, so I posed for a few more shots, and then with us laughing at my wicked wantonness, we all made our way home for a nice cup of tea and a warm up and left the villagers festering in their hatred, to choke on their celebration dinner and make up more stories about me.

CHAPTER NINETEEN

The calendar debacle fizzled out as these things do, although I'm sure many of Brickhill's worthy citizens had been unable to make any plans for the early spring 2005 as they'd torn out the April daily planner and thrown it with me attached onto the fire.

'Madam Becky's' had been uneventful for a few months which made a change. The girls were happy and the clients were still enjoying our laid-back version of comedy prostitution with their tea and biscuits. We could have been busier, but we got by just about.

The only disaster was that Mr North's gimlet-eyed whippet had murdered Sooty one afternoon when left alone in the house with the orange furred object of his master's affection, and jealousy had got the better of the rejected canine. Sue, the whining lady bear had survived with Sweep, but without their muse the two remaining plushies had little sex appeal.

'I've looked on line,' I said after Mr North had tried and failed to have an enjoyable visit with just Belinda, and no 'little friends'. 'The most universally popular stuffed critter in plushidom is that Meeko thing from the Disney Pocahontas film.' Belle and Mr North gawped at me as if I'd gone mental. 'Mattel make Meeko. It's that racoon thingy, and according to those chat rooms you hang out in, some loopy person has devised the 'Meekometer' as a standard unit of measurement to convey relative sizes of bonkable teddies.' I tried not to crack up laughing but it was impossible, as I went on to explain how people who enjoyed sex with toys estimated the size of their lovers by comparing them to a fictional animated rodent. 'For example,' I continued, trying to breathe and speak through my hysterics, 'one Meekometer is five hundred centimetres.' I held my hand from the floor. 'About so high.' Mr North was not looking convinced or aroused at all. 'I'd reckon that Belinda, who is vertically challenged, is about three Meekos tall, and Sooty, God rest his little soul, was about half a Meeko if that.' I thought it was all hilarious but Mr North looked slightly offended that his hobby should be the subject of such mirth. Later, he searched the internet for pictures of Meeko, and confessed to Belinda that the racoon reminded him of a Philippino bride and was really not his thing. To appease her client's grief and frustration Belinda kindly donated a tatty looking but pleasingly silky monkey puppet that we wittily christened Spanky, and put to work as Sooty's X rated understudy.

We'd had a few new clients who were generally wonderful characters and every one of them had a different story. Stanley made Mr North and the newly employed Spanky Monkey seem like easy money. Stuttering Stanley, as he was known by us all, was a delicate, slightly slow-witted man with a speech impediment. He used 'Madam Becky's' as often as he could afford to after diligently saving up his NCP attendant wage. Although married, Stanley's wife seemed totally unaware of his predilection, which was fairly unique.

St-St-St-Stanley had a boxing fetish of sorts. Unable to drive due to a head injury he'd received at work a few years previously, it was necessary to collect him to save him the struggle on the bus with his huge amount of equipment. Swamped by a bag which included boxing gloves, PVC evening wear, shin pads and thigh boots, we clambered, puffing, up the stairs to the flats for an afternoon of Stanley's particular 'Rocky' style of pleasure.

Stanley would layer up. Against his white flaky skin he wore his boxing shorts and vest. Then thigh boots over woollen work socks, and underneath his boxing gloves, he pulled on his long PVC evening gloves, which elegantly reached to the elbow. Tightly, over the top of his boxing shorts and vest, as layer two, he tugged a glamorous evening gown also in PVC to contrast with his other boxing ring regalia.

PVC clothing and boxing gloves as separate items can get very whiffy, but worn together, the result was a dreadful nasal assault. Clouds of odour wafted from the empty mildewed gym bag, and the girls would drag it into the en-suite, and saturate it with air freshener before pulling the door tightly shut, in a bid to keep the nasty niffs in their work room to a minimum. The quickly sweaty and stinky St-St-St-Stanley proceeded to do twenty star jumps and some deep knee bends as a warm up. His ankles would twist dangerously in his six inch heels, as he got his blood pumping for his first three minute round with the lady who had drawn the short straw.

Not that we didn't like Stanley, he was sweet. But a booking with him was hard work, and not altogether easy on the senses. Luckily for everyone Darren, my new admirer, taught boxing, along with his other strange techniques to disable and disarm an opponent in the shortest possible time. Happily for Stanley, Darren's students included my girls.

Stanley particularly enjoyed being punched in the head. Something I wouldn't allow as I was sure it wasn't a healthy pastime for someone who had suffered a life threatening brain injury. The girls were instructed to be very very careful.

Stanley would fight like a true warrior for several frantic minutes. His PVC frock restricted his movement and his kinky boots made him stagger. But he always gave it his best shot, jabbing and upper cutting as if his life depended on it.

Sometimes I would stand outside the room in the hallway, lean towards the door and listen. I would hear him panting and shouting. 'Yo, Adrian! It's me, Rocky,' in his best Balboa drawl. 'Yo, Adrian, we did it.' I'd smile to myself and wonder why he didn't stutter when he was being Sylvester Stallone. I'd leave them to it, knowing Stuttering Stanley couldn't take too much excitement. Usually after five minutes of the action beginning, he had a tendency to collapse diagonally across the bed.

He would just freeze in the middle of a right hook and fall on the bed fast asleep. If the poor girl moved, or tried to escape back to the kitchen for a cup of tea, St-St-St-Stanley would wake up instantly, and the cycle would begin all over again for up to six hours at a time.

I had to charge him the going rate as the girls couldn't do anything while he slept. It was a strange booking for them. Whenever Stanley called to make an appointment, many of the girls suffered sudden headaches or received urgent calls from child-minders and were forced to rush off home as fast as they could.

So it was a mixed blessing then, when Stanley was eventually awarded a very large sum in compensation for his accident and resulting disability, and he set out to spend it all boxing with prostitutes.

Stanley's session was well-paid, but exhausting and always extremely smelly. Now he had so much money, it seemed to go on forever. Sometimes it would be all day, every day for a week. He never asked for anything explicitly sexual, so I assumed that he replayed the session in his head once back home and got whatever satisfaction he needed then.

Who knows, but I did know Stanley was in danger of spending all of his money very quickly. We were worried about him, so I tried to tell him that he should be a bit more restrained in the number of times he visited. Pace himself, save his money. What would he do when in the months to come he felt the urge but had run out of funds?

Tipping his head to one side, Stanley looked me square in the eye and in an American accent said '*I think we make a real sharp couple of coconuts - I'm dumb, you're shy, whaddaya think, huh?*'

'Pardon?' I said, totally confused.

'Rocky, 1976.'

'Oh, ok.' I wasn't getting through to him. 'But I am serious Stanley. You do need to think ahead a bit, and save your money.'

He looked at me, and almost word perfect, in a passable impression of his idol, Rocky Balboa, without the hint of the crippling stammer, he quoted, '*Let me tell you something you already know. The world ain't all sunshine and rainbows. It is a very mean and nasty place and it will beat you to your knees and keep you there permanently if you let it. You gotta be willing to take the hit, and not pointing fingers saying you ain't where you are because of him, or her, or anybody. Cowards do that and that ain't me. I'm better than that.*'

He paused for breath then continued, 'Rocky to his son in 2006, but I ch-ch-changed it a b-b-b-bit. I l-l-l-love Rocky.'

Good lord! I gave up. Best mind my own business then.

Darren took Stanley home. Now officially my boyfriend, Darren was a huge Stallone fan, and knew all the Rocky films word for word. So he and Stanley were kindred spirits, spending the drive back to Stanley's house sharing dialogue and squabbling over the best sequel.

Darren was a kind, thoughtful man, so allowed Stanley to win the debate and always have the last word.

The girls had finished for the evening and gone home when Darren returned from delivering Stanley, but Wiggy was still at the flat. He was carefully taking off the last traces of his lipstick so his wife wouldn't notice even the smallest amount of rose pink gloss in the creases of his dry mouth.

Darren had only been into the flat on a few occasions, as the girls' nudity made him feel awkward. He wasn't a ladies' man, more of a man's man - football, fighting and politics. His long career in the masculine, egocentric world of Post Office Unions and industrial relations hadn't prepared him for chattering girls in camisoles and their endless stream of banal banter, so he kept his distance.

Darren, Wiggy and I sat at the kitchen table waiting for the kettle to boil. The flat was wonderfully quiet and peaceful without the staff. Wiggy scrutinised his face in Belinda's small mirror, while Darren picked at the tufty bits in Spanky Monkey's fur.

'You don't want to do that really.'

Darren looked up at me.

'Mess about with Spanky,' I continued, nodding towards his fingers plucking at the toy, but he wasn't getting the message. 'That sticky stuff under the monkey's chin,' I pointed, 'it's not where his ice-cream's melted. That's where Mr North, his owner, has been, how can I put it? Been *loving him*.'

Darren shrieked like a teenage girl who'd just stood on a rat and hurled poor Spanky across the kitchen, leaping up to wash his hands, groaning.

Laughing, I picked up the abused plush, and placed him gently in the washing machine for a de-spunk and a freshen up. 'It's called Yipping, or Yiffing, I can never remember which, shagging your toys.'

Darren still looked horrified.

'You'll get used to it if you hang out here long enough,' I said, sitting back down. 'It's all in a day's work here you know.'

The three of us sat and shared a convivial tray of tea and a nice Victoria sponge as Wiggy talked Darren through his need for cross dressing and proudly showed my bemused boyfriend photos I'd taken of him as a slut and a bride.

Someone knocked on the door, and bemoaning the tardiness of punters I got up from the tea table and went to answer it.

It was the police and the Inland Revenge who arrested me instantly and dragged me away, still with crumbs on my chin, whilst I complained bitterly of injustice and inconvenience as I'd only half finished my slice of cake.

Across a desk in a sweaty room I was handed a folder of my press cuttings.

The tax inspector wanted to know where the money was. If, as the papers had stated, I was providing the royal family with domination services and spanking the bottoms of regal princes then I must be earning millions and hiding my loot. The News of the World had printed a story cleverly headlined 'Whores and Hounds', which exposed my organising orgies in stately homes, surely substantially adding to the stash I was avoiding paying tax on.

I did have an accountant who submitted my end of year accounts in exchange coincidentally for bum smacking, so as far as I was concerned my dues had been paid.

'Anyway,' I protested, 'how come as I'm running an illegal business I have to pay tax at all? Shouldn't I be exempt?'

'Tax is a civil matter, not a criminal matter,' the inspector informed me, 'so the exchequer will want to collect on all the profits.'

'So if I was mugging old ladies or nicking tellys, I'd have to pay tax on that as well?'

'That is correct Miss Adams.'

'Drug dealers?'

'Even drug dealers, and we will investigate them if we catch them.' It had all got very Al Capone.

'How come you're just focused on me then? Milton Keynes is full of villains.'

'It's impossible to miss you these days Miss Adams. You've foolishly brought yourself to our attention, and questions have been asked. I am planning to find all the answers.'

I was surprised that a professional organisation was using over-egged media gossip as evidence for arrest, and I explained to my accusers that the tabloids weren't always entirely honest, and that it was, in my opinion, somewhat naive of the Inland Revenge to rely on the Sunday Sport strap line as proof of earnings. The only royalty I'd been near were drag queens, but the man in the suit seemed quite determined. Darren was asked to rummage through the kitchen drawers at the flat, which doubled as my filing system and bring in bits of crumpled paperwork that would hopefully prove I was pretty much skint.

Eventually, after many hours of debate, they let me go with the threat that they'd be keeping a very close eye on me from then on.

CHAPTER TWENTY

I was lucky to have Darren who was a strong steady chap, with very little interest in half-naked girls and baby oil - the best sort of boyfriend to have in my circumstances. So when, a few days after my interrogation by the Inland Revenge, a lady called and asked if 'Madam Becky's' needed a receptionist, I asked her to come in for a chat thinking it would nice if I could employ someone sensible to leave in charge whilst I took my new fella away for a few days.

Diana, the lady I interviewed as a receptionist was South African, well over six feet tall and almost circular. She told me she'd been managing a smart, very successful brothel in Bournemouth for the past so many years. She cast her judgemental eye over 'Madam Becky's' and found us all sadly wanting. I ran through the basic operation and then wished that I hadn't.

'Close at six uh?' she asked incredulously in a thick Afrikaans accent. 'Eeeish! Then you miss all the night customers? Shame uh?'

I stared into her piggy eyes. I wasn't sure what colour they were beneath the heavy lids. She really was seriously fat.

She stared at me like I really was very stupid and tutted loudly. I really should have sent her packing. But for some unfathomable reason I didn't.

She shook her head, an action that set the multiple chins off in a jelly like wobble. 'So, you are telling me you close at six in the evening uh?'

I nodded and apologised for having family to attend to.

She cut me off and started a tirade. Why were we not open through the night like her previous establishment? Why did we not have TV's and porn in all the rooms? Why do we not do out-calls and party-orgy bookings? Where are the contracts and the paperwork?

'And look at these girls. Shame uh?' she added, pointing a fat finger at Belinda, who stopped combing Spanky Monkey's matted fur and stared at her. 'How do you sell these girls to men uh?' she demanded to know. 'Eeeish. They play with toys like children. And where are their stockings uh?'

I glanced at Belinda and she pulled a face quickly before Diana's glare refocused on her.

'You need to brush your hair girl, never mind that monkey and look, she has a broken nail. Shame uh?'

The attack went on and on.

Belinda sat Spanky gently on the kitchen worktop and left the room. I almost got up and followed her out. But something made me sit still and listen while the whale of a woman tore my business to shreds.

'Eeeish. That girl should be fined or sacked for looking like that. Don't you know how much money you're losing uh?'

Her slitty little eyes moved from the recumbent monkey to me. 'Ja, are you stupid uh?' she rudely asked.

Was I? I'd never thought so. Daft maybe, and slightly quirky but not stupid. But as I sat and took the verbal beating the penny dropped.

She was right. The horrible harridan was right.

We may be infamous locally, and invited to all the best parties. But truthfully, as a profit making operation we were rubbish.

'My last place in Bournemouth uh, would earn ten thousand British pounds for a weekend's trade.'

I nearly spat my tea at her. 'Ten grand takings?'

'No, not takings, profit for the house after the girls have been paid uh,' she said, folding her arms across her enormous chest, satisfied that she had my proper attention.

I would have died of shock if we took just one grand in total. Yet she was telling me that I could be clearing ten times that as house profit. She must have seen the doubt and disbelief on my face.

'One hundred to one hundred and twenty clients a day uh,' she added, nodding to herself.

What? She had to be kidding. That was impossible. I began to wonder why she'd left such a successful place and why she'd turned up at my door. Dear god alive. But now I understood why the Inland Revenge pestered me, convinced I'd hidden countless bundles of twenties under the floorboards. I'd thought numbers at 'Madam Becky's' were the massage parlour norm; our record to date was twelve gents in one day. That caused a serious towel shortage and Belinda to have a nose bleed.

If Diana was for real then I couldn't afford to let my dislike of the woman dictate my actions.

Wiggy arrived half way through Diana's guided tour of the flat. She had a derogatory comment about everything from the beds to the decor. Wiggy proceeded to have his make-up applied by Belinda who was still offended from her dressing down, then squeezed himself into a leather mini dress. He had a cross dressing competitor, Barry, arriving that afternoon, and wanted to be on top form. Even so, I knew he was half listening to Diana's contemptuous commentary. I was interested to hear his opinions, but they'd have to wait as Barry was ringing the bell.

Wiggy and Barry sauntered into the kitchen, their heels clacking on the floor, to show us how fine they looked. Wiggy was sporting silver buckled thigh boots to complete the mini dress ensemble, and closely resembled Dick Whittington. I watched a sneer cross Diana's face as she looked them up and down, like a playground bully. I could almost see the unkind taunts forming in her mouth, but she stayed silent. As they walked out with a tray of tea, she shook her head and laughed.

'Eeeish. Two old queers uh? How much do you take from them?'

'They're not queers,' I snapped back protectively. 'One lady is a close personal friend, a guest, more part of the furniture to be honest; the other taller lady pays about thirty pounds for the hour, but we don't rush her.'

She shook her head in disbelief. 'You could be making a fortune here, it's perfect uh, what's stopping you? You too lazy uh?'

'We've always done ok. It's about the girls really, not the money.' I was defensive and upset at her attitude to Wiggy. He was my friend, the 'Madam Becky's' mascot.

'Ok, so where's the paperwork and safes uh?' she asked, dismissing my defence of my cross dressed chum.

'Well, we don't really bother with paperwork,' I said. 'The girls remember what they've done, and we poke the money in an envelope in this drawer.'

She shook her head again and threw in a tut or two. She came straight to the point.

'You give me a month uh to turn this place around. You pay me the minimum wage and commission on the jobs uh? If I can't earn us both money in a month then it's a shame uh I'll leave. You've got nothing to lose.'

I thought about it. She was really grim, and very mean, but she was right, I had nothing to lose. I wanted to talk it over with Darren. He'd had years managing in the upper echelons of Royal Mail before following his heart and becoming a self-defence instructor. I valued his calm, sensible opinion. I also wanted to talk to Wiggy, and see if he had felt the bad vibes that she'd sent him.

'It sounds great,' I said with a fake smile. 'But I have to get ready to pick up Stanley, a disabled client, now for his appointment, so can we talk again tomorrow?'

The ugly head nodded agreement, and several chins and jowls collided. I showed her to the door and wondered how she had the gall to criticise Wiggy and Barry for looking dreadful.

Wiggy hadn't noticed how unpleasant she was, as being more beautiful than Barry had been his main focus, but he'd not been able to miss her considerable girth.

'She should offer a face sitting service, she's got to be a hundred stone or more,' he said grimacing.

'Be sensible please Wiggy. I'm confused, and I need your advice.'

'I am, she should. She'd make a fortune. Big girl like that.'

'It's not important for everyone to like you if you're doing your job properly,' Darren said having arrived just as I'd returned with Stanley. At least he was paying attention. 'A manager isn't there to make friends, they're there to manage, and you'll always find people who are unhappy when you implement a new system. People hate change; it's just how it is in any work place.'

I nodded. 'I've been thinking so much lately about the risks from the police and the Inland Revenge. Truth is, running 'Madam Becky's' the way I'm running it, it's just not worth the risk. I'm making almost nothing but the Old Bill and the tax inspectors are after me. I need to decide if I'm prepared to go for it, and make more money, or close down completely and get a proper job.'

Wiggy raised an eyebrow. 'Proper job? You? Like what exactly?'

I had no idea what I would do if I closed 'Madam Becky's'. I was very tempted by the big bucks that Diana had bragged to me were possible by re-organising my brothel properly.

'If I see Diana again tomorrow, will you meet her, and tell me what you think?' I asked Darren. 'She's really scary, and it makes no sense to me why she left Bournemouth. Something's fishy.'

'Fishy top and bottom that one,' Wiggy joked. 'If it's fishy down below, would she charge extra to sit on your face? Is fishy an extra fifty thing, or a bad thing?'

'Wiggy! Please! Be sensible, this is important.'

He laughed at his own humour, and apologised that he couldn't make it tomorrow.

Darren was free, and he agreed to meet the monster with me. Leaving Belinda to answer the phones and one of the other girls to erotically punch Stanley in the face, I went home.

I needed to go to bed and sleep on it. This was a huge decision to make, but I had no idea just how disastrously huge it would end up being for us all.

Darren and I had a long chat and I decided to employ Diana the Devil Woman, and implement her ideas. I'd give her a month to see if she could make a difference to the income, and take it from there. I was prepared to consider the changes she deemed essential. Darren, a compiler of lists and lover of forms was in his element.

He sat at the table discussing paperwork and statistics with Diana the next day, the smile on his face showing that he'd found his true calling. He nodded sagely to the incredible hulk and began a mantra of, 'If you can't measure it, you can't manage it.' - his decades of post office management training coming in useful at last.

Darren and Diana Devil Woman headed off together down the hallway to decide which of my rooms they were going to commandeer and turn into their office.

I wasn't so happy. It became clear to me, watching, as the two of them discussed what needed to change, that I wasn't as clever as I thought I was. Although always a good hostess who could be relied upon to provide for everyone else, it seemed that I was not a natural business person.

Mr Pip was always saying he could see my potential, but I couldn't.

I struggled with the organisational aspects, and I wasn't meticulous with the daily facts and figures. A creative person, I was easily bored with the small details like income and expenditure. In some ways it seemed pointless to try too hard when you were continually being closed down and moved on.

If I was honest with myself, I really needed help from Darren and Diana to take 'Madam Becky's' forward, and part of me loved the idea of facing up to the challenge. My gut and my heart told me she was trouble.

Everything was changing.

Large safes were purchased to hold all the money Diana promised me would be flooding in. They were screwed into place in the kitchen, which after a decision about not wanting to lose a working room, was now officially the office, security station and bastion of the reams of paperwork she and Darren were inventing. No client was allowed to step foot into Diana's organisational hub on pain of death.

The wobbly kitchen table had been promoted. It was no longer a friendly mantel over which, aided by gallons of tea, working girls could trade tears, laughter and secrets. It was the nucleus of the 'Madam Becky' expanding empire according to Diana, and as such must not be approached by anyone other than management.

She would have banned the girls from the kitchen altogether if she could. But then she'd have to prepare the tea trays and fill out the forms herself, so she conceded, and allowed them in, begrudgingly, watching their every move.

We were busier weekly. The graphs proved it. But the money still went one way, and that was the wrong way, into new furniture, bedding, TVs, porn and printing all the bloody forms we filled in.

Mr Pip was once again required to use his marketing skills. Eye-catching and very expensive full colour adverts went into all the papers. He was still disapproving, but was pleased we were being more professional.

'If you can't measure it you can't manage it'. And, 'you have to speculate to accumulate', were phrases that were quoted at me all day everyday by Diana and Darren. I did my best to appear interested in tick boxes and spread sheets, but it wasn't easy, and it didn't come naturally.

As the efficiency rose, the laughter declined, until it was noticeable in its absence. The girls were used to the old laid-back ways of doing things and were getting very unhappy. Muttering and grumbling could be heard around every corner as the girls voiced their dissent about the new rules and regulations. The fact that they were earning more didn't seem to matter to them; I'd heard rumours that a few of them were planning to leave.

Wiggy stopped coming to see us as much. He had been told off by Diana once too often for leaving his stockings on the floor and messing up the massage room.

Feeling a bit low myself I picked up the phone and rang him. I missed our tea and chats.

'Just not the same anymore Becky,' he said, telling me what I already knew.

'We couldn't carry on as we were,' I replied, trying to justify the situation.

'You have to do what's best for you Becky. But I'm not paying to get shouted at and humiliated. That's not my thing.'

'I'll have a word with her. Come in and see me, we'll get glammed up and go for a night out in Pink Punters together.'

I heard him sigh, 'sorry Becky, I'm just not up for it.'

'Oh Wiggy...'

'That dreadful woman's done me a big favour. I think she's cured me of cross dressing and hanging out in brothels.'

I put the phone down with an overwhelming sense of sadness. Diane was costing me on so many levels. But I really had reached a crossroads. I couldn't have continued indefinitely as I was. I had a reputation and a client base that was the envy of every Madam and pimp in the area, and probably beyond. But I was permanently broke. Everyone made money but me. If it went wrong, I'd be the one banged up in the ol' pokey for years. I owed it to myself and to my family to make the business work, or walk away.

Diana had the answers. I didn't. I might not like it but I had to live with it.

At least, for the first time ever, the location of the flats wasn't causing me problems.

Migrant workers of various nationalities lived underneath us; they were busy when we were busy, and didn't seem to be bothered by us at other times. We noticed our Thai and Oriental neighbours seemed to have their fair share of white, western gentleman callers, and I kept an eye out for John from Northampton sneaking in to have some fun. It was an easy and peaceful co-existence, a case of live and let live that worked for us all. For once in my life I wasn't going to be bothered by the locals, and that felt good.

Diana inevitably got her way, and we opened twenty four hours a day, seven long days a week. That was a whole different ball game, and took some getting used to. It's obvious if you think about it, that escort agencies would be busier at night. But what I had never expected was that the busiest times would be from one to five in the morning. Of course Diana knew. It was exactly what she had expected.

The flats were in a perfect location for being open twenty four seven, with a private staircase that was easily secured. It was brothel heaven, and Diana was right, we needed to make the most of it. Security still worried me; I didn't like the thought of the girls having to work through the night.

'What if someone turns nasty? I don't like it, it's not safe.'

Diane tutted.

The three of us were in the kitchen. Her bulk made the room seem small, cramped and hostile.

Darren gave me an encouraging smile. 'Any trouble and I can be here in five minutes.'

It was true. Since separating from his wife, Darren lived with his friend just a few minutes away, and would be on call if a problem arose.

'You get more drivers. No problem uh?' Diana said, speaking down to me like I was a child with learning difficulties. 'We start doing out-calls. Between bookings the drivers can stay in the flat.'

'They'll act as a deterrent for anyone who wants to start any trouble during a visit,' Darren added.

I still wasn't convinced but felt outnumbered. They seemed to have it covered and my opinion was surplus to requirements. The pair seemed to have struck up an alliance and I felt pushed out and a little jealous.

Up until that point at 'Madam Becky's' we'd just dealt with nice chaps who were popping in to see us in their lunch hour. Now we were inundated by all the drunks and over-excited party animals as they fell out of clubs at dawn, much the worse for wear - full of lager and cocaine, and not the least bit discreet or compliant.

The girls would lie on the sofas to catch their breath between rounds with substance-fuelled virile players. I would hear them reminisce back to the good old days when they'd just had to entertain portly, middle-aged businessmen in the afternoons.

All this extended activity obviously required a greater number of staff. Girls, drivers, security and receptionists, all needed to be found from somewhere and interviewed. The recruitment adverts, on top of the new towel and tea tray expenditure, were costing every penny I had, and these new staff all still needed to be paid somehow.

I thought being more successful would be less stressful and more profitable.

I was very, very wrong.

The new flats felt so safe that I made a conscious decision to reinvest as much income as possible into creating a fine, traditional knocking shop. I decided that these flats over the converted Lloyds' bank in Bletchley were where 'Madam Becky's Gentlemen's Club' would be staying. I put everything I had into it.

In a moment of madness, I fitted Jacuzzis. They may as well have come straight from the pits of hell for the amount of trouble they caused - regularly pouring boiling water over the ever-patient neighbours below, and never doing a proper day's work in their wretched lives.

Winning the hateful things on eBay was the easy bit. The hard part was getting them up two flights of narrow twisting stairs, over a high banister, through the security doors, and past half a dozen semi-naked young ladies. They giggled and squealed with excitement at the idea of a hot bubbly free for all and distracted the delivery men, which caused the whole lot to go crashing back to the bottom hallway - twice.

After trials and tribulations, injuries and incidents, when they were finally installed, the plumber gathered the girls together. He diligently instructed the staff on the care and careful usage of such expensive pieces of equipment.

'No bubble bath,' he said sternly.

'No bubbles?' a half-naked Belinda looked surprised.

Everyone looked disappointed and confused.

'Not under any circumstances,' was the firm reply.

The girls were all chattering and arguing and touching the new apparatus.

I was very impressed at how calm the plumber remained as girls in see through lace pants twiddled with his knobs.

'Girls...' I said, shushing them back into attention. 'Listen to the man please.'

'The results would be dire, not only for the internal workings of the tub itself, but for the flooring, pipes and the residents below.' He looked around the gathered faces, 'Ok?'

'Ok,' they all replied.

I'm not sure if it was one hour or two after the plumbing contractor had left, that the first bubbles were visible under the door of the ensuite.

It was definitely still the same day. And it was one of the very girls who had stood and nodded sweetly through the Jacuzzi lecture who then went and upended two bottles of fragranced bath essence into several hundred litres of oxygenated water, and turned the motors on to the highest setting.

Diana sacked her.

When the sodden carpets had been replaced, I created a pole dancing lounge, painted deep red, with a stage, mirrored walls and disco balls that reflected their magic across the ceiling. Big comfy sofas lined the walls. As money was still very tight, I'd bought the furnishings from a local charity warehouse. I just shrugged my shoulders in an apologetic way when the volunteer delivery drivers humped the things up the stairs, and stood, jaws on the floor, staring at the room and the staff.

A domination chamber was next on the list, and over time I had beautiful hand crafted furniture purpose built to suspend chaps from or spank them over. We always kept a tranquil massage room with a treatment couch, for the clients who wanted to lie back and let the lady do all the work, and we still had a few of those. Diana moved herself into the second flat and the clients came flooding in.

The girl's complaints became louder. They didn't like being told what to do by Diana; they didn't like being fined for turning up late for their shifts, keeping clients waiting in the process. They thought she was unreasonable when she told them they could not drink the complimentary refreshments I'd bought for the gents. They moaned like hell when she took a booking from several men who were bored with their 'boys' own adventure' of night fishing and wanted to reel in something more appetising.

Broaching no complaint, money was money at the end of the day. Diana marched four grumbling women across several fields, through the cold drizzling rain and alarmed sheep, to a dreary cluster of saturated saggy tents, on the banks of the river Ouse near Olney. She then stood guard, shooing away cows with her umbrella for two hours while the girls floundered around in the torch light, and tried not to catch anything.

The following day, still fuming about the forced frog march through mud and manure in the Northants countryside, the girls had a union meeting and, in a show of hands, votes were cast, and they staged a walk out.

Darren, an industrial relations expert, wanted to discuss their issues and try to find a way forward.

Diana, tutted, shook her head and said to me in front of the entire gathering, 'Man, what's with these lazy bitches uh? They lay right on the furniture. Moaning there's no work uh, then you give them the chance to earn dollars, they moan like children uh? Eishhhh, it's a shame.'

She had a point.

Darren and I had our first huge argument. He wanted to call a meeting to allow them to put forward their grievances, but I knew what their grievances were. I'd been listening to them for weeks, and it had been pissing me off.

'Madam Becky's' was still my business; I was still Madam Becky. I was throwing everything I had into these improvements. They were all earning more money than they could have ever imagined and ended each week with much more cash than I ever saw. I was still the one who ran the risk. I was the one who would be going to jail for the pleasure of them earning a fortune, and bitching about it. The flat was beautiful, the clients were arriving in droves, I was bending over backwards trying to keep everyone happy, and all I got was aggravation from the staff.

Sod them.

Why should arriving for work on time be an impossible task? Why, when you'd said you'd work on Wednesday, could you not arrive for work on Wednesday? That was all I was asking. I had spoilt them all for far too long.

One thing I'd learnt over the years was that if you had a problem in a brothel, you had to be prepared to deal with it fast, and with as much force as necessary to keep risks to a minimum. As good as Darren was with paperwork, this wasn't an environment that allowed three written warnings and a disciplinary hearing. Difficult decisions had to be made on the spur of the moment, before things escalated, and people got hurt, or arrested or both. There was no place in the sex trade for indecision or miserable, sour-faced, grumpy girls, whose malcontent would drive my hard won punters into the arms of another agency.

The way the girls were carrying on, I wouldn't pay tuppence to spend time with any one of the woebegone harpies so why should anyone else have to?

So, quoting Mr Pip...

'If you can't change the people...' I said glancing at Diana, 'then let's change the people. That's what I reckon.'

She looked at me, pleased and nodded. 'Yaaa, sack the lazy bitches uh?'

Darren wasn't pleased. 'Come on baby, we can sort this. Let me go and talk to them, find a compromise.'

My stubborn streak asserted itself. I folded my arms and shook my head. 'No. No compromise. Let them go and find somewhere else to be late. Find a new boss to moan about. I'm done with them.'

'Eishhhh, ah shame uh but they gotta go,' Diana said smugly.

In shocked silence the girls packed their belongings and all left together. Darren kept staring at me silently willing me to relent. But I wouldn't, I couldn't. I felt let down and betrayed by the whole ungrateful lot of them.

As Diana locked the security door behind them as they struggled down the stairs with their boxes, I heard her muttering. 'You lazy bitches. You were warned uh? Off you go you pieces of shit.'

My beloved Belinda was the only one left. She sat there at Diana's office table with me, looking balefully at a list of new girls due to come in for interviews. Diana waddled back up the hall from the front door, still muttering curses to herself.

'Hope you don't regret this baby,' Darren said as he walked off.

'Move yourself,' Diana demanded, rapping Belinda's chair leg impatiently with her foot.

Lowering her immense frame slowly onto Belinda's vacated seat and pulling the list of escort applicants out of my hand, she proceeded to plan the re-staffing of 'Madam Becky's' properly, the way she wanted it.

The unease that I had felt about her right from the beginning flooded through me again. Her fat, piggy eyes glanced at me and a shiver slid down my spine. I'd been out manoeuvred and manipulated into handing over the control of my business.

I just hoped I'd done the right thing. It was all feeling very wrong.

CHAPTER TWENTY ONE

An extensive recruitment campaign was launched, orchestrated mainly by Diana. Girls of all shapes and sizes turned up in droves. I was amazed how many ladies wanted to be escorts, or were already providing services on the sly around full-time jobs and families. I sat with Diana at the kitchen now office table and listened to their stories.

Many girls were cagey about their real names and addresses, and I understood why it would take a girl a while before she trusted people like me who ran agencies. Diana tried to make them fill in forms, and show ID. But as long as they were obviously well over the age of eighteen, and fairly able bodied, I was happy for them to remain anonymous, and gave everyone a chance to fit in.

Sadly, there would always be companies out there that would willingly use all the information they could get about their staff to control and manipulate women into complying with dangerous or unreasonable demands. If I was a new girl, about to start working at a flat, with people I didn't know, then there would be no way on God's earth I'd tell them where I lived.

People point the fingers of dishonesty and infidelity at married clients. But the more working ladies I met, the more it became obvious that the women were telling as many fibs as the men about their time spent having sex in brothels.

A number of these ladies who were applying for jobs in the newly reorganised 'Madam Becky's' already had very good jobs in the real world. Accountants, solicitors, public sector workers, benefit agency staff, wives, mothers and grandmothers - they were all at it. Women who've worked in the care industries make the transition to sex work very easily, and are often the most popular and highest earners.- used to dealing with all the machinations of the human body, good and bad, a comforting, genial bedside manner, soft touch, and realistic uniform was always a money spinner.

Many husbands and partners of working girls seemed to live in blissful ignorance of where the money was coming from. But with most ladies being the ones who run the household finances, duplicity became second nature.

Helena, a new recruit, was the perfect example of a lady leading a secret life. A charming, softly spoken coloured South African girl from Botswana, she instantly got up Diana's white Afrikaans' nose. I liked her, she was one of the sweetest, most gentle people I'd ever met, with the voluptuous full figure of a real woman, and I knew she'd make the clients feel comfortable and they'd enjoy her company. In her late twenties, she'd lived in the UK for a year - a married Christian lady with two small children, who, unbeknown to her husband, had been earning an income with sex work since she'd arrived in the country. She always pretended to have a job that involved shift work, so she could explain being called in at odd hours. Large supermarket chains had provided good cover, the large number of staff made it almost impossible for her husband to contact her on a work number. Now Helena was worried that she'd used the supermarket ruse for too long, and her husband was getting suspicious.

'I think I need to tell him I work in a different place Beeky? Tesco you know, I don't think it's so good to tell him there again. I think George will find out about me being a whore soon.'

'Have you tried using the Royal Mail as a cover?' Darren suggested. 'They have shifts, and overtime, I was a manager there for years, they do have a uniform though. You'd need to get one of them to be convincing.' He paused to think it through. 'It could work. They move you about a lot, so you could pretend be anywhere if he tried to find you.'

'Hey! Thanks Dirren. That's good I will. What is this royal male place please? George drops me off there, when he drives away I'll get a cab here.'

She was so sweet, and so easy to like, I knew she would be popular with the punters.

'Maybe I can say I start there tomorrow if I can find a uniform yes?'

'I'll get you from the Bletchley sorting office, if you tell me what time,' he offered with a friendly smile.

'Hey, thanks Dirren, let's do that.'

The following morning, I went off to stock up with condoms and gingernuts, Diana was covering the phones. Darren went off to pick up Helena from outside the sorting office for her first imaginary day as a 'mail handler'. I suppose she was only half lying to her man, as she was in fact going to be handling males, but I doubted the homonym defence would stand up in the divorce court if her husband found out.

As I wandered around the shop, basket over my arm, picking up supplies for work, Darren phoned. 'What's up?' I asked, he sounded a bit strange. 'Are you laughing or crying Darren? You sound a bit peculiar.'

'A bit of both,' he snorted... 'Jesus, these girls!'

'Did you collect Helena Ok?' I said concerned. 'Did she find a uniform? What's happening?'

'She hired one,' the strange choking noise started again.

He was laughing loudly; he could barely get the words out.

'What?' I shouted. 'What's so funny?'

'She's not English is she? She doesn't know what's what, so she'd gone in and asked for a Royal Mail uniform from the fancy dress place,' he paused to catch his breath and let the laughter calm down. 'So when I pulled up at Dawson Road sorting office, she was stood there, in a bright blue padded suit and a little hat, kitted out as Postman Pat.'

He lost control and started howling with laughter.

'Darren stop! Is she ok?'

Pulling himself together he added, 'some of my old mates from the Union were there, outside having a fag. I had to tell them she was a stripper, a 'Pat O Gram' and I was picking her up to take her to another job. Ah, their faces! It was the funniest thing I've seen in years. They tried to get her to do her routine for them, out in the car park.' He dissolved back into hysterics.

I pictured the scene and smiled. It always amazed me how well Darren had slipped from normality into 'Madam Becky' world.

'Where are you now?'

'I'm at me mam's trying to dig out old uniforms for her, she can't wear that shite again,' he was still struggling to contain his laughter. 'Ah dear, I'm crying here.'

I could hear him sniffing and wiping away tears of mirth. Great, so much for Helena being discreet and keeping a low profile.

After lunch Darren arrived back at the flat with an arm full of blue Royal Mail shirts with red piping.

'They're really old ones, so they'll be way too big, but it's the best I could do. Sorry.' He placed the shirts on the sofa in the pole dancing lounge.

'Don't worry Belle and I can take them in for her,' I said turning to face Belinda. 'Belle honey, grab the sewing kit out of Spanky's box and give me a hand darling, we can just take these shirts in at the sides.'

Kneeling on the floor, with a selection of pins in my mouth, I waited for Helena to slip into Darren's old shirts. Diana lent in the doorway giving directions into the phone and watched the proceedings with a look of condescension.

Maybe Darren used to be smaller. Helena was a curvy lady; it quickly became obvious there wasn't much surplus fabric to take in.

'Eishhhh, it's real tight uh' Diana gloated. 'You're the size of a man Helena. Shame uh?'

I pinched together the very small amount of spare shirt at Helena's waist and felt her sag with humiliation, deflated by Diana's spiteful comments. Christ Diana was a vile hag.

I looked up from the floor, straight into the fat woman's eyes, and smiled. 'Better than being the size of a house Diana, uh?'

She turned around and stomped out.

After some tweaking, the disguise served Helena well. On many occasions, just as she got her Post Office outfit and sensible shoes back on in readiness to get dropped back off at the sorting office by Darren, to be collected by George at what he thought was the end of her mail handling shift, another male would come in and require handling. Not wanting to turn down the money, off would come the Royal Mail garb (no one ever had a sorting office fetish) and Helena would have to lie to her hubby as to why she was an hour late finishing her work, slightly flushed and shiny with baby oil.

I wasn't comfortable with the girls deceiving their menfolk, but I certainly couldn't judge, nor could I advise my staff on how to make a long term relationship work. I'd always considered the fact that couples could live together, day after day, to be a miracle that the Vatican had overlooked. My capacity for bloody mindedness had brought most of my romances crashing to an end, so who was I to comment.

Mandy, an older lady who'd recently joined us, described the girls' double standards perfectly. 'When the sun comes up I have morals again.' She'd say laughing.

Mandy had spent years expertly servicing men from 8.00 in the evening until the early hours with several different out-call agencies. A former nurse, she worked hard with us whilst her hubby thought she was on permanent nights in the maternity wards of MK General Hospital, bringing babies into the world. By night she was a bewitching vamp, a blonde, buxom femme fatale, a sexual enchantress in thin heeled, red stilettos and lace topped stockings. But with the coming of the dawn, like Cinderella the spell would break, and once again she would be Maureen, the fake ward sister in flat shoes and shapeless knitwear.

Another of the new recruits was Lexi - a tiny, slim, pretty, brunette girl in her late twenties with an all over tan. Kind and funny, in a slightly dim, dappy sort of a way.

Lexi had only ever worked for out-call agencies and was really nervous about working in a flat with a host of other girls. She was fabulous, and I knew she'd be very popular. I did my best to reassure her that having other girls as competition wasn't going to be a problem, but she didn't look totally convinced, and I was worried she was going to walk back out.

With out-calls, the driver takes a girl to a client. Unless they're as fussy and particular as John from Northampton, ninety-eight percent of the time the client will let the girl in, pay her and have his wicked way with her, even if he's not too keen and she wasn't really what he ordered. I always tried to avoid it, but when it happened, I called it, 'the wrong pizza,' scenario.

The pizza arrives and it's got anchovies on it. You hate anchovies. But you're starving, so you snatch the pizza from the driver, slam the door, flick the salty, fishy bits of shit off onto the box lid, and just stuff it down your throat.

Well, that's how it was with out-calls.

The bell rings, the expectant client nearly snaps his ankles dashing to answer the door, and there she stands. Too fat, too thin, too old, too young, not really his idea of what a lady should look like, even if the agency has tried hard to find his perfect match.

He's hungry for love, she's female, and guaranteed to have sex with him, so although he's disappointed, he lets her in, pays up and hopes for the best.

Looking at Lexi, I knew she had no worries about punters not thinking she was delightful. She was stunning and sexy, but I knew it was a common anxiety, and I was keeping my fingers and toes crossed that she'd stay and uncross her lovely legs at 'Madam Becky's'.

I showed her the working rooms, and the pole dancing lounge. A client was shown in by Diana. Walking past Lexi and I, he made himself comfortable on the edge of the bed, and helped himself to a mint humbug from the complementary sweet dish.

'Who have you got for me today Becky?' he asked with a big smile.

'Belinda,' I suggested, knowing she was the only one available and ready to roll.

His smile slipped.

I knew he'd seen her several times for a massage, but it wasn't a rub and tug he had in mind that day.

'Isn't this gorgeous young lady working today?' he asked, smiling hopefully and lecherously at Lexi.

'Leave her alone you naughty man,' I chided. 'Lexi meet Reg, he's one of our more frisky gents.' I rolled my eyes heaven ward in a parody of exasperation. 'She's only here for an interview Reggie my love, and I don't think she's too keen.'

'No! Don't say that Becky. My life will be ruined if I can't see her! Oh, my lovely, lovely Lexi. You'll break my old heart if you don't stay with Becky, she'll look after you, won't you my dear?'

Reg fancied himself to be a bit of a thespian.

'Of course I would, she's wonderful,' I replied smiling at Lexi. 'But she prefers out-calls Reg, so don't bully her, or I'll smack your bum and toss you down the stairs.'

'Bum smacking and tossing with the lovely Lexi. Becky, you know me so well. You're a star!'

'Reg! Behave. Are you staying to see Belle?'

'I don't think so Becky,' he said, getting up from the bed. 'I'm going to save myself for Lexi.' He winked wickedly at her. 'Who was that dreadful beast who let me in?'

I laughed at his observation.

'She is a bit scary isn't she? That's Diana, she's helping me get the place sorted, and keep all you lot in line.'

'Well, don't send her in! She'd kill me!' he replied in mock horror. He blew Lexi a kiss and headed for the door.

'I don't mind seeing Reg now Becky, if it's ok with you.'

Reg stopped in his tracks and span around excitedly.

'Ooh yes please,' Reg said with utter delight, grinning from ear to ear.

'Really?' I said, my mouth open with surprise.

'Really?' Reg gushed. 'Really?'

'Yes, if you don't mind me looking like this. I have none of my things.'

'My dear girl! You are a vision. You've made my day. My year.'

'Well, that's that then,' I concluded merrily. 'Do you want a nice tray of tea and a bourbon Reg? I'll leave Lexi with you to discuss details.' I walked out, closed the door behind me and smiled. I knew Lexi would be staying. She'd be worth her weight in gold that one, I just knew it.

The interviews continued, and it became obvious as we recruited more girls that Diana had favourites, and only wanted to take on women that she could push around. If she liked you, you'd be given the best shifts on the rota which were Thursday, Friday and strangely Sunday nights, and the pick of the jobs. If she didn't like you, the spiteful comments and whispering in corners made life a misery.

This troubled me, and upset me, but I tried to push it to the back of my mind. I thought that eventually, once she had made her presence felt, she would wind her neck in and running a knocking shop would good fun again like it always had been.

Concerns about Diana were still running through my head later that afternoon as I took a break from interviewing and collected my daughter Emilia from school.

Stood at the gates, a mother in her forties approached me, dragging a low slung border collie along on a lead. She stopped next to me, and smiled. Bending down, I chatted to the dog about its splendidly fluffy hair, and gave it a good scratch around the whiskers. She told me the dog's name was Ami, and that she was obsessed with trying to corral inanimate objects, and spent most of the day whining and frustrated that nothing moved when she wanted it to.

'I know how she feels. She should come and work with me,' I suggested. 'See if she has any luck speeding my lot up with a nip on their heels.'

She asked if I was the person who'd been on the ITV program a few years ago, and recently in the newspapers.

Standing up, and brushing dog hair off my trousers, I laughed, and admitted to being that very Madam. After all the years of media excitement and finger pointing, I was quite happy to have an open discussion in the street about what I did and why I did it, and defend my ladies to the last.

'I wondered if you might need a receptionist?' she asked quietly.

We had Diana on reception, for better or worse.

I shook my head. 'Sorry I've got that covered. What I really need are escorts.'

I expected her to walk away. But she didn't.

'Can I come along for a chat?' she said, lowering her voice discreetly, 'see if it's something I might be interested in.'

The nice lady from the school gates arrived the next morning with Ami Dog, who got parked under a chair in the kitchen. She'd decided she'd like to give it a go, and wanted her working name to be Diane. I squealed so loudly in horror that it startled the collie, who shot out from under the table and started barking at me, fearing its mistress was under attack.

Lexi explained to her that if men confused her with the incredible hulk that answered the door to them she'd never get any work. So she settled on 'Kate' and we added her name to the rota.

Kate and I sat at the table drinking tea, with Ami Dog, pretending to be dozing underneath, but still on guard, ready to dash out on the defence if there was any more shrieking. Lexi, exhausted, but full of a new found confidence, leant against the kitchen units, sipping coke, getting her breath back. Since her initial hour of high jinks with Reg the previous day, Lexi had been flat out, quite literally; she'd seen six punters that first day, and was back for more. She'd certainly taken to working in a flat. I knew she would.

'How long have you been an escort Lexi?' Kate asked.

'For about six years now I think,' Lexi replied. 'I like it. It's better than working for a living.'

'How did you start? Were you scared? I'm terrified. I don't know if I'll be able to go through with it when the time comes.' Kate reached under the table and stroked Ami Dog's head, comforting herself with the touch of the soft fur.

'It's like committing murder I reckon,' Lexi laughed. 'Once you've done the first one it's easy. My friend got me into it. She'd been working to pay for uni. My first one was as scared as I was and talked most of the way through, and I just kept thinking about the money and wishing he'd shut up and get on with it.'

I looked at Kate. I'd seen that initial fear often.

'Maybe you should start with the massage service,' I offered. 'Keep your undies on if you want, and just do a massage with Belinda so you can see what she does. If you want to leg it, then just walk out. No worries. Belle can finish him off.'

Kate liked this idea and seemed to relax slightly, knowing that she could just leave when she wanted clearly had made her feel better.

'Just take it slowly,' I added. 'Don't do anything that makes you feel bad. If you can't you can't. It won't be a problem. It's not a thing everyone can do. I can't do it. I'd make a crap escort.'

'Have you ever worked Becky?' Lexi asked.

'I tried,' I said, remembering Chinky Charlie and our not so romantic episode on the shoe rack under the coats all those years ago. 'I'm not a tactile person. I'm not even very cuddly with my kids; I'm really uncomfortable having people in my space. I made inverted commas with my fingers.

'If a customer wanted to get close, and grabbed me, I'd get panicky and poke him in the eye, so I'd not be very popular. I do some of the humiliation stuff, and shout at them if they're naughty for an extra fifty quid, but I'm better on the phones than in the room.'

Pointing to a box in the corner that was home to Mr North's Spanky Monkey and his new plushie friends, Tranny Tedward and Lady Lima, I said, 'Belinda, the massage menace, and I do a thing with glove puppets, but that's just hilariously funny.'

Kate looked understandably confused.

'Puppets?'

'Don't worry,' I laughed. 'You'll get used to it! It's all in a day's work here. Don't put yourself under any pressure, that's the key. If it makes you feel bad, don't do it. Promise?'

'Thanks Becky, but I think I should be ok.' She smiled, but it didn't really reach her eyes. 'It can't be any worse than sleeping with my husband.'

Lexi and I looked at each other.

I raised an eyebrow. 'Oh dear! That doesn't sound good.'

She shrugged her shoulders, the laughter was gone, she looked sad. 'I want to leave him, but he won't let me, so I'm going to do this and save enough money to rent somewhere he doesn't know about. Then I'll just take the kids and the dog and go.'

'Blimey,' was all I could think of, not wanting to pry too much, but sensing that she wanted to talk. 'Like I said, take it one step at a time, you'll soon know if it's for you or not.'

'I'm forty this year, aren't I too old?' She glanced from Lexi to me. 'Let's face it, I don't look like her. I'm twice her size and I've had three kids so I've got the whole wobbly belly thing going on. Do you think anyone would pay to see me?'

I could see her confidence ebbing away. This was one of the most common misconceptions - that men only want to have sex with frisky young girls with big boobs and bodies that look like match sticks with the wood scraped off.

'The most popular escorts are often in their thirties and forties Kate,' I said. 'Clients will see the cute young things once, but what does a self-centred teenager know about pleasing a man time after time? They'll be wanking him with one hand and texting with the other.'

'No!'

'Yep, and be nattering away about how big and rampant their boyfriend's todger is, while the poor punter is trying to motivate his flaccid member into action and failing miserably.' I dunked my digestive into the fresh tea that Lexi had just made me and bit off the soggy half.

'You'll earn the decent money from your regular regulars, men who will come to see you week in, week out, bring you pressies at Christmas and champagne on your birthday,' I explained.

'To keep those men cumming you need to be attentive and interested in them as people. Prostitution is a service industry, just like any other, and your gents will be expecting value for money, which strangely includes companionship and empathy as well as enthusiastic sex.'

I could see her thinking and reasoning it out. Lexi was nodding in agreement; even the dog wagged her tail.

I showed her around the flat, and explained how it all worked.

The phones rang all day every day, and they were answered by the receptionist, who ran through descriptions of all the girls that were working, and what services they offered, and if they specialised, and what if anything we charged extra for.

Lexi explained to Kate as the three of us wandered room to room followed by the collie, that 'specialising' meant that you offered services that are not included in the price of the booking, French kissing, water sports, hard sports that type of thing.

'O levels and A levels are popular,' Lexi added.

Kate cheered up. 'I have a degree in English, will that help?'

Perturbed Lexi looked at me.

'O levels and A levels are pseudonyms for Oral and Anal sex Kate. Not further education,' I said, remembering my 'annual' experience.

Kate looked blank.

The speciality requests are strange and varied, and not wanting to freak her out with images of peeing in a man's mouth, having a cucumber inserted up your bum or fisting an OAP, I glassed over the specialising conversation with 'Oh, I'll explain all that later.'

Belinda wandered out of the massage room with Wiggy, who was looking summery and divine in layers of chiffon and a big straw hat, and I introduced them to the new lady and her dog.

Amazed how relaxed it all seemed, and how nice the girls were, Kate decided that starting tomorrow she'd work the day shifts while the kids were at school. I knew she'd be good, different to Lexi, but just as popular in her own way; it was proving to be a good week for new ladies.

It was vital that Kate kept everything secret. She'd planned to take the kids to school then come straight to the flat, then leave in time to collect them in the afternoon. Diana wouldn't like the fact that I'd allowed Kate to work a short shift, finishing at three rather than six, but Kate needed our help, and I was still the boss as far as I was concerned, so Fatty Arbuckle would have to lump it.

The animal was the other problem. Ami Dog was always with Kate, they did everything together and her husband knew it. She was worried that leaving her faithful friend at home would give the game away, alert him that she was up to something. I suggested that she brought Ami along to work. We were all looking forward to it.

Diana sat in flat two like a fat spider in the centre of her web, weaving some kind of vile mischief, pulling strings and brewing malcontent. She was now on a big wage plus commission and free accommodation. I was penniless, hoping that she'd get the promised results. Mr Pip and I changed all the adverts in the papers again making them bigger, funnier and glossier than ever, and with the new marketing and the new girls the punters started rolling in.

T, a huge lump of surly Asian bodyguard joined forces with Darren, who was also larger than average and just as surly when needs must. Their job was to take the girls out to clients and keep everyone safe and sensible. Opening through the night could be a tricky business, with large groups of drunken customers needing firm handling at the weekends, and bored girls needing firm handling when it was quiet during the week, but they left that to Diana and I. You never knew what you're going to be faced with and we were all learning fast.

Diana haggled like a market trader when five girls were required to perform at a stag party; she was never willing to pass up business if there was a shilling to be made. Darren and T raced around the Home Counties growling and flexing their muscles at new clients who may have considered taking advantage.

To squeeze every last quid out of the clients, Diana insisted that girls, who couldn't dance for toffee, performed on the pole in the lounge. We didn't have any trained dancers, so if an easily pleased chap was prepared to pay money to watch a shoddy show, then they had to all take a turn. This was a woeful experience. Darren and I listened shamefaced to Lexi's heavy, flat footed clumping as she hoofed it across the wooden stage to which the pole was attached. She came crashing, cursing to the floor at the end of what should have been a seductive spin.

It was all too audible through the wall, as we stood in the kitchen grimacing, feeling the girl's failure. Even the long suffering Thai lady from downstairs was forced to come up, and politely bowing over clasped hands, asked if we were moving a piano and when would the noise stop?

Lexi was devastated by her lack of prowess, and she was one of the more accomplished ones. Determined to assist their plight I hired a pole dancing teacher who could help them hone their skills.

A slippery pole is a disaster waiting to happen, and the close proximity of baby oil and lubricant in the establishment didn't bode well. Kate who had embraced pole dancing as a way to lose weight was the first casualty as she gained momentum for a backward helicopter. Centrifugal force is a powerful thing and the speed at which she took off across the room was quite remarkable. She landed on the edge of the stage, took most of the skin off her thigh, and kicked poor Ami Dog square in the nashers. It ended her work for the day, and sent the dog howling back under the table. The instructor suggested we buy a bottle of cheap vodka to clean the pole with between dances, she swore by it, it was the best thing.

Unfortunately Lexi drank the cheap vodka when she was bored working through the night. And then became the next victim as pissed, she span off, belly flopped hard onto the carpet and broke her ankle, which relegated her to plying her trade in the missionary position for six weeks whilst plastered to the knee.

Resigned to trying to tantalise punters in slippers and a support bandage from weeks seven to twelve of the healing process, Lexi had learnt her lesson. We lay on the sofa laughing uproariously as the dance teacher tried to get Darren to hold himself upside-down at the top of the pole, and erotically mime the removal of his imaginary tasselled bikini, and throw it into his invisible audience.

The doorbell rang and a minute later Darren froze in mid-comedy spin as Diana walked into the lounge followed by the police, and council officers.

They'd arrived to arrest me again. This time for not having an entertainments licence.

CHAPTER TWENTY TWO

I sat in the overly hot, stuffy room at the police station and read the posters on the walls which urged me not to inject drugs or let my dog plonky on the pavement. Two men from the council's licensing department and two CID officers shuffled chairs and made themselves at home around a tired Formica table.

One of the chaps from the town hall opened a file and produced a large number of my new adverts. They really did look great. Mr Pip was a genius of design, and this man must have spent weeks collecting them. The campaign had obviously worked, as everybody had seen the ads, and this chap had even taken the time to cut them out of the paper.

I smiled.

He didn't.

Pointing to the advert with a quality pen that he appeared to keep in his top pocket for the sole purpose of officious pointing, he said, 'Is this your advertisement?'

I in turn, pointed with my long fake nail to the large picture of myself in glorious Technicolor, on my hands and knees, breasts bursting out of the black PVC cat suit that took up half the advert and replied.

'I'm not sure. Do you think that looks like me?'

Banging the saucy exhibit down onto the table with an over dramatic exhalation of stale coffee breath he said, 'Yes Miss Adams, I think it looks like you.'

'Ah, that's really sweet, thank you, sometimes I feel such a mess though, and it's really not easy being glamorous when you're trying to juggle a family and a business.' I smiled sweetly at him.

The quality pointing pen was once again utilised to bring my attention to the words in a bright pink blocky font that read, 'Gentlemen's Club,' and the sentence causing the most offence, 'New Pole Dancing Lounge'. So distressing was this wording it appeared, that it warranted not just pointing at, but being tapped repeatedly with the springy button at the top of the haranguing ballpoint.

'Do you have a licence...?'

'For that minky?' I chimed in, thinking of Spanky and sliding effortlessly into an Inspector Clouseau parody.

If he had a sense of humour he'd left it at home.

'You are in a lot of trouble Miss Adams; I suggest you take this more seriously.'

I answered his frustration with a nonchalant Gallic shrug.

'Do you have an entertainments license for your new pole dancing venture?'

'Do I need one?'

'The Council is a licensing authority and as such exists to carry out licensing functions under the Licensing Act 2003. The local councils are responsible for licensing the sale and supply of alcohol and the provision of regulated entertainment. It also states in your advertisement the provision of complimentary refreshments.' Clicking out the nib, he underlined the words 'complimentary refreshments' in black ink.

'You must by law apply for an Entertainments License if you wish to play music to the public and perform dancing.'

'Ok,' I said, deciding to join in. 'I run an illegal business, but I still need a license?'

'Yes, that is correct. You must apply to the Licensing authority for a license.'

'And if I apply for one, will you grant me one?'

'No,' he said, 'we won't.'

I couldn't help it, I laughed, you gotta love these guys.

'Ok, so why would I apply for a license I know you won't give me and waste your time and my money?'

'If you wish to entertain the public, you must hold a valid license.'

'That you won't give me. Even if I apply and ask nicely? Well that sounds fair enough.'

I was getting hot, and bored now. The police weren't saying a lot, but I was getting the feeling they were finding it all quite amusing.

'I hear what you're saying,' I continued, 'but with all due respect, you and your colleague attended my flats with the police earlier today. You witnessed at first hand, a six foot, slightly badgery- looking man in his forties, wearing jeans and knitwear, clinging to the pole, in what could loosely but officially be described as an erotic dance move.'

They looked at each other, and the two police officers coughed and shuffled to hide their titters.

'Well,' I continued, 'he's the best we've got, our piece d résistance.'

The man stabbed his pen at the advert, he was getting rattled. 'You have ladies.'

'True,' I said. 'But have you by any chance seen any of my ladies dancing?'

They shook their heads and looked confused.

'No, I thought not, because if you had, you'd realize that none of them are the least bit entertaining, and therefore, to my mind, do not require licensing.'

They stared in stunned silence.

Leaning forward across the table I continued: 'I think you will find they are 'practicing' under the watchful eye of their instructor, for health benefits. And we do not play music, we make our own entertainment at 'Madam Becky's', we are like a big family, we work in harmony, we all sing along together, like the Waltons.'

'I don't think 'practicing' or harmonious humming requires any paperwork.' Silence filled the room. 'If a gentleman wishes to torture himself and watch them 'practicing' then we feel obliged to let him,' I continued. 'People are free to watch all types of horror these days; the most dreadful sights are readily available everywhere in various formats.' I rocked back in my chair and folded my arms defiantly in front of myself.

Down but not defeated, he leant across the desk and tried to out stare me. 'There is still the issue of the complimentary refreshments. You require a liquor license if you are providing alcoholic beverages for clients, even if the client is not paying for said beverage. If the alcohol is purchased with profit from the business, then you must apply for a license by law...'

I held up my hand, palm facing him, to signal my intention to speak.

He paused.

'Sadly at present there are no profits to purchase anything much,' I said. 'My boyfriend Darren, the pole dancer...'

The CID chap barely managed to hide his smile. I had a feeling Darren's sexy turn up the pole would stick in the poor man's mind for quite awhile.

'...used some of the rent money to buy six bottles of lager to share with his friends when they visit, does that count?'

Their faces showed they felt this one slipping away.

I pointed at my very classy, professionally designed advert. I tapped the words 'Gentlemen's Club' with a long, red fingernail.

'You gents are as bad as the Inland Revenge, guilty of believing the hype, falling for some snazzy marketing. Not everything you read in the papers is true you know. It's just an old fashioned knocking shop - nothing to get excited about.'

I knew I was pushing my luck, but they were so pompous and ridiculous, I felt it my duty to be annoying.

'You are correct though in as much as I do provide complimentary mint humbugs and boiled fruit sweets in all the rooms. And every visitor is offered a variety of English or fruit tea and quality biscuits, so I would be more than happy to apply for a tea time selection license if there is such a thing?'

Wankers. I sat and stared them out.

'We will be keeping a close eye on you from now on Miss Adams, now you've been brought to the attention of the licensing authorities.'

'Great,' I said as I stood up. 'Join the queue.' Politely I offered them my hand to shake. 'You know you're always welcome to pop in whenever you're passing. You never know, Darren may have learnt some new pole tricks by then, you can watch him practicing, have a nice cup of tea and a sit down with a complimentary garibaldi.'

They all ignored my out-stretched hand, and the main protagonist, wielder of the pointing pen, laid a sheet of paper on the desk.

'You'll need to sign this to say we've cautioned you about this matter,' he said and clearly without thinking he went to hand me his precious pen. Checking himself, he made an exaggerated show of clicking the nib back in loudly, and clipped it safely into his top pocket, then gesticulated to CID to find me something cheaper to autograph the form with.

I signed my name and date on the official warning in splotchy blue ink from an old chewed biro fished from the sagging trouser pocket of the Old Bill, and walked out to phone Darren and inform him he'd just been promoted to the position of 'Madam Becky's' most talented and prestigious erotic dancer.

CHAPTER TWENTY THREE

Business was booming and the flats became more manic daily with girls and clients. It was like a revolving door of staff and one in one out, one in one out. It was enough to make you dizzy and drop the tea tray.

Some of the women worked for specific things - family holidays, credit card bills or just to keep the wolf from the door, but for others there was an element of enjoyment, camaraderie or even revenge. Many a lady started escorting after she'd discovered a loved one's infidelity.

With a secret life similar to Helena's, one slightly odd apprentice pretended to her husband that she had a part-time job as a fitness instructor. Her excuse to her family for disappearing off at odd hours was short staffing for aerobic sessions. Darren was dispatched again to pick her up from the gym car park where her husband had dropped her off. At the end of her fake classes he'd return her back again. She'd carry a small portable CD player around the flat. Whenever her husband phoned, she would shush everyone frantically, turn the music on, flick the volume up loud and start running on the spot.

'I can't talk now babe,' she would pant into her mobile. 'I'm teaching a boxercise class. Give me an hour and I'll call you back yeah.'

We'd all be breathless with laughter at this bizarre apparition.

'Can't you just turn your phone off?' asked Lexi when she'd stopped laughing.

'Jaa, what's the point in lying eh? You never do enough in the room to get out of breath anyway. Too bloody lazy eishhhh,' Diana added, ruining the moment as always.

Some recruits just didn't work out. I had to sack one girl who said she was determined to be a successful escort. Trouble was she'd hurl herself sideways off the bed, thudding onto the floor screaming when anyone tried to touch her, exiting the room cursing and spitting abuse at the bewildered bloke over her shoulder.

We talked it though, and I made her see that attacking customers and calling them 'filthy bastard shit pigs' came under the 'speciality service' heading and was charged as an extra. Greatly enjoyed by some, but wasn't really the done thing in a standard booking. Eventually she saw my point and went home.

I arrived the next day at lunchtime to find the previously dismissed lady back in the building, sunbathing on the roof terrace, covered entirely in gold paint. Enquiring at her presence I was informed she'd come in to work her shift. We went back through the previous day's conversation, regarding her unsuitability to the task. I pointed out that in addition to terrifying the clientele, the wearing of perfume, strong deodorant or anything else that could be indiscreetly transferred onto a client was unprofessional. A thick metallic waxy gold coating, added to her hatred of men, would have made it even more improbable that she would have a successful day on the job. Once again she agreed and went home.

She turned up every day for the next week on time and enthusiastic to work her hours. Accepting the fact that she was obviously even more bonkers than the rest of us, I let her stay and hang out with the girls, painting herself daily in a variety of different hues. Diana was all for having her committed, but she was harmless enough if she was never allowed to set eyes on a man, and really quite entertaining in an endearing, glittery sort of a way.

A firm favourite of everyone's was a Cuban stunner who laughed and chirped incessantly in Spanish, but spoke not a word of English. She arrived for her interview with an interpreter and, having checked out her credentials, she was introduced to the girls as Carmen, and was quickly taken under the corporate wing. A week of tuition from the girls and Carmen was swearing like an Irish navvy. Unable to ask for directions home, or book a cab, by the end of the month she was fluent in sexual positions, penis descriptions, pot noodle flavours and pizza toppings.

The flats had got far too busy for endless tea drinking and sewing so Belinda and I had a break from making costumes and repairing puppets. Our previous efforts had resulted in most specialities being catered for and the dressing up box was pretty full with spangles and feathers – until Duncan appeared - a tall, well built, handsome and charming man, with soft wavy blonde hair who worked in finance, and loved to be humiliated.

Dunky, as Belinda had abbreviated him to, was particularly taken with horse riding – with him as the horse, and me as the rider. Luckily, as a keen horsewoman, in the traditional sense, I had all of the requisite paraphernalia, so a mad dash to the stables and a quick rummage around in my bag of manky leather odds and ends meant that I was able to fashion Dunky-Donkey a nice bridle and harness.

An old saddle was dug out from my shed, the mould wiped off, and as I changed into my jodhpurs, Belinda was busy cutting lengths of beige wool, chosen to blend in with his hair, and sticking it on the old headband and cardboard ears set up.

Belle's arts and crafts had given my new pony a mane and forelock he could toss, and he was delighted. As I fastened my spurs, I could see him trembling with excitement, metal bit in his mouth, and reins round his neck, he started to prance on the spot snorting.

It was only possible to walk or trot on hands and knees, with me sitting astride him swiping at his flank with my whip. To canter or jump he needed to get up onto his hind legs, while I held the reins and cantered behind him. His balls were strapped up with leather, which in turn was attached to his girth which held the saddle in place. This tightened when he stood up for a good race about, and he seemed to prefer it that way as tighter strapping created more friction, and got him even friskier.

Memories of being a small innocent child flashed through my mind - playing horses all through lunch break, with a jumper for a bridle tied around the waist of my best friend, prancing together across the rounders' field, whinnying and nickering when you saw someone you knew. Who'd have thought I'd end up like this? Certainly not all those nice girls I'd gone to school with, that's for sure. I looked at myself, two decades later shouting, 'giddy-up Dunky.' Or, 'trot on dear,' to a naked banker, whilst his willy turned blue and his ears came unglued.

Whipped when he didn't perform well and given a rosette when he was calm and pleasant to ride, I took Dunky through his paces. I'm sure the British Horse Society would remove me from their list of instructors if they saw how

I spanked my little pony. It did make me wonder how these chaps discovered that they liked this sort of thing. It baffled me.

A course of show jumps was constructed around the apartments, ingeniously created from mops, brooms and the ironing board. Dunky was a natural steeplechaser, but he became overly excited by show jumping and went too fast and bounced off the walls. Ami Dog, who usually lurked unnoticed, took great offence to Dunky-Donkey's whinnying and ricocheting, and as a Border collie felt duty bound to pen him with bared teeth into the en-suite.

When his hour was up, exhausted Duncan tried to return to his suit and tie in the bedroom, but Ami Dog rushed forward and bit his fetlocks quite ferociously. Brothels aren't big on public liability insurance, so she was banished to the kitchen for Dunky's prize giving and lap of honour.

Unperturbed by being attacked by a dog, Dunky returned again later that week. As a reward for being so good and jumping a clear round, we tied a small metallic dildo to his forehead. It perched just in front of his stuck on ears and woolly mane, and for a brief time, with some Christmas angel wings, he was transcended into Pegasus, a shimmering, mythological creature, horse of the Gods, flying carefree through the clouds.

Diana was not overly pleased to have a naked unicorn piaffing around her paperwork and made it clear that the dressing up clients, dogs, ponies, maids and slaves were becoming a major hindrance to the sausage factory sexual services that were making the money. The more sensible visitors became a little disconcerted when they caught glimpses of Wiggy pow-wowing as Pocahontas, bearded and tattooed French maids making beds, a sheep dog rounding up fallen women and the rhythmic bobbing of Duncan's well-polished horn.

Comments were being made on the internet about the uniqueness of 'Madam Becky's' and the more staid patrons preferred to take their business to our main uber professional competitor. Luckily, there were enough fun loving guys looking for some entertaining action for our sales figures to continue to climb weekly.

The slightly odd visitors tended to frequent the flats during the daytime, escaping from work for an hour to be transformed into princesses, poodles or pantomime dames. I usually looked after the day shift and Diana the night shift which was mainly out-calls and straightforward shagging which she preferred to the quirky stuff. The night shift always seemed a bit more risky, with the drunks and groups of men out looking for fun or trouble. T, my Asian heavy, was doing a splendid job alongside Darren keeping everyone safe and happy. But Diana was proving to be a typical bully, and whilst enjoying picking on the girls, she seemed unable to deal with even the smallest fracas if a man was involved.

At the slightest hint of trouble, she would phone Darren, hysterical with certainty of her imminent murder and mutilation. In hindsight, this was probably her guilty conscience. She'd have known, even if we hadn't, that her previous employers from Bournemouth were systematically hunting her down. We just saw her terror at every shadow that crossed the window as an irritating over-reaction, night after night.

Twenty four hour opening meant being on call for twenty four hours out of every twenty four. My last contact with Diana would be at about two am to check all was well. Then I would try to get a little sleep before she phoned me and demanded Darren went to the rescue as something untoward was occurring.

One night as I was lying in bed with Darren, dozing, trying to unwind after a difficult day, I took a call from the office saying that two pissed up, mad men had tried to set the flat alight. Darren leapt up, got dressed and headed off to do his duty, phoning T on the way for back up. T was already there, having received a similar panic stricken phone call, and believing that catastrophe was imminent, he arrived half dressed. As usual Diana had over- egged the danger. Her arsonists were two inebriated Russians who had tried to smoke in the massage room. A tissue in the bin had been set alight in the process, causing a bit of smoke and commotion.

When Darren arrived, T informed him that one of the blokes was 'fucking massive,' which, coming from T who was at least eighteen stone of bad tempered, gym-honed Pakistani beefcake was not something to be taken lightly.

Diana immediately started wittering and flapping, describing the situation loudly and frightening the girls. She made it sound like a mixture of the Russian invasion of Afghanistan and Paul Newman's Towering Inferno.

Darren tried to calm her and the situation down, before Diana caused a much bigger incident with her incendiary racial expletives.

'They're just a pair of pissed idiots,' T explained to Darren. 'But they're refusing to leave. They wanna talk to management. They wanna know why the ladies wouldn't see them.'

Darren, the master of arbitration, explained to the grumpy guests that he was the manager, and if they wanted to talk they could talk to him outside, but they would be leaving forthwith, that was non-negotiable. There was no way he was getting into a debate with inebriated visitors and taking up a working room on a busy night shift.

T was right; one of them was a monster with a big, bald head and shoulders so wide he had to go sideways through the door.

T and Darren allowed the two gents to walk down the stairs and once outside led them away from the other flats. At this point Darren explained politely that we did not entertain drunks.

'You're not banned,' he explained patiently, whilst poised and ready to defend himself if it kicked off. 'You're not in trouble and you are welcome to return but not until you have sobered up.'

'We see ladies now?' the Russian giant said, focusing past Darren and fixing his gaze on the entrance to the flats.

'No,' Darren said firmly, standing his ground. 'Not until you can behave properly. Come back sober and whatever ladies you choose will then be available. Treat the girls with respect and everybody can have a nice time without any problems.'

The two soviet man-mountains left with surprisingly little argument, and after returning to the flats to reassure the girls that all was OK and the culprits had agreed to visit another day, when sober, to resume their pleasure, Darren returned home whilst T took Carmen, who sportingly was happy to do anything to anybody for the right price, to see John from Northampton and his wife.

'I'm glad that didn't go pear-shaped.' Darren flopped back into bed. 'Whilst I had no doubts we could have handled them it wouldn't have been pretty. The one guy was almost twice the size of T, almost as huge as Diana!'

I laughed. He flipped the pillow over, pummelling it into a hollow so he could lie knackered on the fresh cold surface.

'T really hates Diana,' he mused sleepily, 'it's only out of loyalty to you that he answers her calls at all. I think he'd be happy for her to be burnt at the stake.'

That made two of us then.

About an hour later, when he was in a deep sleep, Darren got another call. The same blokes were back. Diana had refused to let them in this time, and they were trying to kick down the security door. Poor Darren, back up, dressed and at the flats in under three minutes, only this time much more grumpy, tired and on edge. He phoned T to learn that back up was unfortunately still on an out-call with Carmen and miles away, so Darren was on his own.

When he arrived at the flats, Darren quietly ran up the stairs, trying not to make any more noise than necessary to either alarm the neighbours, or alert the intruders. Very much aware that he was outnumbered and would be confronting two, (four if you counted the big bloke three times) alcohol-fuelled, nutters who, in Darren's book were obviously looking for trouble, having come back when they'd specifically been warned not to.

He stopped when there was half a flight of stairs between them. The protagonists became aware Darren was there, watching them. They turned around and groaned theatrically. They kept calling him boss man and saying they just wanted to see a woman for sex. Once again, attempting to diffuse the situation so as not to disturb the people in the other flats, disrupt the business, distress the girls, not to mention avoid a potentially problematic confrontation in a confined stairway, Darren very politely explained to the blokes that they needed to come outside again so that he could talk to them.

Amazingly, they obeyed for a second time that night, and followed him down the stairs. Darren calmly led them outside and again discreetly away from the other flats.

Putting on his best assertive voice and body language he explained to them that they were now in deep shit. He'd phoned the rest of 'Madam Becky's' security and they were on the way. They were now banned for life, and if they ever showed up again at the flat they would be dealt with accordingly. Even more drunk than the last time, swaying back and forward as Darren pushed his finger into their faces, he explained that they should go home whilst they still could.

Again they tried to talk their way back into the building, to have sex with a woman. But the conversation was shortened as, thinking on his feet, Darren 'answered' his non- ringing phone and made imaginary arrangements with his non-existent security team to have these boys properly taken care of.

Concluding that the game was up, the bolshie Bolsheviks decided to head for home, and staggered off across the car park.

Darren dragged his exhausted and sleep-deprived self back up the stairs to the flat.

'All sorted,' he said to Diana and the girls. 'That pair are now on the banned list.'

He didn't stay to listen to one of Diana's tirades. He just wanted to get home to his bed. On his way back down the stairs he realised that the evicted men had not phoned for a cab or got into a car. So there was a distinct possibility that they would either be hiding waiting for him to leave or that they lived locally, too close for comfort. Darren, having a nasty feeling brewing in his waters, silently caught them up and followed them at a distance for a couple of streets. Turning a corner he was hit by a crescendo of trash metal music coming from a small, unkempt, terraced house.

In the front garden, the big guy and his side-kick had re-joined about twelve of his mates, who were having a 4.00am barbecue.

Ducking down behind a wall, Darren watched the big guy talking to his lads with a horrible feeling in the pit of his stomach. He watched the group down more and more industrial strength hooch and become more and more animated. There was no doubt in Darren's mind that things were going to get very ugly indeed.

Darren legged it back to the perceived safety of the flat and phoned T. 'Mate, you better get back here as soon as you can and bring some help. Your bro and your cousins. The bigger and meaner the better. I'm gonna call Becky's mental mate Keith as well.'

Darren took his cricket bat out of his car, along with a metal bar and his extendable baton, which he tucked into the waistband of his trousers. He took up a position in the car park and waited for the advance of the Red Army.

He waited about half an hour preparing for the onslaught and then… nothing happened, then nothing, then nothing. Darren was raising up a prayer for the soporific effects of homemade Russian brew just as T and the Asian cavalry arrived, followed by Keith and his cattle prod.

There's an old Samurai saying, 'when the battle is over, tighten your chin strap!' After a few days, when we thought we'd seen the last of him, Darren got another call - this time from T saying that the bloke had come back, this time on his own. T had taken him outside where the guy had pulled a gleaming machete from his jacket, and proceeded to threaten T in broken English with various forms of cold war torture and decapitation. T, not one to take such bad manners lightly, took out his baseball bat and proceeded to chase the oaf through the car park and away.

Some people never learn.

A couple of weeks later, again in the early hours, Darren answered another call from a hysterical Diana who shrieked that the big bloke was outside kicking the door again. Good old Darren was up, dressed and in the car in a record ten seconds. As he ran up the stairs, the delinquent intruder turned to look at him, again trying to explain that he just wanted to see a woman for sex. Ten out of ten for effort and perseverance, but this guy had crossed the line several times and this needed to be ended fast.

Again, not wanting a confrontation on the stairs in front of the other flats, Darren explained that as usual they would be going back outside to talk. Walking down the stairs first, Darren made sure he kept far enough ahead so he wouldn't get stabbed in the back. At the bottom of the stairwell Darren stepped aside so the big man could pass, and as he walked through the exit door Darren pulled out his extendable baton and flicked it sharply out to its full length just as the Russian reached inside his coat for his weapon. Darren flashed the baton hard and fast inches from the end of Rasputin's nose.

'Keep your hands still and don't move,' Darren ordered.

Surprised, he almost laughed out loud, when the Russian told him to be quiet, and urged my boyfriend not to be frightened and that if he retracted the baton, he wasn't going to get hurt.

Darren pointed out to his confused companion that he was feeling a lot of things at that point, but fear wasn't one of them, and he was fighting and losing an overriding urge to cave the man's skull in.

At the critical moment of the car park confrontation, Darren got a call from Diana upstairs. The daft cow had panicked, wound the girls up into mindless hysteria and called the police.

A multitude of sirens were audible. Darren pushed the end of the baton hard under the man's chin and, as threateningly as he could, he recited the fellows address. This had quite a sobering effect on the prisoner as Darren pointed out in easy to understand basic English that the entire security team knew where he and his friends lived and that they'd be getting a visit in the very near future. As the sirens from the police cars got closer Darren advised him to bugger off but promised that he'd be seeing him again soon.

The warning must have worked. That was the last we saw of our friend, but there were always plenty more where he came from.

CHAPTER TWENTY FOUR

Rumour has it that the British are very uptight about sex, but the truth is Britain is statistically the most promiscuous country in the western world. The British have wonderfully vivid imaginations, and it's not always kept behind closed doors.

The younger generation, motivated by cheap booze and pop videos, have embraced recreational sex and binge drinking with delirious abandonment. There's a whole randy world of sex out there, ordinary people doing their thing. Fetish scene, swinging clubs, massage parlours and domination chambers, sex shops, amateur porn, dogging, reader's wives, on and on it goes; I'm surprised we've not all gone blind, together as a nation.

There were many evenings when I was leaving one of Milton Keynes' trendy night spots in the early hours after a good boogie, that I would cast a sober, critical eye over the beer-soaked, staggering proletariat and despair. Young men pissing up police vans and shop girls vomiting in doorways, no knickers, gravity defying shoes, the geisha shuffle, shivering coatless into oblivion, I would think if God doesn't destroy the towns and cities of Britain, then he owes Sodom and Gomorrah an apology.

Sex workers are condemned by many as depraved and lacking in morals, but I have found that ladies who work in the sex industry are often the least promiscuous of all the people I know.

As if I didn't have enough on my plate running a busy brothel, I decided to branch out into the realms of more public sexuality, and open an adult shop - not quite a sex shop, but nearly - selling lingerie, basques, sex toys and the other accoutrements that contributed to successful fornication. It would be a legal business, in case 'Madam Becky's' landed us all in the clink and destitute. When the locals discovered I planned to open on the high street, there was a public outcry, culminating in petitions to the relevant authorities. Apparently I was opening an Amsterdam-style whore house, right on the pedestrian crossing, complete with naked Go Go dancers in the windows, and masturbating midgets to render the surrounding property worthless. I've never really known what Go Go dancing is, but we did have a dwarf on the books, so I was half way there. Despite the rumours and hysteria, I went ahead and opened Foo Foo in the Milton Keynes suburb of Fenny Stratford just before Christmas 2006.

Foo Foo is a French slang word for a lady's private parts, and I thought it was a perfect name for a naughty knickers and fanny paraphernalia outlet.

The shop was sensational, even though I say so myself. Using all my design and decorating skills, it had an air of Versailles about it, with huge chandeliers, marbled walls and gilt mirrors reflecting the classy British underwear and corsetry we were specialising in.

An area was partitioned off for the ruder items to be hidden behind a curtain, to avoid the shame if you were bra shopping with your grandmother or maiden aunt. But many of the silly sexy gifts had been dotted around the shop to tempt the browser into buying over-priced secret Santa tat for the forthcoming festive season.

It was the first time I had dealt with the dildo buying populace, and I was shocked. The general public were far more badly behaved and depraved than prostitutes. Working in Foo Foo was the first time I had blushed in many years, and lo and behold, my friends from the council licensing authority were back.

My crime du jour it seemed was the illicit and illegal trade of milk chocolate willies on sticks.

Standing in front of my counter were two seedy-looking men. They'd had a good poke around in the vibrator and cock ring cupboard, and were now standing before me so shiftily that I was expecting them to ask me if they could be fitted with stockings and crotch- less panties. Nervously fiddling with the impulse buy comedy items on the counter, a small rodent-looking chap was over fondling a chocolate penis, welded by its balls to a lolly stick, and gift wrapped in cellophane.

Up the road in the brothel the customers weren't allowed to mess about with the merchandise before they paid up, I was going to have to get used to customers wandering around, fingering my goods.

'That willy'll go soft and your hand'll get sticky if you hold it that tightly.' I gave him a wink. 'Didn't your mum ever warn you about that?' A couple of days behind a counter, classy as it was, and I was turning into Barbara Windsor.

He seemed to be reading the ingredients on the back, studying them carefully.

'You'll absorb fewer calories if you suck on a real one, but maybe your friend's isn't quite so tasty!' I said, hoping to tease a laugh or a smile from the two sour-faced men. 'We have a full range of low calorie, sugar free, fruity lubricant to cheer it up a bit if you fancy a lick?' I winked at the other chap, and handed him a pina colada flavoured anal lube tester.

Giving me a withering glare, the rodent placed the chocolate willy on the counter and reached into his briefcase.

Great, I thought, my cheeky banter had resulted in a sale.

While the rat man rummaged through his briefcase for his money, I glanced at the price sticker on the chocolate knob, and mentally ran though how to use the till in my head. The sodding thing was still getting the better of me, technology really wasn't my thing, and an impending sale was making me anxious.

Instead of handing over £2.50 and putting his willy in his bag and heading home, the man presented me with a pile of forms and unbelievably asked, 'do you have a licence?'

Bugger me, here we go again! This had to be personal.

'For this confectionery?' he said seriously. 'You need a licence from the council to sell confectionery.'

'I need a licence to sell novelty chocolate cocks?'

'Yes, indeed you do.'

'Nipples?' I asked innocently.

'I beg your pardon?'

'I have chocolate coated nipples.'

Well I'd embarrassed him, so that was a small victory.

'I really don't think there's any need to get quite so...' he stuttered.

I cut him off and held up a tiny film covered box, rattling it at him. 'I have chocolate coated nipples as well as a willy, do my nipples fall foul of the letter of law, or will more leniencies be shown to them as they cover less surface area?'

His mute mate alternated between staring at the floor and staring at my chest. Neither of them seemed to see how ridiculous the situation was.

'You must fill out these forms, and pay the fee, and we shall return to inspect the premises before we can issue you with the required paperwork,' the rodent said in a sour tight voice.

'But I only have two nipples, and a few pricks on sticks,' I said. 'Just to see if anyone fancied them, but they are not all that nasty. I'm not applying for a licence for a few foul tasting dicks and a box of booby buttons.'

'If you are planning to sell them, then you have no choice,' he said stubbornly. His silent sidekick nodded in agreement. 'Even if you have only one food item, the licensing laws must be adhered to.'

They were getting way too much satisfaction from my novelty nipple problem for my liking.

Smiling at them, I lined up four willies and two nipples on the new shiny countertop in front of me, the chocolate nipples resting on top of his official forms perkily.

Quickly, starting with the willy closest to hand, I tore off the cellophane and stuffed the milk chocolate members into my mouth, one after the other without chewing.

Four sticks protruded from between my lips, and I struggled to breathe as I forced the nipples past the willies down into my cheeks like a bulimic hamster.

The men from the council stared at me in horror.

I was a bit horrified myself. It was that awful cheap waxy chocolate of Christmas tree decorations. It tasted like the inside of pet shops, and was just disintegrating into small clumps like damp sand in my mouth, before solidifying again, and threatening to cut off my windpipe.

Their look of utter disgust and disbelief made me giggle, and I started to dribble. Big blobs of chocolate splattered my top. My saliva was unable to find a way past the chocolate flavoured chemicals that had formed a tight ball at the back of my throat. I was teetering on the narrow ledge between asphyxiation and hysteria, something had to give way. With little choice if I wanted to stay conscious, I leant forward, opened my mouth, and gagged the entire revolting dark brown sludge, sticks and all, onto Milton Keynes Council's pristine licence applications.

'Oops!' I said wiping my lips with the back of my hand. 'Sorry about that. Can't sell them now can I? Was there anything else I can do for you gentlemen before you go?'

Small victory to me I think.

Meanwhile, back at the ranch, I desperately needed help to cover my reception duties at 'Madam Becky's'. One of my girls, who we sold on the phone as a Billy Piper looky likey had told me that her friend was really interested in being a receptionist and would be perfect. I arranged to meet them later, and then turned my attention to locating Belinda, who'd been on a hot date with a new lad the night before and was now late for a session with Mr North and Spanky Monkey. Diana had set up a system of fines for tardiness, and Belinda was her main target.

Belinda was the only one left from the old days, and I think Diana was threatened by our friendship. Belinda was unreliable, winsome and as daft as a brush, but I loved her, and there was no way Diana was going to push her out. It was tricky though, the rules needed to apply to everyone equally, but I just couldn't help being more lenient and forgiving with my little pal. I'd sacked her too many times to count, for all manner of misdemeanours - generally all round laziness and absenteeism, but she always phoned and said sorry, and we always kissed and made up. No one else ever got a second chance.

Mr North was on the bed in the biggest working room with the Jacuzzi, and talked to Kate about her awful marriage while he waited for the puppet mistress. He was such a nice man. Just my type, but I don't think I could be bothered with the whole Plushism fetish thing outside of work. I didn't have any fetishes or fantasies. I suppose when you're surrounded by a bit of everything all day every day, the mystery soon wears off and it just becomes another day at work rather than an exciting scenario played out in your head for sexual gratification.

Kate, to her surprise, was doing amazingly well. Her confidence, ruined by twelve years in a bad relationship, was growing daily. She was astounded by how men would want to pay money to spend time with a frumpy and slightly plump forty year old mother of three.

Many times I had explained to her, that good escorts give a little of themselves to their clients, and a warm, caring and genuine personality will make you more money than an expensive boob job. Finally she'd started to believe it. Kate was finding it hard to hide the new skip in her step from her husband, but her running away fund was growing rapidly, and she'd planned to leave him after Christmas.

Ami Dog was a regular feature under the bed in the main room. The other bedroom had a large round bed that sat directly on the floor with no hiding places, so it was useless as a canine retreat. It was a receptionist's duty to remember to whistle her out of the bedroom before the action started; she was often forgotten if we were busy. Our Asian gents were none too keen on dogs, and many a time a disgruntled shout would proclaim the emergence of a wet nose, appearing at face level when at the peak of activity the bouncing bed slats drove Ami out into the open seeking a quieter refuge.

'How long can you wait?' I asked Mr North, as he drank his second cup of tea.

'Not much longer Becks, I've got a meeting at lunch time in St Albans.'

Bloody girl. She'd known for days that Mr North was coming in. Only yesterday she'd brushed out Spanky's mattes, dried from a previous encounter, and had a practice play with Tranny Tedward and Lady Lima, the new puppets. I knew that she knew she was meant to be here. So much for managing girls in flats being easier than managing girls on out-calls; they could drive you to an early grave this lot. If the worst came to the worst. I'd have to dig out my Rolf Harris costume and see to Mr North myself.

'I'll call her again and see if we can get an ETA,' I said calmly, none of my irritation showed for the customer. 'Kate honey, can you come here a moment?' I walked out of the room.

'Do you think you could do the Spanky Monkey thing if she doesn't show up?' I asked Kate quietly outside the room. 'Maybe just half the monkey thing if he has to rush off? Just give him a quick Anne Frank with the puppet? Not the whole squeaking and silly voice stuff. It seems such a shame to waste his time. Bloody Belinda, I'll have her guts for garters when she finally gets here.'

The way she looked at me didn't make me think she was up for the job.

'Becky, I can't, it's too weird!'

'Kate hon, we're in a medieval castle-themed brothel, with men dressed as women, randy puppets and a sheep dog... it's all weird. It's what we do. We're all very weird.'

'Fair play,' she conceded with a smile. 'I'll give it a go. I'll laugh though.'

'Yeah, laughing's expected, we all do. Thanks Kate, I'll ask Mr North if he's ok with you stepping in. Diana's stuffed Spanky and his mates back in the broom cupboard, so you'll have to fish him out, but he's had his hair done yesterday by Belle, so he's ready to roll.'

Darren walked out of the kitchen, holding the land line handset.

'Belinda's just called the work phone, she's trapped.'

'What?' I shrieked. Memories of Tasha's kidnap years ago were flashing through my mind.

'She stayed with that bloke she met last night; he went to work at stupid o'clock this morning and has locked her in by mistake. All the ground floor windows are locked as well, so she can't get out. Oh, and she's lost her phone, so she can't call him or you. Luckily she knew the reception number from memory and he has a land line.'

'Give me strength!' I leant against the wall and closed my eyes.

Darren looked amused.

'I'll go find that monkey thing,' Kate hurried away.

'Can we do anything?' I said looking at Darren as I tried to formulate a rescue plan.

'I'm going there now to try and get her out,' he said putting down the phone and picking up his car keys. Then kissing the top of my head he walked out of the flat chuckling to himself.

'Where is she?' I called after him.

'Somewhere called Gardenia Gardens in Walnut Tree. That name rang a bell for some reason. Hopefully I won't be long.'

As he pulled into Gardenia Gardens, Darren realised why the road sounded familiar. One of his best mates from his Post Office days lived there, just up the road from where Belinda was leaning out of the bedroom window waving frantically, like a budget version of Shakespeare's Juliet, her weighty chest threatening to tumble her forwards to her death at any moment.

'He's gone off and locked me in. I've tried all the downstairs windows, but I can't open them,' Belle shouted down.

'You can't have made much of an impression on him if he's forgotten about you already. Does that window open fully?' Darren asked.

She nodded that it did.

Darren jogged up the road to his mate Browny's house. He rang the doorbell and desperately hoped that Browny's misses wouldn't answer. Darren's luck held out as his best friend of years before came to the door. He looked quite grumpy and sleepy; Darren had forgotten he was the night shift manager, and that he would have been deeply asleep.

'Darren,' he said surprised. 'What you doing here, come in.'

'Hello mate, how's it going?' Darren replied, staying on the doorstep. 'Don't suppose you've gotta ladder I can borrow?'

'Ladder? Sure no problem,' he yawned. 'What you need it for? Taken up window cleaning?'

Darren shook his head. 'Nah mate. I've got to rescue a daft tart whose been locked in a house round the corner. I've got to get her back to work, she's got a punter and a glove puppet waiting, and if I don't get a shift on, Becky's going to kill her.'

After a couple of seconds of open-mouthed silence Browny just smiled and said, 'I fucking love hearing about your life. I bet you're gutted you left the Post Office! Can't wait to let the lads at work hear this one, it's almost better than the 'Pat O Gram!'

Darren gratefully borrowed the garage keys and left his mate to go back to bed whilst he located a ladder and jogged back down the road with it.

Belinda's tears flowed loudly, and people started to come out of their houses to watch.

'Hang on, I'll come up to you and help get your leg over.'

'It's not flaming funny,' she wailed.

Realising what he said and apologising Darren climbed up quickly and tried to calm her down.

As she timidly stretched her leg over the window sill and inched out backwards, her ridiculously short dress, perfect for a night of seduction, but not ideal for escaping down ladders, was hitched upwards leaving her bare arse, and everything else, showing to the world and his wife. Screaming with terror at every inch of movement, six inch platform shoes floundered in mid air trying to find the first rung of the ladder.

'Jeez Belle, you could have taken your shoes off you dozy bint. Hold still, you'll kill us both like that.' Twenty foot in the air, carefully, whilst trying to cling on to the ladder with one hand, Darren pulled off Belinda's shoes and threw them behind him into the bushes.

She screamed very loudly all the way down. .

After returning the ladder, they made it home in time for tea and medals, but way too late for Spanky and Mr North.

Things had calmed down slightly by later that afternoon, and I looked at the kitchen clock and realised the new receptionist candidate would be arriving shortly; although how any normal person was going to keep this lot under control I had no idea. I saw Gemma, the Billy Piper girl whose friend I was waiting for, as she pulled into the car park and I turned away from the window to put the kettle on.

Gemma walked into the kitchen, followed by a tall, good looking dark haired man in his twenties, who smiled widely at me his eyes twinkling.

'Don't let Diana see you with a strange man in the kitchen,' I joked. 'She'll burst into fairy lights! I think the massage room is free now if you'd like to show sir into there.'

'He's come about the receptionist job; this is Luke. Luke, this is Madam Becky.'

'But he's a man.'

'He's a gay man Becky,' she said looking crest fallen.

'A very gay man,' Luke added, still smiling. 'Very very gay!'

'It's good to be gay,' added Gemma.

Luke gave her an affectionate squeeze.

'What do you do at the moment Luke?' I asked whilst quickly working through the possibilities in my mind. Could it work?

'I'm a magician and children's entertainer. Oh, and I make balloon animals,' he told me.

'Seriously?'

'Yep, I've done it for years. I love it. The kids are great.'

I sat down at the table and looked him over - a few inches above six foot, with dark wavy hair and an open endearing cheeky grin. I could imagine that kids loved him. I liked him instantly. But I am always wary of men in this business. Many get involved for unpleasant ulterior motives, be they sexual or financial. Girls know if they're being letched over, and it makes them uncomfortable. They come to work to feel safe and relaxed, not ogled and mucked about with by the management. Darren and T had no interest in the girls, and from what Luke said nor would he.

I wasn't sure if the clients would be happy with a man answering the phones, or opening the door. On the odd occasion Darren picked up the phone, the client would often hang up. A male receptionist could be bad for business, but I liked Luke and wanted to give it a try.

'Ok,' I said, making a decision. 'One week trial.'

It worked wonderfully. He was just camp enough to make the punters feel relaxed and welcome, and, better than anything, he had OCD. He was as obsessed as I was with tiding the rooms, folding towels, making beds and having everything looking just fine and dandy.

'Why don't you do male escorts?' Luke asked one day.

'Women won't pay for sex Luke, if they have a spare hundred quid they'd rather buy shoes or have a hair do. I've tried it before, there's no customers. No matter how grim looking a female you are, at 2.00am after ten pints of lager some bloke will shag you.' I thought about my night receptionist and grinned. 'Even Diana could get herself some action. Anyway, men are like dog turds; the older they are, the easier they are to pick up; it's no problem for a woman to get laid.'

'Not for women,' he said, shaking his head. 'I mean male escorts for men. Gay boys.'

'Really?'

'I'll run it,' he reassured. 'You don't need to do anything. I think it'll work.'

Luke's confidence and enthusiasm was infectious, so I thought why not?

Within a week we were ready to launch a new website for Madam Becky's Boys. Thanks to Luke I had several lads working for me, and a photo shoot was organised with all the Gayz as they were now called. They were buffed and gleaming to drum us up some business. They were all quite young or young looking, but there wasn't enough of them to make the website look established, so poor Darren was coerced to step in as an honorary gay and make up the numbers.

Laughing uproariously, Luke and I posted his profile as 'Sidney' on the new site. The young gayz laughed and winked at him making saucy comments about him being a hunky bear, which seemed to be the name gay men give to older, slightly portly, hairier chaps.

'You've got to chop his head off that photo; he'll have a frigging fit if he sees that,' I said, dabbing at my eyes with a tissue. 'Everyone will recognise him. You'll cause the Royal Mail to empty their sacks in protest!'

Luke was photo shopping Darren's images while I was clinging onto the edge of the desk crying from laughter. Darren being outed as a gay prostitute was almost worse for his family than him dating a notorious Madam.

'He's way too old and plump to be a rent boy; he'll have to be the rent man,' I laughed as we tweaked him on the screen.

'Oooh! He looks super against the red background in the pole lounge.' Luke was excited. 'Can I keep just his chin? It's a good one.'

Stripped to the waist and posing as if his life depended on it, Darren and his badger- grey chest hair became a hit. He got quite a few enquiries from other bears or chickens which is what the younger gay men are apparently called. Each time a client called to book him, I would have to say that he was on his holidays in Egypt and the others would fall around shrieking with mirth.

Luke re-named Darren, Fanny Dazzle, and the boys printed off pictures of him and stuck them to the walls covered in love messages. Poor Darren would sit beside me at the kitchen table, red-faced and terrified that he would be pressed into active service during one of our many unexpected staffing shortages.

The gayz, 'Madam Becky's Boys' provided gay massage for men, and were surprisingly busy. The regular clients found them a bit shocking, and we had to push the lads squealing into empty rooms when straight gents were shown in. What I found most surprising was the number of straight dads who had been seeing my ladies for years, who decided to give a boy a try once in a while.

Who'd have thought it?

Luke had, and it all worked splendidly well.

CHAPTER TWENTY FIVE

At Christmas lads and lasses were flat out. If we ran out of rooms I just pushed everyone into the pole dancing room together and they all had it off willy nilly, where ever they could find a space. The clients loved it, and everyone would swap half way through, it was great value for money.

Kate complained that she always ended up shagging on the wooden dance stage and had splinters in her buttocks. She'd saved five grand already, and had plenty of money to start a new life away from her husband; she just couldn't seem to make the break. The fear of the unknown, and the fear of being single again after so long crippled her. She was actually in a position to have changed her life; she hated herself for being, as she thought, so weak and pathetic. We had so many different ladies, from so many walks of life, that there were wise words and advice on tap, covering all scenarios. I was an expert in staying in unhealthy relationships for way too long, and knew how hard it was for even the most determined of people to break free of their comfort zone.

Christmas was the time when all the gifts arrived from the regular regulars, given to their favourite ladies for services rendered. Champers, chocolates, gold chains and flowers all came flooding in.

Punters were in and out all day, as they sloped off, escaping their family duties for a festive frolic. I provided a steady stream of tea trays piled high with mince pies and fancy shortbreads. Ami Dog looked splendid, sneaking around the flats stealing tasty left-overs, wearing a little Santa outfit I'd bought for her when I'd bought one for Dogbaby, my terrier.

Gemma our Billy Piper tribute had become a fighting favourite of St-St-Stanley's and she'd earned enough from her bouts for a very good Christmas, thanks to her left hook. She was halfway through round two, when I heard her shout loudly, swearing and cursing. Wondering what Stanley had done to upset her so vocally, I ran down the corridor and burst into the room.

Ami Dog was cowered under an occasional table, ears flat to the sides of her head, eyes wide with fright. Gemma attempted to haul the dog across the room by the Santa Paws costume whilst cursing her loudly. Stanley, dressed as always in his boxing gloves, PVC dress and thigh boots had collapsed on the floor with his legs waving in the air like the childhood parody of a dying fly. The usual aroma of sweat, both stale and fresh, mingled with halitosis, and hot PVC - Stanley's trade mark scent - filled the room. But there was something else, an undertone of something altogether meatier but no less unpleasant.

Stanley started to cry, howling pitifully, his legs still held aloft, as he strained forward at the waist in an odd version of an abdominal crunch, flapping his boxing gloves fruitlessly towards his shiny boots. I just stood and stared. This was a new one on me. I had no idea what was happening.

'That filthy hound was under the bed, it came out and sodding well chucked up everywhere.' Gemma was furious. 'It looks like it's stuffed about a thousand bloody Yule logs. I hate this sodding animal, and then he......' still clutching the dog by the scruff, she nodded towards the prone Stanley, '...went and stood in it, and slipped over. It's all over his feet and up his boots. I'm not sodding cleaning it up. Frigging stinking thing.' Letting go, she aimed a kick at the dog's backside as Ami made a bolt for it out of the open door, and back into the kitchen to hide under a chair until the fuss died down.

Kate cleaned up the mess.

'Your bloody dog, your bloody problem,' Gemma had said to her, as she led a distressed Stanley by the gloved hand into the other room, to re-start round two from the beginning.

Kate's husband had gone to his work's Christmas party and her kids were with their grandparents, so she'd decided to work in the evening which was unusual, and the evening clients weren't used to seeing a collie on the premises.

A Friday night before Christmas in the height of the party season was going to be bonkers, and we needed all hands to the pump. I was in helping Luke with the phones and my elder daughter Abi, who'd now turned eighteen, was in the work kitchen keeping the refreshments flowing. Belinda had called in sick, half dead apparently from typhoid, rabies or something or another.

No secrets in a brothel; it was common knowledge that she was on another date with the young man who'd accidentally locked her in the house. She was smitten and I was happy for her.

A group of six older, rather tipsy gents were in the pole dancing room, watching Lexi 'practicing'. We were playing for time, as most of the girls were returning back with T from an out-call. They were only a few minutes away and I was confident that Lexi, her toned, tanned and much improved twirling and grinding would keep the waiting customers entertained for a while longer.

T phoned to say he was just pulling into the car park with the girls, so I gave Kate a silver tray of cold beer, and asked her to serve the patient partyers.

'Assure them that the girls will be with them in the next few minutes,' I said. 'Tell them that they are just freshening up.'

The main office kitchen was next to the pole dancing lounge, so I heard the shout of 'you vile disgusting animal!' clearly.

Oh no, not again. She was going to have to take Ami Dog home if this carried on. The angry shouting got louder, and I heard an answering whimper coming from under the table.

Eh Ami? She was in the kitchen with me, looking even more terrified than previously, the fact she was still dressed in red velour with a white fur trim making her look even more cowed and unhappy.

Who the hell was Kate screaming at then?

I dashed in and discovered Kate hysterically slapping a client around the head and neck, having previously thrown the tray of beers at him. Unfortunately Lexi, catching her breath between dances, had been sitting on his lap at the beginning of the onslaught and was now soaked and smelling like a pub carpet.

As I dragged Kate off her victim, shaking with rage, it was obvious that we had just met Kate's husband. Of course we all felt we knew him already after eighteen months of hearing about his antics - always nice to put a face to a name, but maybe in slightly less disruptive circumstances.

The gentleman in question had now come to his senses, and surprised at seeing his wife in a basque and stockings, carrying a tray of complimentary drinks into a brothel dance lounge, had started to shout back. Luckily T had just entered the flat and heard the commotion and moved in to separate them.

Poor Kate, weeping and shouting, was bundled into flat two and the entire party of revellers, their ardour now severely dampened by flying alcohol and fists, were shown by an irritated T out of the building.

We refused to let Kate go home that evening without T and Darren going with her. She went to collect her clothes and stayed with the kids at her mother's for the night.

I took all her details off the website, and we waited for the fireworks to start.

I would always defend my staff, but the double standards were obvious. Who should be more hurt and angry, the woman who finds her husband visiting a brothel, or the man who finds his wife working in one?

Needless to say that was the end of that marriage, and Kate's time at MB's. Fearing a custody battle, the risk of working as an escort was just too great for her, and not something she wanted to defend in court. She had shared part of her journey with us and was now moving on to other things. We wished her and Ami dogspeed, and we all got back to what we did best.

The New Year of 2007 got off to an emotionally rocky start. Kate had left us, and the fight with her hubby in the pole dancing room, and Stanley's slide into the dog sick had become the stuff of legends. Abi my daughter was helping Luke more and more on reception, the girls treated Abi like a pet. Carmen, the Cuban hotty, who seemed to have stopped bothering to go home at all, and was now living in the flats as a permanent fixture, adored her. Carmen was as obsessed with everyone else's appearance as she was her own. She spent hours each day brushing Abi's hair and trying to pluck her eyebrows as she squirmed away, attempting to escape the tweezers.

'Ah, ah, ah baby girl! No cry! I know baby girl it pains, I stop now eh? We go for a smoke?'

The plucking and squealing would be postponed as the girls pulled on their coats or thick dressing gowns over their lingerie and stockings, and trouped out, shivering, nearly naked onto the frozen roof terrace to puff on a fag. Then enrage me by flicking the lipstick smeared butts off the roof onto the staff of the restaurants below.

Belinda had come to see me at home in the week between Christmas and New Year, and told me she was going to quit. She wanted to settle down with her new man, and they were considering moving away, to be nearer his family. He knew what she did, and didn't much like it, and I got the feeling he was keen to distance her from us all, and her previous life. It was a difficult heart-breaking conversation. I was happy for her, but Spanky, Mr North and I would miss her dreadfully.

Diana was fining the girls for every small indiscretion; £5 was taken from their money at the end of their shift for leaving a client's tea tray in the room. Another £5 for not washing the tea pot. £5 for not washing out the bath and a whopping £20 for being late. Some of the more unreliable girls had slipped into negative equity.

In some ways I understood what she was trying to do. I was as frustrated as she was. The girls were a nightmare, and it felt like we were running a playgroup - chasing round trying to clean up after, referee and organise two dozen people who behaved as badly as a group of under fives who'd been filled with fizzy drinks and e-numbers before being shaken up at the fun fair. Wiggy's theory all those years ago about having the girls working from a flat would make management easier, was so wrong. Sometimes I shut myself into a room and cried.

Then one cold day, money went missing from the safe, about six hundred pounds. Diana and I were the only people to have had access at the time. I knew it wasn't me. She caused a massive fuss, saying there were girls in the kitchen spying over her shoulder and peeking at the digital code as she opened the door.

'It's her,' the witch said, pointing at Helena the Postman Pat-O-Gram.

Diana grabbed Darren's arm. 'You go to her house. Search it. That lazy Kaffer bitch yah, she's hidden it.'

She emptied all the girls' bags and boxes on to the floor, and tensions were running high. Girls shouted and jostled, and called her a fat cow. Poor Helena was beside herself and couldn't stop crying.

'I haven't Becky. I wouldn't,' Helena sobbed at me. She was terrified that Diana, who she knew hated her, would go to her home and tell her husband everything.

I hated bullying, and I hated dishonesty. Diana had crossed the line between running a tight ship and terrifying vulnerable people, my friends, and I wouldn't have it. Escorts are notoriously difficult to deal with. It's like spending your life pushing a piece of string uphill, but that's how it is. You can't bully and fine them into submission.

I protected Helena from the incredible bulk, but the money was never found.

The discordant mutterings soon started again and there was about to be another mutiny. I struggled not to take sides. Coming to the boil, I had a sneaky feeling that it was all a smokescreen, and Diana had helped herself to my takings. She had recently moved out of the adjoining flat as we needed the rooms for the Gayz, and she seemed cagey and distant. None of us minded her being distant; in fact, the further away she was the better, but I felt she was up to something and had a bad feeling about it.

The accusations had caused bad feelings within the group. Luke came to me with the girls' issues, and Darren decided that to arbitrate properly we needed to hold weekly meetings so grievances could be aired and dealt with quickly and satisfactorily.

We sat on the big round bed in the working room and had a management conflab, Diana, Luke, Abi, Darren and I, followed by another parley with the girls and the Gayz. Darren took down the minutes while we listened to their ideas and suggestions on improving working relations and productivity. The main and oft repeated request seemed to be the swift and permanent disposal of Diana.

One change that we did make, after a suggestion from Luke, was to use the pole dancing lounge for clients requiring domination services. He noticed that he took far more calls for sadomasochism and bondage appointments than he did for pole dancing, and as we had nowhere to accommodate such adventures we were losing money.

With the festive season over, the clients didn't seem to be in the mood to have their visual senses abused by Lexi or Carmen's version of erotic dance.

A dungeon and the most beautiful torture equipment was made for us by a specialist carpenter, whose main business was the construction of spanking stools and suspension frames.

Mistress Matrix joined us. It was her duty to flay, spank and pee on those who required it. At her request I went on line to purchase some interestingly bizarre electrical gadgets. She assured me these strange items were very popular in certain circles. A very large power pack arrived, with a strange looking thing called a pin wheel, some clamps and most outrageous of all, a violet wand.

The pin wheel was attached to the battery pack as were various clamps, and the whole lot and the client were plugged into the mains. I had a mistrust and terror of electricity, and these preferences revolted me in a way nothing had ever done before.

I had no wish to see a demonstration of the violet wand. I thought that when it was inserted up a consenting bottom and switched on, not only did the client get an electric shock, but he glowed in the dark like a 1970s bedside lamp.

Luckily this wasn't the case. Mistress Matrix explained that the wand was a hand held electrical transformer created for kinky play. She lost me at that point.

'When they are set to mid-range, they can feel like holding a firework sparkler when the sparks nip at your skin.' I still wasn't getting it.

'At low settings,' she carried on, 'they are gentle tingles. At the highest settings, they can feel like cutting or burning.' Nice.

Sounded like hell to me. Apparently clients love the various sensations on the skin, or when inserted up inside, and get turned on by the fear of crackling electricity moving over their bodies. It looked a bit too much like Keith's cattle prod for my liking, and brought back some unpleasant memories.

Each to his own, but this was all too much for me. It was all in a day's work at the revamped 'Madam Becky's', and Diana was happy since Matrix, the electrocutioner, was charging them extra. Quite a lot extra.

Domination services were doing a brisk business and Diana, always keen to increase the size of everything, planned to expand her own wallet by providing her much discussed 'face-sitting service'.

If Diana sat on me I would be dead. That was a fact, but we all knew that there was a market for everything, no matter how uncomfortable. So she talked to Mistress Matrix about it in hideous, stomach turning detail. The image of a knickerless Diana, as she lowered herself onto my face, was beyond contemplation, and I was forced to run from the room in disgust.

The busier we became, the more we came to the attention of other agencies and the authorities, who were both keen to see us closed down. Our client numbers were up twenty percent each month, and these were all patrons who we'd taken from other establishments. We were making enemies fast.

CID dropped in to check us out, as they'd had a tip off we had children and animals plying their trade. It was obvious that they weren't taking the accusations seriously, and they implied it had come from someone whose own immoral earnings were being disrupted.

'Ami Dog has gone,' I explained, 'and she only participated in the one booking with Stanley, which was accidental and ended in tears'. Someone sniggered.

'But we do have a lady who's only four foot eight tall and she could easily be mistaken for a child from a distance.' I paused and smiled at them. I wasn't bothered; I could see they had no interest in causing us trouble. 'She is in fact in her twenties.' I added, 'you can meet her if you want?'

They soon left, having done what was required, investigated a malicious complaint and conceded that all was well. I was slightly concerned that again a rival had deliberately tried to shut me down. There had been several plans previously to have me robbed, maimed and closed.

Luckily my heavies were heavier than their heavies so robbery and violence had been avoided by a strange underworld weighing in, at which I was deemed to have the most clout, and therefore left alone for the time being.

I was confident that I could look after myself, but I hated the thought that the girls would be hurt or scared by any incidents. My friend Sharon had never mentally recovered from being slashed across the face and arms by the Bedford maniac and I didn't want anyone to suffer anything like that just because they worked for me.

Diana had proved herself worse than useless at dealing with such things and now Abi and Luke were working full time on reception. They couldn't be expected to handle altercations, safety was my main priority.

I needed to make the place safer, that would put my mind at rest when Darren, T or I weren't there holding the fort. As luck and good timing would have it, I was approached by a company who arranged product and services swaps between businesses.

Bartercard was a strange concept new to the UK. It was complicated and made my brain hurt, but theoretically it meant that I could have a state of the art security system fitted, by paying for it with blow jobs, dildos and the naughty limo service we were now offering, so that was exactly what I did.

Early in January 2007, the local paper ran a scoop, which saw me looking fancy on the front pages, this time wearing clothes, and the headline 'Bartercard businesses spending 'pounds' on MK Madam's services.'

Great free publicity.

The local parlour competition was furious. They were convinced that I was being given special dispensation by the powers that be, as well as from the wider business community. More rumours reached my ears about their plots to overthrow me and close me down for good.

The security cameras arrived not a moment too soon.

I heard on the subterranean grapevine that Diana was spending a lot of time in Luton, hanging out with Albanians. She'd not discussed her new friends with me, over a cup of tea as girls would, and my internal psychic alarm was sounding. When quizzed she said she had a new Eastern European boyfriend, and was very much in love. She brought him to meet us. The happy couple never exchanged a word or a touch during the visit. Diana's new love spoke very little English, but managed to check the place out thoroughly before they left. They were not convincing - her over six foot and thirty plus stone, him five feet and a fag butt with the body of a racing worm. I was sure it was a sham, and she was up to no good.

Spiritual advice via the tarot had been somewhat neglected, but when it came to a big decision the cards came out. Diana had made a huge difference to 'Madam Becky's'; it had changed beyond all recognition. Takings were going up a minimum of twenty percent a month and we ran a professional and orderly operation.

The Tower and Death had come up in the cards. The situation could only end one way, whatever mediation and middle ground Darren proposed.

We were out bulk buying condoms when Darren took a call from Luke, and informed me that Diana had placed an ad in the paper for her 'face sitting'. But the ad was for a different business, her own business, and she had clients arriving at *my* flat.

'Matrix is going wild,' Luke was panicking. 'Some of her clients are visiting Diana. She undercut Matrix's basic fee. You better get back here...'

'You're joking?.'

I could hear the girls wailing and crying. Mistress Matrix on the warpath was enough to terrify anyone.

'The girls are hiding behind the sofa,' Luke was wailing, 'I don't know what to do.'

I stood in the cash and carry, holding two trays of condoms.

'Has she lost her mind?' I demanded of Darren. 'Seriously, how can she think she can get away with this?'

The camel's back was broken by the straw. The boxer stood off the ropes, Darren went pale. I put down my Johnnies and ran back to the car.

Face-sitting does exactly what it says on the tin, and when I kicked in the door of the domination room, aided by a vengeful Mistress Matrix, Diana was trying to haul her enormous sweating bulk off her victim who was prone on the floor. I pushed her sideways hard, she rocked once, then toppled over, lying like a knickerless turtle on her back, legs kicking.

Swearing commenced and I let rip with a vengeful tirade, based on the facts that we all hated her and wanted her gone. She was fired, and told to dress instantly and leave. I have no idea how long it took to get herself upright, but she was gone in under ten minutes.

Well, you would have thought we had just won the world cup if you saw all the cheering and back slapping.

Ding Dong the witch is dead.

Intelligence soon arrived via Keith that Diana had been trying to open an agency in Luton with her drug-dealing Lothario. Dastardly Diana and Co had also been bragging to anyone who'd listen about their planned takeover of 'Madam Becky's' and, more alarmingly of a plot to bury me in the woods.

The troops were rallied. Death threats had been made to me and I had to take them seriously.

Contacts were contacted and favours called in. The flats quickly filled up as all types of nefarious ner-do-wells were summoned. We were expecting Albanians with guns, and Keith's army was ready to deal with whatever arsenal arrived at my door.

They manned the battlements and waited for the enemy to appear over the horizon.

An hour later I took a phone call from some bloke we'd never heard of, in Luton. He claimed he was a punter, and had booked one of my girls. He said he'd been robbed in his home by a hugely fat South African woman and a swarthy foreign dwarf. He told me he was being held hostage by the pair who were waiting in his front room whilst he cowered in the toilet. He had already been forced to send a friend out to the cashpoint to get the large lady more money.

I also discovered from this conversation that Diana had set up an escort agency, also called 'Madam Becky's', but based in Luton with a different phone number, and it was that new number Diana's hostage had called initially. It seemed she was using my good reputation to rob and extort terrified Lutonians.

The day had become more and more surreal. If Diana and her sidekick were in Luton, sitting on a couch demanding money with menaces, they wouldn't be in Bletchley anytime soon. Not unless her new operation was bigger than I'd been led to believe.

The 'Madam Becky' boys and girls who'd chosen to stay to watch the ruckus ran into Diana's old flat and started rooting through all the stuff that she had just walked out and left. I tried to make them bag it up and leave it for her to collect, but they had turned into a frenzied mob, looting and laughing and taking turns to carry her belongings out into the car park and set them alight.

Watching my gleeful staff capering around a pile of smouldering clothes on the tarmac, I called and texted Diana several times. I was polite and requested that she came and collected her oversized outfits, as I couldn't vouch for their safety. Everything had been torched, but at least I had evidence of my innocence if she wanted to cause a problem.

I went to find Keith and tell him to stand down the troops. There'd be no Battle of the Bulge, no Bletchley blood bath. We could all relax and put the kettle on.

CHAPTER TWENTY SIX

I had a real problem now. Not the police, Albanians with guns or wayward fatties, but my own personality and failings. We were all glad Diana had gone, there'd been no alternative, but I couldn't argue the fact that she had made a huge difference financially to 'Madam Becky's'; I knew I didn't have the skills to carry that on. My paperwork, book keeping and attention to detail were all but non-existent. Although I didn't trust her as far as I could have spat a rat, I trusted Darren, and I'd just left him to get on with it.

I had foolishly allowed other people to understand my business better than I did. They had made a better job of running it properly than I ever had and now without that back up I was weak, disorganised and terrified.

I'd left Darren and Diana to deal with the statistics which gave me a headache. I was better at chatting up the clients, dealing with the girls and irritating the authorities.

So many new forms had been created, so much information gathered. Darren and Diana had monitored and measured everything meticulously down to the last broken gingernut. It just swam before my eyes.

Each girl was given a daily job sheet when she started her shift. I leafed miserably through them; the girl's listings of the guys who came in to see them cheered me up a bit and made me laugh.

They had to write in a box who each visitor was. But as we didn't know who they really were anyway, they were given nicknames, or descriptions so we remembered vaguely who'd been in.

I scanned down the lists - Super Shag, Mr Multiple Orgasm, Dave Blue eyes, Fat Andrew, Pants on fire Paul, Bovril. I recognised most of them from their pseudonyms; fondly I pictured their faces and their preferences.

'What happens to all this stuff?' I asked Darren, whilst doing a calculation in my head. If we had fifteen or more girls working over a twenty four hour period, that added up to a lot of evidence to illegal activity over a week.

'I file it, so I can do the figures at the end of the month,' he said, pleased with his efficiency.

'Is that wise?' I wondered aloud. 'It's a hell of a risk. If we get raided, then the Old Bill's going to know exactly what the girls have been up to. They're meant to pay their own tax and stuff, but I'd rather no one could prove anything one way or another.'

'How are we going to measure everything then?' Darren was horrified; my concerns threatened his paper empire.

'Is measuring everything that important? I think we need to get rid of all this stuff immediately.'

'All of it?'

'Yep,' I nodded, 'you never know what shit Diana will be stirring up. We need to expect trouble of one sort of another, and reporting the girls to the Inland Revenge would be the easiest way for the stinking old trout to get her own back.'

He looked at me unconvinced, unwilling to see all his hard work rendered pointless.

'It's not that I want it to go back how it was,' I said, trying to reassure him. I didn't want to return to the chaotic ways of the past any more than he did.

'We have to think of a way to hide the evidence, I don't want anyone to point a finger at the girls and gayz and be able to say, "we know what you're doing, and how often you're doing it." They need to be able to deny everything if they want to.'

Darren wasn't happy. He loved his filing system, but we had so many people out to get us that I didn't want to give them any more ammunition.

It was with a sense of bereavement that Darren deposited armful after armful of incriminating facts and figures into the black bin bags I held open.

I watched out of the window as he lugged his beloved calculations into the car, and away to meet their Waterloo. It was sad, but having all that information readily available would get us all hung.

After much thought, we'd come up with a code, a new secret system, a cipher of sexual encounters, so that Darren could do his bit, satisfy his need for order, and hopefully the girls and I could stay out of the clink.

It wasn't long after I'd watched my crestfallen boyfriend reverse his cargo of culpability out of his parking pace and pull into the traffic that the doorbell rang.

I was short of girls; many of them had taken a few days off to let the Diana dust settle. I glanced down at the current job sheets to see who I had available for this customer who was impatiently buzzing the buzzer to be let in. He was going to have to wait for at least half an hour before anyone was free.

'Alright, all bloody right, I'm coming,' I muttered as I hurried to the intercom and electronically allowed him through the outer door. A few moments later the interior security door buzzer was pressed, and not bothering to look at the newly installed cameras I sauntered down the corridor to the door, fixing my hostess with the mostess smile into place.

'Well helloooo.......' my greeting fell hard and flat as I was faced by two miserable uniformed bobbies who looked as if they'd been sniffing arses all the way up the stairs.

'We've received accusations from a Miss Diana Farine regarding the theft by you of various items of clothing and personal belongings,' one of them said.

'We'd like to come in please,' said the other. And in they came as always.

I was very glad I'd just watched Darren and the paperwork drive off down the road.

There were still a few bits of Diana's in the flats, stacked against a wall with a picture.

'I did ask her to collect her bits and bobs,' I smiled innocently, showing them the evidence from my saved text messages.

'She say's...' Bobby One flipped open his notebook, 'that you have stolen her underwear.'

'Knickers!' I laughed at the absurdity of it all.

They didn't see the funny side and dragged me off to the police station as always.

Sitting in the interview room across the desk from a pleasant enough police inspector, it became obvious that they were really more concerned with the imminent threat of vice induced turf wars on their patch. I understood the inconvenience that would be caused by a pitch battle between Keith's Milton

Keynes mafia and eastern European hoodlums. They weren't really interested in Diana's outcast, outsize undergarments at all.

'Were you aware that Ms Farine is an illegal alien?' the inspector asked.

Good lord and I just thought she was a morbidly obese tyrant with bad skin and no people skills. Would you believe it, despite a warrant for deportation the cheeky cow was harassing MK police on a daily basis from a secret location demanding I was remanded in custody until I guaranteed the safe return of her rancid skivvies.

Once I had made it clear that I didn't want a turf war any more than the police did, the inspector became quite chatty. He disclosed to me that as well as being on the run from the border agencies for out-staying her visa, she was wanted by the police in Hertfordshire for theft and kidnap, and in Bournemouth for stealing a very large amount of money from her previous south London gangland employer. I stayed quiet about her face-sitting crimes against humanity.

The woman I concluded really was utterly bonkers. She'd earned me a few quid, but 'Madam Becky's' had definitely had a very lucky escape.

When the police had done with me, I had to ring Darren to ask him to collect me from the nick, as they showed no interest in returning me back to work. He was on his way to the train station in Bletchley to collect a client, which as luck would have it was right next to the cop-shop.

Getting into the car the punter, a distinguished looking guy in his fifties, started telling us about his life and his wife.

'I'm still very much in love with my wife; it's a shame, she has been ill for some time and just cannot do the things that a married couple need to do,' he nattered on, 'and I am more than happy to look after her but I am still a man and I do still have my needs.' Justifying his reasons for visiting 'Madam Becky's' behind his wife's back, he prattled incessantly all the way back to the flats. Darren held the door open for us and shook his head with a smirk as he met my eyes.

'Yes I still have my needs, my poor wife, she's just so ill...' the monologue continued down the corridor and into the room.

Settled into a chair, still professing his love and adoration for his wife, I offered him refreshments and told him that the ladies would be in shortly to introduce themselves.

I returned to the kitchen to fill out the paperwork and Darren asked, 'which of the girls is going to be filling the needs that his wife can't then?'

I shook my head. 'That poor woman's got no hope. However much better she gets, she's obviously got nothing that he's interested in. He's just asked to see the youngest looking boys, and he's having three hours of fisting with Shaun.'

It's a funny old world.

Darren checked the job sheets and put the money in the safe, and then he turned to me.

'I've brought you a present.' He handed me a small yellow book. 'It's called the Richest Man in Babylon, and it's brilliant. It's basically a tale about how various poor, useless people learn how to make themselves wealthy and successful by following the example of the man in the story. It's about learning how to be rich even if you're skint and crap at business.'

I smiled, not sure whether to be touched or insulted. 'Thank you darling.' I turned it over and read the back.

'I learnt what I know about management from doing courses over the years,' Darren said. 'If you want to get better at running MB's, you can. You just have to learn how. Step by step.' He pulled me close and hugged me.

The thought of losing everything we'd built up was far worse than the prospect of learning new skills, so I clung onto the book, and made a pact with myself to set about changing my unhelpful personality traits and make my enterprise a success.

The tarot cards were replaced by bank cards and business cards. I started meditating to keep my mind clear and manifest wealth as Dr Wayne Dyer, Deepak Chopra and Brian Tracy were all telling me to do.

It appeared to me, from reading these books that financial success is like making a cake. If you follow the recipe, put in the correct ingredients and cook accordingly you will by default get something that resembles the picture in the cookery book. It may take some practice, but in time you'll get it right

Learn and do, learn and do.

I read books on, 'How to be a good manager'. I studied things and wrote things down. I found an amazing life coach who helped me set goals, and NLP'ed me into a new state of mind, and very quickly I started to see results. Ticking things off my goals' list as I achieved them, I was so pleased and proud of myself, that I thought it was only fair that the girls and gayz should be given a similar opportunity to understand the power they had over their own financial and personal destiny.

To a man with a hammer every problem is a nail. Like all those newly converted to anything, I was an irritatingly passionate zealot, preaching financial independence, premium bonds, focus and goal setting to anyone who would listen, and everyone who didn't.

Many of these ladies earned more than bank managers and politicians. They could earn five hundred, a thousand pounds cash in a day, and know if they worked tomorrow they would earn the same again. Escorts very rarely looked to the future or planned ahead. I always thought the main reason to do a stint in sex work was to give yourself the quick money that if invested wisely could then create long term choices. Many ladies started that way, with good intentions of thriftiness, and steady saving, but continued to spend daily, always thinking there would be a tomorrow.

Belinda and I once sat down and worked out that in one year she had spent a staggering eighty thousand pounds on shoes, taxis and alcohol poisoning. At just twenty one years old that was crazy. She could have passed her driving test for three hundred quid and put down the rest as a deposit for a house. Instead she still lived part time with her mum and had put on a stone from pot noodles and an ocean of alcopops.

I asked my life coach, Mr Chip, if he would come in and talk to the crew. An ex-pro footballer, he was working as a motivational coach to premier league players, so he was used to wastrels, and had seen most types of lewd folly. I was keen to share his magic with my staff.

Mr Chip visited once a week, and would sit in the pole dancing lounge come torture chamber surrounded by nearly nude people and domination apparatus. LouLou, a young English girl, was always naked, and I do mean always totally naked, when she was at work. A favourite of the gayz, she would lie, totally in the buff, across their laps as they sat on the sofa, insisting they stroke her back whilst she listened to Mr Chip imparting his wisdom. Unabashed, the boys would be listing their goals, where they wanted to be in five years' time, while balancing their handy notepads on LouLou's naked thighs, and trying not to lose their pens down the crack.

Mr Chip would spend a whole afternoon with us. Not wishing to turn away punters, the girls and the gayz would pop in and out to service their regulars during their NLP sessions, then return to the discussions on meticulous attention to financial planning thirty minutes later, slightly dishevelled, moistened and ragged round the edges.

I bought a wonderful book on carrot and stick management, and as we had both carrots and sticks available for clients it seemed a perfect way to boost my staff's motivation. I created the 'Madam Becky Bonk-o-Mometer'.

The Bonk-O Mometer was a large brightly coloured graph nailed to the wall in the kitchen. At the end of the month the person who'd done the most bonks won a prize.

Lexi worked so hard and was so popular she almost always won. One hundred or more bonks per month was normal for her. It became so repetitive, that I'm ashamed to say we knobbled the Bonk-O-Mometer and fixed the results once or twice to give someone else a chance to win.

It seemed unfair that the clients should miss out on my newly discovered positive mental attitude. So to reward them for their efforts I created the loyalty scheme, which was advertised as the best thing to happen to escorting since the fall of the Berlin Wall.

Clients were given a small card with ten squares marked on it. Each visit the receptionist stamped and signed a square. After he'd filled in ten holes as it were, the erstwhile gent was entitled to a very generous free half hour with the lad or lady of his choice. It was massively popular, so popular it cost me a fortune. One recently separated school teacher become so obsessed with a new, tiny, outrageously sexual Thai lady, that he spent all his family's savings in under a week, and claimed his free go in just over twenty four hours.

'Madam Becky's' was back on track.

CHAPTER TWENTY SEVEN

In the midst of running a brothel, a lube and lingerie outlet, wrestling with my personal development, hiding paperwork and looking after kids and horses, I had a litter of puppies. I worshipped my dogs, and the arrival of a new litter of Jack Russell cross Bichon pups to Dogbaby and his lady love Mrs Dogbaby was an eagerly awaited event.

Excited to be able to give everyone the happy news, I bounded up the three flights, and opened the security door with my little electronic fob thing.

Out of breath from leaping up the stairs two at a time, I pulled open the heavy door, and stopped dead in my tracks. The thirty foot, bright pink hallway between the two flats was full of people. Even when ten girls on a busy shift went out to have a fag on the terrace, the corridor was never this full. So I calculated there must have been at least twenty five men and women, who all turned to look at me as puffing loudly from exertion, I appeared in the doorway.

A square-shaped, mannish woman, in black jeans and a leather jacket, with short ginger hair, and the look of a PE teacher was nearest to the door. She leant against the window frame that overlooked the smoker's roof terrace as I made my entrance, and looked me up and down.

'Bloody hell,' I panted as the door banged shut behind me. 'Is this the queue?'

As she stood upright she addressed me, 'I take it you've just had a phone call?'

'No,' I looked at her bemused, 'I've just had puppies.' I had no idea what she was on about and, unable to hide my pride, I added with a smile, 'Five little smashers.'

'Who are you?' asked the next in line, a tall suited man in his fifties.

'I'm Madam Becky.'

They looked at my frizzy hair, pasty make-up free face, council house leggings and bobbly knitwear and were clearly unconvinced.

Slightly offended by their disbelief, I justified my shoddy appearance. 'What? You think it's easy having five puppies in an hour?'

I pointed at the larger than life, seven-foot photographic image of me in the skin tight, black PVC cat-suit, my 34 GG's bursting from the struggling zip that filled the far end of the corridor. 'Sometimes I look like that....' I said before I straightened the bottom of my oversized grubby sweatshirt, emblazoned with a threadbare panda transfer with three dimensional wobbly eyes, and tipped my head coquettishly....'and sometimes, I look... like this.'

'We are here....'the woman continued, ignoring my attempt at light-hearted banter, 'to look for anyone who is working here against their will, anyone who would rather leave, and is being prevented by members of staff from doing so.'

'That'll be me then,' I offered 'I'd love to leave; you have no idea how much. You've come to save me. How kind. I've been trying to get away from this bloody place for ages. I'm a slave to it.'

They seemed very annoyed with my saucy attitude. A third visitor pushed forward and waved a search warrant in my face.

'We are part of Operation Pentameter, and we have a warrant to search these premises for trafficked or illegal workers,' he said pompously, like I should be impressed.

Operation Pentameter, ah yes, we had been expecting them for a while.

This wasn't the local plod or the council, who I would happily back chat, irritate and push my luck with. No this was the Labour Government's heavy mob, which under the guise of the battle against sex trafficking was systematically travelling the country raiding all establishments that sold or rented sex in any form.

All fifty five UK police forces had amalgamated into a joint venture - their aim, they insisted was to rescue women and children forced to work in the sex industry and prosecute the gangs who profited from the abuse of the victims.

While recreational sex, promiscuity and underage pregnancies in the UK were at their highest level ever, the women of New Labour announced that they were going to eradicate the sex industry and all forms of commercial lustiness altogether. Every penetration was an act of aggression they told the nation, and all women needed saving from the filthy men who wanted to poke things into them. I wasn't sure what Harriet Harmen was doing wrong with her penetrations that caused her so much upset, but I enjoyed mine. I was sure we had something fruity in the Foo Foo stock that could help her out. She and her cronies were determined to stop the British public thinking for themselves and Operation Pentameter was their answer.

As an industry, we were all horrified by sex trafficking, and did what we could to prevent it.

I knew of clients who'd seen girls in flats and parlours that had worried them, and they'd immediately contacted the police. Trafficking revolted us all, and we all wanted it stopped as much as the government. But they had the ulterior motive of winning votes, and tainted the facts, blatantly lying and trying to hoodwink the public. We in the trade felt the women of New Labour were personally putting our sex worker friends in danger and it seriously pissed us all off.

I knew the hallway activity was Operation Pentameter, and we had been expecting them. I knew we were ok, at least theoretically. We never had any underage girls, trafficked or otherwise, drugs or alcohol and the local police kept an eye on our behaviour. But this lot would still have me arrested if it suited them, but there was something about arrogant, rude, authoritative figures, who get a thrill out of frightening and bullying the public, that brought out the minx in me. I just couldn't help it. I was on their side, we all were. There was no need for the condescension and the threats that they were levelling at my staff. I was happy for my, and every other parlour in the country, to be raided on a weekly basis if it meant that trafficked women were rescued and helped. But I knew a national hysteria had been built on the government's lies and falsified statistics, and Pentameter and the Labour Party were hindering more than they were helping.

At one stage a report had been published stating that there were eighty thousand trafficked women in the UK, and these were being forced at knife point to service up to forty men a day each. The general public were justifiably horrified, and the idea of saving these women was winning votes for Labour. It was only those of us involved in the industry who were being vilified and judged by all sides who actually bothered to do the maths.

If what the Government was saying was true, then over the course of a week, almost every member of the British male population above the age of eighteen was having at least one vicious tryst with a half-dead, female sex slave.

Purveyors of this vile social outrage statistcally must therefore include my elderly dad, my gay brother, all my gay staff, Darren, T and every other man I knew.

We wrote to MP's, blogged, campaigned and protested about this falsehood. Added to our clamour were the blatant, published facts that over five years Pentameter had rescued barely enough women to start a football team, let alone a hundred, and most of these rescued women were consequently deported home back into poverty or ran away from the Old Bill who'd just rescued them.

To add an additional insult, the Government refused to acknowledge that any woman entered escorting as a choice; they said that women like Kate, Lexi, Belinda, Carmen and the others didn't exist. They labelled all female sex workers as victims, and all customers, Wiggy, Stanley, Spanky and Mr North as violent aggressors who were abusing us all mercilessly.

We tried to explain in letters to The Times, that ladies like Mistress Matrix earned a politician's wage abusing men for a living, but they said that wasn't true and ignored us. The happy hooker, with the nice clothes, reliable car and well fed kids was like the Yeti or the city of Atlantis, a myth, a fantastical story that only a fool would believe.

These female revolutionaries in the seats of power told us they were true feminists, and as such were going to stop all these vile men paying for sex, and therefore save us girls from these filthy animals who wanted to stick their willies in us. We argued that surely the feminist movement was based on giving women the power of choice, the power to make their own decisions, and wasn't it a human right to be allowed to have sex or just a massage, cup of tea and a cuddle if you wanted to with someone who wanted to do it with you? They ignored us a bit more, obviously as we didn't exist anyway and carried on passing laws that were sure to get us all maimed and killed.

The raid was well under way when I arrived, and I'd not received a phone call. Luke was on reception duty and was in a right flap. Officers were in the working rooms searching through bundles of towels and bedding. Quite how many eastern European sex slaves they expected to find in a stack of laundry I have no idea. The untidiness was sending Luke into an OCD dicky fit. Launching himself at the mess like a pig at a potato he was berating the policemen for their tardy tidying. As I walked down the corridor and into the flat I heard him call the new staff into the wrecked bedroom and say, 'Well, now they've ruined it all, it seems like a good time to show you new people how Madam B likes these towels folded, no point in standing around doing nothing.'

I do love staff with a touch of a tidying disorder.

I'd missed the initial police pep talk when they'd quizzed the staff and let the punters leave. The place was in turmoil, and as I walked into the domination room, which was full of plain-clothed officials from the police and border control, I was horrified to see Mr North standing half- hidden behind the dressing up and fetish outfit wardrobe.

I took hold of his arm protectively and said, 'I am so so sorry, I had no idea you would be here today.' I looked at one of the officers. 'Do you think we can let this poor chap leave? I've known him for years. He only has a quick massage and some other stuff....'

I heard Mr North groan and thought it best to keep Spanky and Rolf Harris out of the situation. 'He's certainly not fourteen and vulnerable,' I continued, wondering why the officer looked so confused. 'Please let him go, he can't tell you anything.'

Mr North reddened dramatically and tried to back away from me into the closet again. Determined to get him out safely I tightened my grip on his arm, pulled an apologetic face and tried to manoeuvre him to the door.

Straightening his shoulders, Mr North looked me directly in the eye. 'I'm with Customs and Excise Miss Adams, I need to see your statements and returns immediately.'

Momentarily speechless, I recovered enough to splutter, 'Sorry. My mistake, you're the Inland Revenge? Ah yes, so you are dear, so you are. I was confusing you with an old friend who I thought worked in the fur trade.'

I stepped over an abandoned Spanky Monkey who had tumbled from his ransacked box, and without an incriminating downward glance, I led Mr North, the Tax Inspector, off to find some non-existent paperwork.

The chaps from Operation Pentameter were very thorough. They measured the inside and the outside of the building and subtracted one from the other, searching for secret rooms and sex slave hidey holes. They searched and questioned for nearly three hours, before leaving satisfied.

As the Detective Inspector walked passed me on the way out he said, 'It's so nice to see a well-run, old fashioned brothel. It makes such a change these days.'

My heart filled with pride, I was finally getting some recognition as a business person, and it made it all worth it.

All my money and time had been invested into the two flats, and it was a shame, but a fact of life that we could be closed down over night. I accepted I was running an illegal business, even though I didn't accept it was morally wrong. I had no working capital; if they closed me down I'd lose everything. I had all my eggs in this basket full of holes, and as no one knew where these new Labour laws would take us, brothel life looked extremely precarious.

I watched our official visitors climb back into their vehicles to leave. Luke was still flapping and folding towels behind me. The weakness of my position was evident, I was hanging on by the skin of my teeth.

CHAPTER TWENTY EIGHT

It's a fact of life that nothing stays the same forever.

The restaurants below us had closed down, and new neighbours had moved into the complex. Most were on housing benefit, and many were struggling to bring up large numbers of over-active kids in small flats with no gardens. The communal areas had become tatty, full of abandoned bikes, toys and exploded rubbish bags. Several times I'd paid to have all the hall and landing areas cleaned and re-decorated, as they were the first point of contact with the clients. I seemed to be fighting and losing a very depressing battle.

Shortly after I'd paid the decorators, the new kids on the block wrote badly spelt graffiti over the fresh paint, and clients started to complain. Darren went several times to speak to the other residents about the mess, but they had no interest in creating harmony.

As the weather improved throughout the spring of 2007, they sat on the pathway to the front door competing with each other in lager drinking and fag end flicking competitions. Picnic type benches were purchased with bingo winnings, and the ever increasing group would sit night and day at tables laden with Stella cans while tiny children weaved between them like shaven-headed sharks.

Drug dealers were seen visiting some of the other flats, and punters started to discuss the distasteful surroundings on the on-line forums and punting communities.

It was heart breaking for me. I had tried so hard to build the business. It was a constant battle against so many different things and I was getting sick of it. To have other residents ruining everything by being revoltingly slovenly was so upsetting.

Many people would equate massage parlours and brothels with the more seedy areas. But in fact, most clients would not feel comfortable and safe visiting such places. They'd not leave their cars for an hour or so on grotty streets.

The walk from the rubbish strewn car park to the main entrance was often accompanied by the soundtrack of shrieking, swearing mothers as they hurled insults at small children who sobbed pitifully in reply, and then escaped to run around the lawn areas with full nappies dragging along the ground. The growth figures had stopped improving, and if we weren't careful we'd lose all our clients to the competition.

One not so sunny day, one of the soiled slatterns from the adjoining block came to the front door and asked for a job. At MB's we had ladies in their sixties, and up to a dress size twenty eight. There was a market for almost everything, but not for foul tempered drug addicts who'd lost their smile and their marbles to substance abuse.

I heard the doorbell ring. I was engrossed in cleaning the flat, so left it for someone else to deal with. Luke had a day off from his reception duties, the girls were all lazing around waiting for randy men, eating pot noodles and putting make-up on the gayz. I tried to encourage them to help me tidy through the flats, but quickly realised that they were more of a hindrance to me, so I'd let them return like roosting starlings to the sofa.

I heard chatter and suppressed laughter and assumed it was a punter and the girls, all bored and ready for action, were vying for his attention. An illusion quickly shattered when Lexi came running down the hall.

'It's her!' Lexi declared dramatically. 'She won't go. They're all with her.'

I got up from the floor and turned the electric toothbrush off. It was one of Matrix's torture tools, but I was using it for scrubbing skirting boards.

'Who?' I asked warily, wondering if we were being raided or visited officially again. I had seen more of the police lately than I had my own mother.

But it wasn't the police or the council or even the landlord that had got my girls in such a flap. It was the neighbour from hell - the mad woman from number eight, and behind her, like the cast of Oliver, were five or six of her multi-coloured, multi-cultural brood.

I had only ever seen her from a distance before, a fact I was grateful for. Lexi was rudely walking around the hallway spraying a scented air-freshener. The other girls hovered in the kitchen doorway, and stared at the woman. The laughter had been replaced by morbid curiosity. I could hear them whispering. I understood. They spent hours making sure that they all looked and smelt fabulous. The woman standing in the doorway was as alien to them as Diana had been.

'Hello,' I said, forcing myself to smile, 'can I help you?' thinking that maybe she'd run out of sugar or heroine.

'I know what you are,' she said.

A horrible waft of rotting teeth assaulted my nostrils. I gripped the toothbrush and resisted the temptation to shove it into her hand. Up close, her clothes were as grubby as her teeth. She was sweating and her eyes were glazed and unfocused, I didn't need to be a genius to realise she was off her head on some form of contraband.

'Gimme a job and I won't call the cops.'

I was speechless. Surely she wasn't serious?

It seemed she was. She became very aggressive and abusive when I politely explained that I had no vacancies. Aside from the fact that none of my punters would pay to see her, I had a strict 'no drugs' rule. A part of me felt sorry for her, but it wasn't possible to have her in my flats.

With teeth like a row of condemned houses, filthy hair, and an odour of fried food, mixed with that musty biscuit smell that makes you back away from people in shops, there was little I could do to help her out.

Darren went to speak to her an hour later, to check she was ok. She was confused and spaced out with no recollection of having been near 'Madam Becky's'. She swung at him with the nearest weapon, which was half a loaf of cheap bread. The bag burst on impact with his arm, and scattered white squares all down the hall. He came back to our flats annoyed, frustrated and crumbed like a turkey drummer.

Later that evening after another ranting session at a child / dealer / boyfriend, the toothless wonder opened her window, lent out and threw a bucket of water over my accountant who came to help some girls fill in paperwork. That, it transpired, was her declaration of war.

Every day there was trouble. The mad woman from number eight would stand outside on the path and shout and swear at the girls as they came into work. She would call them filthy prossies, slags and tarts. The girls had been used to popping out to the local shops at various times during the day for sandwiches, fags or condoms; now they had to run the gauntlet of verbal abuse every time they left or returned to the building.

She grabbed Lexi one afternoon and pushed her against the wall, slapping her hard around the face. When Lexi came back into the flat, bruised and in tears, Darren went straight to Monster HQ, as we called Flat number eight, to speak to her.

Mouldy, disintegrating white bread still carpeted the hall outside her front door. Several of her youngest children were climbing up and down the stairs to her flat. They were naked from the waist down, the metal strips at the edges of the stairs scraping their bare bottoms. Stepping over them, Darren banged on her door, trying to make himself heard over the booming music coming from inside. There was no answer, so he climbed back over her children and came back to our flat. He tried again an hour later. The toddlers were still on the stairs, just sitting now on their cold bums on the wee soaked carpet, nibbling on stale breadcrumbs. He knocked again. Nothing.

'She's left those poor kids outside on the stairs, the stupid bitch,' he fumed as he came back the second time. 'Do you think someone should call social services? She may have OD'd and killed herself. Selfish witch. I pulled the outside door shut, but those babies could easily wander out into the car park and get hit by a car. We need to call someone.'

I looked out of the window, checking the car park for wandering babies, and noticed the mad woman's older son coming home from school.

'Her lad's just arrived, that older mouthy one that kicked the football at Wiggy's head. Go and speak to him, see if he's got a key. Maybe you shouldn't let him go in first in case she's lying dead on the floor.'

She wasn't dead. But she was out of her face on something. The older boy let the younger kids in, and Darren found her sitting barely compos mentis on the sofa. She threw an overflowing ashtray at him and accused him of trying to steal her telly while she was asleep.

At some point during the following day she called the police, and said that one of our clients had knocked on her flat door during the night. The man had apparently then tried to rape her and molest her children. The police didn't seem to take this very seriously, but we did. Darren and I were both horrified that such a thing might have happened. Although she was a liar and a nutter, she did have kids, and we did have some weirdo's visit us occasionally and we couldn't vouch for all of them. If there was even a tiny chance she was telling the truth, we had to make sure the children were safe.

We both went round to see if she was ok, and to get a description of the attacker. She was sleepy and confused again, but let us in to her filthy hovel. Balanced on the edge of a sofa, covered in dirty nappies, food wrappers and stuff I didn't recognise, and had no frame of reference for, we tried to work out what had happened.

Her story kept changing, but the man she described sounded worryingly like the big Russian who we'd had trouble from before. Our security cameras covered most aspects of the building, and Darren was sure if she gave him an approximate time that he could go back through the recordings and identify the culprit. We invited her up to the flat to go through the video footage so we could give the details to the police but she refused.

With no time frame to work from, Darren diligently sat through hours of digital images, but no one other than her usual dealer had been near her flat all night. It was very strange. We had to conclude that she had made the whole thing up.

A week or so later, a lynch mob of her friends arrived from the beer garden of the pub next door, furious and seeking vengeance. This time she'd accused Darren of molesting her and her children. She was one hundred percent certain it was Darren, as he was always turning up at her flat trying to get off with her; she'd know him anywhere.

The police, summoned by her, arrived close behind the shouting rabble, to be told that Darren and I were in France, and had been for days.

When we got back from staying with my friends in the Dordogne, I contacted the people who owned the building to see what we could do about the mad woman from number eight. I wasn't overly surprised to hear that they'd been trying to get her out almost since the day she moved in. They'd already been to court to get an eviction notice. The council wouldn't re-home her as she had previously attacked members of their staff in the housing office. She had also punched one of our landlord's secretaries who went round to hand her a letter about rent arrears. Because she had kids, there was little they could do about moving her until it was ordered by the courts. They were as stuck as we were.

Her next trick was to set off the fire alarms in the whole building. This she did several times throughout the night for a week or so. Each time the fire brigade arrived with a full crew, only to have their patience tried and their time wasted. Eventually the maintenance man came out and disabled the alarms - illegal and dangerous but she had driven everyone to the brink of desperation.

With no working fire alarms, the crazy cow set the staircase in our block of flats alight. She closed the external doors, and removed the door handles, so there was no means of escape.

We sort of understood why she would want to burn us to death, but she had friends living in the flats below us, not to mention her own kids next door. You just couldn't reason with that sort of insanity.

The fire brigade called the police as it was obviously arson, with the intent to endanger life. We were told it carried a stiff prison sentence but the police had been taking dozens of calls every day from this wretched woman, and they had stopped listening.

I tried to keep the girls as calm as I could. Wiggy, who'd only returned since Diana had left, and half of the punters, stopped visiting. It just wasn't worth the agro for them, and I could understand it.

'Ignore her,' I pleaded with the girls. 'They are trying to evict her, it can't take much longer.'

'We should call the police whenever she does something,' Lexi suggested.

'We'd be on the phone all day Lex; we'd need a separate phone line just for that silly old bat.'

'We should move out,' Gemma said, joining in.

'But she wins then Gem,' said Lexi, 'why should we leave?'

'I think Diana's sent her,' Lexi laughed. 'To punish us for burning her fat pants.'

'Gemma's got a point,' I said. I had been thinking about it a lot. 'About moving.'

I walked to the kitchen window and looked out over the car park. It was strewn with rubbish and supermarket trolleys. The mad woman from number eight had made a barricade of push along plastic kids' toys and a sand pit across the path to our door. I watched Carmen, coming back from having her nails done in Bletchley, as she picked her way through the mess to get into work.

'I think the clients have had enough of this place. Even if she went tomorrow, I don't think the punters will come back. Why would they? It's gross.' I sighed, leaning over the sink I peered further out of the window. I watched Carmen hitch up her expensive silk dress, as she tried to negotiate her bags of shopping over a bright red and yellow bike with stabilisers.

'These flats were brand new when we moved in. It's shameful what that lot have done to them in just a few months.' I shook my head sadly.

'No! She's attacked Carmen!' I pushed past the girls and flew out of the flat. We all tumbled down the stairs and burst out through the front door.

Carmen and the mad woman were wrestling on the floor, scattering plastic chairs, and secondhand dolls prams as they went.

'Carmen! Stop,' I shouted.

We all shouted. But there was no stopping Carmen; her Latino blood was up, the red mist was down, and she was in it to win it. Carmen was straddling her opponent, silk dress up around her waist, swearing and shouting in various languages. The mad woman from number eight protected her face with her hands, as Carmen's little fists pummelled at her. My girls shouted and yelled encouragement to their feisty friend, three months of suffered abuse rushing to their vengeful lips. Suddenly in mid punch Carmen stopped and sat upright.

'Beeky look,' she held up her hand, her middle finger pointing upward in a rude gesture. 'Beeky I break new nail!' This seemed to make her even angrier. She stood up, pulled down her dress and inspected her damaged digit. Carmen huffed loudly, 'You make me break nail beetch,' She snatched up her leopard print stilettos from the grass, and looked at her friends. 'We go moke now?' and she swaggered inside like Mike Tyson for a fag on the roof terrace.

The police arrived. The mad woman from number eight had made a complaint about being beaten up by a demented whore, and the police gave Carmen a good grilling. They made her find her passport and paperwork, and someone had been sent to speak to the border agencies to check she was legal in the UK. They were giving her loads of hassle. Clearly they hoped for the double whammy of arrest for assault and deportation.

'She was just defending herself,' I said crossly. Why did the police need to behave like dicks on some occasions? 'You lot know what's been going on here.'

'Beetch put potatoes on me,' Carmen stated unrepentant.

The policeman looked up from his note book puzzled.

'Potatoes,' Carmen repeated. 'On me. Look.' and she pointed with one of her unbroken newly painted nails to a stain on her beautiful dress.

'She threw chips at Carmen, when she was walking down the path,' I explained. 'I saw it all. I watch all the girls come and go, as that bloody woman keeps threatening them.'

'She's made numerous complaints about you running an illegal operation here, and that your staff and clients are causing her distress. We have to take the complaints seriously.'

I raised a patronising eyebrow at him; he was in his twenties, eager to make his mark. I knew the type. Give me an old cop any day. The older guys knew how the world really worked and were usually much less enthusiastic and far more reasonable.

'And she now states that this young lady attacked her in an unprovoked assault,' he said, checking his notes.

Unprovoked my arse.

'Did she also mention that her dealer upsets our clients? Or that we feed her kids when she's out of her face on crack and has left them naked in the gardens? Or that she's attacked all my staff on numerous occasions and several of my clients, including my accountant? Oh, and let's not forget that she tried to burn us all to death and accused my boyfriend of being a rapist and kiddie fiddler.'

'Well, you are running an illegal operation here, and we have to take complaints of disturbance from the other residents seriously.'

I was seriously considering adding assault of a police officer to his list, and punching him straight in the face.

In the end Carman wasn't charged and the young policeman left.

The police stationed an officer at the door to her flat, and Darren or T stood on duty at the door to ours as a joint peace keeping force. The mad woman had been warned off. But just in case the troll decided to come out from under her bridge and tried to eat any of my staff as they trip trapped down the path, the constabulary stayed nearby.

Having a bobby in full uniform stationed at the front door of your brothel is no better for business than having toddler poo thrown at clients by a neighbour; it was ridiculous.

Darren spent hours chatting to his new policeman buddy as they stood outside drinking tea together. Eventually CID came in for a chat, and made it clear that they were as sick of it all as we were.

Legally, she was allowed to stay where she was until the court evicted her, which could be months. The police admitted they'd always been happy to leave us working from the flats, as I ran a decent place, obeyed the unwritten rules of no drugs, no drink, no underage girls and no coercion. They knew all about the mad woman from number eight, and had had problems with her in the past, at different addresses. But legally, if they had complaints from a resident about us, they had to be seen to be doing something.

They couldn't look as if they favoured a brothel over a single parent, a member of the community. I paid my taxes and invested every penny I earned back into the business. I provided life coaching, financial management, exit strategies, and now even private health care to my staff. Yet it could all be ruined overnight because I wouldn't give a drug addict a job. As sex workers we had no human rights, no employment rights and no right to re-dress.

It was just all so wrong, and I was sick of it.

It was time to move on.

CHAPTER TWENTY NINE

I put the word out to everyone I knew that we needed to move out of the Bletchley flats as quickly as possible. I was offered the opportunity to rent an enormous eight bedroomed farmhouse located deep in the Buckinghamshire countryside. With no neighbours and at the furthest edge of a smart village, I jumped at the chance. I thought God had been listening to my prostitution prayers. It was perfect.

The existing flats, complete with pole dancing lounge, torture chamber and role play examination room were not easy to re-locate overnight. We dismantled the massage couches, beds and spanking stool, bagged up the puppets and dressing up costumes and prepared to leave the rapidly declining location.

I had always wanted to run a posh gentlemen's club and putting a positive spin on a disastrous situation, I decided the new farm was perfect to propel MB's upwards to new heights. Every cloud and all that.

I felt confident, well, as confident as I could that we would be discreet enough to keep a low profile. We were now just outside of the Milton Keynes police jurisdiction and right on the very edge of Aylesbury Vale. I hoped that we'd go undetected and unmolested by a different police force with whom I'd never crossed swords, and who didn't know that we existed.

Being evicted was an occupational hazard when you own a brothel, and you never really knew how quickly it was coming (if you'll pardon the pun). All in a day's work to us, but what really causes the problems with a moonlight flit is communication with customers.

They don't know you're gone, or where you've gone. Needing to deal with their immediate urge, they'd often go elsewhere on the spur of the disappointed moment for their half an hour of heaven. According to Darren's paperwork and pie charts, every new visitor had cost us nearly fourteen pounds in advertising to obtain, so losing clients needed to be avoided.

We worked through the Friday night, all humping furniture together, and managed to move enough baby oil, towels and tea cups into the new farm to start work at 9.00am the following morning. Since adverts in the newspapers were booked weeks in advance. it meant that the old landline number was still the main contact. So a receptionist was stationed at the old flat, given a kitchen chair, and left with a security chap to dodge the mad woman from number 8, the police, answer the door and re-direct the randy traffic.

The layout of the farmhouse was perfect for a busy twenty-four-seven brothel; there were eight bedrooms, five bathrooms, four reception rooms and parking for endless vehicles, including the Foo Foo Love Limo full of sex toys and pink fluff that I'd bought as a marketing ploy for the shop. The girls now had a separate annex over the garages to keep themselves, and their pot noodles, away from my posh rooms.

The house was isolated on the outskirts of a traditional stockbroker village, on a small local road, with only a few other large properties with well-kept lawns and pony paddocks within a mile.

To avoid confusion, clients were given very specific directions even though the place was impossible to miss with a large sign and jaunty arrow pointing towards the floodlit bordello.

My girls had all been nervous of the move. They'd thought that the countryside location would prove a few miles too far for the punters. But they were wrong. We'd never been busier. Some of my foreign ladies wept with fear, convinced that wolves, and bears, roamed the rural Buckinghamshire hedgerows.

'We are eaten alive,' was the constant moan from Carmen as she sent the other southern hemisphere, hot-blooded ladies into dramatic hysterics. A queue of punters and a pile of money soon quelled their nerves and settled them down.

The first day we opened we broke all previous records, and Lexi's Bonk-O-Mometer had to be fitted with an emergency extension. Our takings for a

Saturday morning had doubled and by 4.00pm had trebled. That shut them all up.

The annex in which the girls made camp was at a separate end of the huge house from the client's reception. So to save his legs I bought Luke a digital doorbell that he could keep in his little plastic box in which he carried the half a dozen phones and his fags. The wireless chime was strategically placed above the mirror in the girls' room so they couldn't pretend they hadn't heard it ring. Luke would repeatedly buzz his buzzer, holding it down irritatingly with his finger, until the girls acknowledged the arrival of a client and dragged themselves off their new sofa, away from the telly to say hello.

It's well known that blood rushes south when a man's excited, and unfortunately, in his wisdom, God did not provide men with enough blood to work their brains and an erection simultaneously. Sexually aroused men are just the stupidest things, and shouldn't be allowed to roam the countryside alone. The full extent of this biological conundrum was a surprise even to me, and was shortly to cause the downfall of the recently opened 'Madam Becky's Country Club'.

The house stood proud in its own land and was perfectly visible and recognisable from the road. The Foo Foo limousine covered in vinyl graphic frilly knickers sat on the driveway. Yet still ninety per cent of our men drove straight past the imposing front gates, the thirty-foot limo and the two large signs.

Despite the painfully clear instructions given to gents slowly over the phone and colourful maps on the internet, almost everyone knocked at the wrong houses asking for sex - houses that even to the untrained, innocent eye were family homes, not knocking shops. Trampolines, bouncing children and dads in cardigans mowing lawns should have been enough to alert the most simple minded punter he was in the wrong place, but it seemed not.

Houses that sadly for me belonged to several very influential pillars of the community.

Clients parked up, knocked on doors and asked if they'd arrived at the newly opened house of ill repute. Unfortunately for the beleaguered homeowners this continued throughout the night as 'Madam Becky's' only ever closed on Christmas Day.

The Sunday evening, just one day after we'd opened, a confused taxi driver dispatched eight loud, drunken revellers, onto the front steps of a very pleasant mock Tudor mansion belonging to a local councillor. Revved up and overexcited, half-way through a stag night, the frisky lads refused to take no for an answer, utterly convinced, as they peered, inebriated, through their beer goggles, that the gentleman's well-groomed wife was one of my strumpets. They spent several loud minutes swaying across the threshold, trying to convince her to let them in and give them a lap dance.

The final straw seemed to be the pissing on her scented roses by the best man, whose lager brimming bladder couldn't be restrained a moment longer. The police were summoned, and the revellers dispatched, frustrated. The village couldn't help but notice that we'd arrived.

Oblivious to the outrage we'd caused, and nightly protest meetings being held in the local tavern, I thought we were doing very nicely. Afternoon tea had been served in the smart drawing room to half a dozen men in frocks, Spanky had his own room, Luke had control of the phones, and as I headed out through the farm's palatial entrance to drive back into Milton Keynes to buy cases of condoms, I looked around myself filling with pride.

This was what it was all about. I'd put escorting on the Milton Keynes map; it was the turn of Aylesbury Vale to celebrate our prostitution prowess.

Little did I know as I accelerated merrily away down the gravel drive that 'Madam Becky's' would be leaving again, sooner than I'd ever imagined.

Returning from the condom buying trip, I found the driveway blocked by riot vans and those saloon cars that the better paid officers are given. Heaving one of the world's biggest sighs, I leant back against the headrest and put my hands over my eyes, despairing at the fact that it was only Thursday. Just five days since we moved in and already we were being raided. I slowly got out of the car and went in to face the music.

Half a dozen uniformed policemen and three council enforcement officers were drinking tea at the kitchen table along with some plain clothes chaps. Luke was in a flap, but even so he had the sense to boil the kettle and crack open some figgy rolls.

The police would have been hyped and high on adrenaline at the beginning of the bust. They'd charge around, checking rooms, being rude and stroppy, questioning everyone, using stilted, robotic language whilst they searched for contraband, sex slaves and piles of loot. I wasn't worried about what they'd find, just very upset that it was all happening again in under a week. Aside from running an illegal brothel I knew they had nothing else on me. This was a different police force to my usual antagonists; I hoped they'd looked me up somewhere and seen that we were generally an ok bunch.

By the time I arrived back from the jonny and baby oil run, they'd searched the house and things had settled down a bit. The lady from the council put her tea cup down and headed across the kitchen towards me. She introduced herself as Ms Shelby and waved a document in front of her like a flag. I knew what it was. She was thirtyish, pretty in an underpaid, overworked, harassed type of way.

'This is a stop notice,' she said. 'We've had complaints.'

I didn't think we would be hurting or offending anybody. That was one of the benefits of the location.

A policeman explained that a magistrate had been awakened three times during one night by rowdy visitors, and that a group on a stag night had offered a lady in the village fifty pounds for a lap dance; I was pretty sure that some of my customers were the self-same local dignitaries who'd been complaining about me. The boys in blue also informed me that previous to our arrival the house was used as a cannabis factory, so was already flagged on their radar.

Great.

'Certain things have been brought to the attention of the council,' Ms Shelby continued. 'Locals walking their dogs or riding their bikes have seen,' She quoted from her notes, 'Naked men and women seen through the windows performing sex acts, a group of girls dancing semi-naked around the fountain near the front door, people tied to furniture, men in dresses and large numbers of vehicles coming and going throughout the night.'

The nearest neighbours were a quarter of a mile away and it would need to be a very sharp sighted dog who could spot, and be offended by frilly knickers or a bare leg at that distance. I suspected there had been a fair bit of deliberate snooping going on.

'They must all have binoculars, or a bionic eye,' I said annoyed with myself that I hadn't anticipated the local outcry better, 'your super sleuth dog walkers.'

'You have to stop immediately,' Ms Shelby said. 'Otherwise you will be arrested.'

'Immediately?' I said. 'Is there nothing we can do?' I was thinking fast. The weekend was our busiest time. I'd spent a fortune getting the house ready and we were already almost booked to capacity. The deposit, the rent, and the redecoration - it had all cost so much money. I'd spent thousands. I had even borrowed some from the girls. I didn't want to be arrested, I didn't want to upset or enrage the locals further, and Ms Shelby seemed like a nice lady, but I couldn't carry the losses.

In truth, I just wanted to lie face down on the floor and have a massive frustrated tantrum. I wanted to shout and cry, beat my fists and bang my head on the ceramic tiles and have screaming ab-dabs. What the hell was I doing? What was I thinking? The temptation was to just say, 'You know what? Fuck it. I'm done here.' I was a split second away from walking out, getting in my car and driving fast, as far as I could, until I ran out of road and fell into the sea.

But I stood my ground, outwardly calm and professional. I had fought for my girls and my business for so long now I didn't know how to do anything else. I was on automatic piss people off pilot. Like a hamster, just running and running on a wheel of pointlessness. I lost money as fast as I could earn it, and got absolutely nowhere apart from more miserable daily. The girls were always fine; they always earned well and had everything they needed. In all the years of aggravation and upheaval, I'd made sure that whatever I went through, they never lost one day's whoring.

Belinda used to say, 'there's no business like ho business,' but I was beginning to think this ho business would be the death of me.

Lexi walked into the kitchen and an idea struck me.

'We will obviously stop immediately,' I said, 'but it's Lexi's birthday tomorrow and we were planning a big party for her. I'm assuming that you'd have no objections?'

Lexi stopped in her tracks and looked at me as if I had gone mad. She obviously had no idea she was celebrating her birthday tomorrow, having generally done so in mid-November. I gave her my sternest of looks, and she played along, nodding.

Ms Shelby looked at me. 'We can't stop you having a party.'

'All weekend?'

'As long as it is only a party.'

'And if the weather is as hot as it has been, then I can imagine clothes might be removed.'

The woman wasn't daft, she knew what I was saying. She nodded her head, 'as long as you stop trading as a brothel then the council have no interest in how you spend your time.'

'The locals and their dogs might not realise it's just a party,' I added, wondering how much I could get away with.

Ms Shelby shrugged her shoulders. 'The council offices are closed over the weekend, if we get complaints then we'll be back Monday afternoon and if at that stage you are still operating as a brothel then you will be arrested. No questions asked.'

I nodded. We understood each other. 'Monday afternoon?'

'Yes.'

'Ok, that's good news. Lexi would have been so disappointed, wouldn't you Lex? We've been planning this for months. Well, thank you all for coming. I'm sorry if we've caused you any bother, but I have a birthday cake to make, I need to get on.' With a smile of finality I opened the door and showed them all out.

The police taped up anything that was stationary. Red and white plastic ribbon was put across the gate, the door, even around the fountain. Large 'illegal business' stop notices printed with bold capital letters were stuck to almost every surface. The girls and a few lingering customers were asked to leave and escorted from the premises.

Ms Shelby and the police finally drove away. As they disappeared around the bend I wound up all the 'scene of crime' bunting neatly into a ball and slam dunked it into the bin. All the distracting evidence of their visit conveniently vanished as if by magic.

The girls returned and the punters poured back in.

I hadn't planned to walk away that easily. The Stop Notices with power of arrest were served on a Thursday afternoon, just five days after we'd arrived. Up to that point and despite a police presence for most of Thursday we achieved daily figures I never believed possible. Up to five times that of our busiest days in the previous flats. The punting world's only topic of conversation was 'Madam Becky's' new gentleman's club out in the sticks. My success must have affected the competition badly.

I figured if we could avoid jail over the weekend, and make the most of the Friday night rush, we would have the deposit money covered by the Monday, and maybe break even. That was the plan. Avoid arrest until Monday.

I imagined running my business from a Romany caravan might be a better idea, and then we could just keep on trucking. Maybe dear old Dunky Donkey could put on his little pony ears and be harnessed up, and drag a mobile bagnio from pillar to post, one step in front of the constabulary.

My mum owned a narrow boat, and we'd seriously considered opening a floating knocking shop. I was told of a palatial barge for sale, complete with Jacuzzi and gold taps. Tempted yes, but I worried those de-spunked clients with trembly legs and stars before their eyes would slip off the gang plank and drown. Actually, I was beginning to feel as if I'd had enough of the entire wretchedly pointless performance.

I'd tried so hard, with the help of Napoleon Hill and his, 'make yourself rich' books, Mr Chip and his goal setting NLP magic, meditation and concentration. I'd overcome the unhelpful parts of my personality and against all the odds, I'd created a booming bonking empire.

Motivational books are not written for illegal business. The better I did, the bigger I grew, the more attention I drew. It looked like a perfect exercise in why not to develop and prosper. I wished I'd not bothered at all.

We had the most amazing weekend. We made enough money to repay the costs incurred moving in, with almost enough left over for a deposit on a new flat in Milton Keynes. Lexi's 'party' was a great success. But I felt like my life was going to rat shit.

Beggars can't be choosers, and the ridiculous place we moved into next was all that was available at one day's notice. I knew the council lady and her gang would be back on Monday to arrest anyone who looked even remotely sexually active, so we had to be long gone.

The new flat was so small that the clients thought they were in some kind of parallel universe. One moment they were in a magnificent eight bedroom bawdy house, with a sweeping gravel drive, and the next in a micro-apartment, bumping their knees against the window ledges if they tried anything remotely exotic on the beds.

If we got busy - that is more than one client at a time, the receptionist would have to move her office and the other girls into the hallway and set up camp outside the lift doors. Her other alternative was to crouch them all down, as silently as possible, on their knees, below the waist high dividing wall that separated the small kitchen from what was officially the living area, and was now a fully operational shagging room. It was her job to make sure everyone held their breath and remained silent whilst all manner of sexual activities happened just a few feet away.

Our miniscule new HQ was the penthouse according to the letting agent particulars, in as much as it was on the top floor. We overlooked a gigantic superstore building development. The teams of builders and scaffolders working on the mammoth construction task were friends of crazy Keith, my security chap, and Darren's boxing buddies - loud, leary and very easily excited.

We begged the girls to keep off the balcony, which was clearly visible from most of the site and the large canteen, and to be as discreet as possible. Our survival as an enterprise relied on us staying in this flat unnoticed.

I was wasting my breath. The lads would line up along the scaffold at lunch time and plead with the girls to come out in their basques to dance and wave. This they kindly did, laughing and blowing kisses to their admirers. I received endless irate calls from the site management and had Keith begging me to make the frisky pests go in and close the curtains as the entire development project had ground to a halt.

Admittedly, the penthouse was almost impossible to work in properly, and the same girls that complained so bitterly about moving into the big farm, complained even more bitterly about leaving it and going back into a tiny flat in Milton Keynes. I stood in the depressingly claustrophobic front room and listened to the endless bitching about the lack of space, the parking, and the small bathroom. I snapped. Enough was enough.

'Right then!' I shouted into their shocked faces. 'Anyone who doesn't like it is welcome to fuck off now.' They stared at me in stunned silence. 'Moan, moan fucking moan, that's all you lot do. I'm not having a good fucking time either. I've just about had enough of all of it, and I'm not sitting here anymore, miserable and skint, listening to you lot slagging off my efforts to make you ungrateful bastards money.' I marched out slamming the door on them.

I stopped outside the lift doors, heavy breathing and shaking with rage. I took a deep inhale to calm and centre myself. Admittedly, the outburst had been totally over the top. I felt shamed and humiliated by my behaviour.

Getting myself back under control, I turned round and walked back into the flat. They had obviously been talking about me as they instantly went silent, and stared guiltily at me.

'And keep off that fucking balcony.' I yelled and stormed back out again.

The new flat and the ungrateful girls weren't the only issue. We still had the problem of what to do with the house. I'd signed up for six months and if we left just one week into the lease then once again we lost all the deposit and rent money. So in the second deliberate mistake of my life, the first - ever opening a brothel to begin with, I decided to stay and live at the farm.

Darren and I moved my daughters into the house. Emilia, my youngest absolutely loved it, showing off to her friends in the multi-roomed grandeur. My dogs, Dogbaby, and his new wife, Precious, a tiny Bichon with very poor genetics, adored it. Abi wasn't bothered either way. She was working a lot of hours on reception, had learnt to drive and was at the age that she thought her mother was a drag and best avoided.

Living at the farm made sense from a business point of view, or so I thought. The drive gave us safe parking for the very expensive Foo Foo limousines. The house was big enough to use as a warehouse for the Foo Foo sex toy stock, with which I was planning world domination through online sales to help boost the shop's income. We turned part of the annex into an office for the 'Madam Becky' operation, and a new gay receptionist, Neil, moved in to the rest of it as a lodger.

With my 'never say die' attitude, the optimistic plan was to open more flats in different areas and play a game of cat and mouse with the Old Bill. Having a central office meant that we could have a single reception rather than placing a receptionist into every location, thus we saved money. Emilia and her visiting school friends soon got used to being surrounded by boxes of dildos, anal probes and fantasy rabbit costumes. The evening I dropped a case of amile nitrate (poppers) on the kitchen floor during a kid's slumber party was a problem. I had to evacuate the house, and take five twelve-year-olds and two small dogs to McDonalds at midnight, to stop them getting their heads blown off by the orgasm enhancing fumes.

On paper, living in the farm and running the businesses from there was perfect. What I failed to take into account – yet again – were the village idiots.

The brothel was gone. Why they were still determined to ruin my life and drive us out of our home?

CHAPTER THIRTY

It had never occurred to me that nobody in the village would believe the brothel was actually gone. They were convinced we were still at it. The village pub had been set up as a command centre for angry residents; and a decision had been made to make my life as tiresome as possible. They'd reckoned without my bloody-minded tenacity, and refusal to be shifted. They wanted me to leave, and thought they'd achieved their goal when they'd had us closed down. They hadn't reckoned on my moving my whole family, yappy dogs and crates of sex aids in.

The girls were not happy being squashed into the smaller space, and discord and grumbling had replaced the laughter and happy banter that MB's had always been known for. The main culprits were a Brazilian girl called Vanessa, who was Carmen's arch enemy, and a very small, pocket-sized Thai lady, Mia, who wandered between all the agencies complaining about everyone to everyone. Even Lexi was getting fed up.

Abi would return from looking after the girls for the day, really miserable and pissed off. 'Vanessa is really shit stirring Mum, she's going on and on about how quiet she is, and how you don't know what you're doing. She's telling everyone 'Madam Becky's' is finished.'

'Just ignore her honey, it can't be easy for them all,' I said trying to calm her down.

'But I hate it when she slags you off, she's such a bitch. Carmen reckons Vanessa is planning to open her own flat and take all your girls.'

I stopped bagging up clean towels for her to take in the next day and looked at her.

'Abs, they have no idea what they're talking about. How often have girls tried to open their own places, and failed within two months, asking for their shifts back?'

'Yeah, I know, but it's awful in that flat Mum, bitching all day, it's upsetting everyone and it's too small to get away from them. I'm stuck listening to their whinging shit for hours on end.'

She was really wound up. We'd had our differences, Abi and I, but she was fiercely loyal, and wouldn't have a word said against me, except of course by herself.

'Vanessa has done eight jobs today, so I don't know how she can say she's quiet,' Abi added, 'and she buggered off up the city for half the afternoon. She was meant to see Howard at four, but she turned her phone off and vanished.'

'For Christ sake,' I sighed. 'Poor Howard. Who saw him?'

'That new older lady, Rosie. She seems ok, but she never stops talking.'

'Did Howard say anything?' I asked worried. If we wanted to stay in business then pissing off loyal regular customers like Howard was not sensible.

'Just that she was lovely, and he had a nice time.'

'Ah, bless him. I love Howard. He must be due his free half hour on the loyalty card soon,' I said relieved.

'Yeah he had it today. Mum, seriously, what are you going to do about Vanessa? I'm sure she's giving customers her number as well, trying to poach them for her own place.'

'Let's wait and see,' I said. I wasn't overly worried. There was always a bit of bitching and backbiting in a brothel. And there were always rumours about girls pinching customers and setting up on their own. 'I'll keep an eye on her.'

'You're hardly ever there anymore Mum,' she pleaded.

She was right, I was never there. I made a point of it. The last lot of drama, and being kicked out of the farm had soured it all for me. I was beginning to hate going in to the flat, happy to do the phones from home, and let the receptionist deal with the day to day grind on the front line.

'You keep an eye on her for me then,' I said, refocusing on my folding.

I had lived and breathed hanky panky in one form or another for the last two decades. Night and day - day in, day out. It had been my life, my love and my vocation. Sadly, I could feel a growing part of me wishing I never had to look at it again. Wishing they'd all sod off with the customers and start their own agencies and leave me with an empty flat and a quiet mind. Just thinking about it, I could feel myself getting stressed.

I finished organising the clean washing, then I shut myself in the office and fired up the internet. Time to book some flights to France for a few days rest, before my brain melted.

When I returned from France after my short break, the police arrived and demanded a list of car registration numbers that belonged to friends and family. They then proceeded to tell me how often each person was allowed to visit me.

They insisted that my mum justify her trips up and down my drive, and logged her turns for the school run and towel collecting for the work flat. They insisted she limited her visits to my house to once a day.

'On what grounds?' I demanded.

They couldn't answer.

'So you're sitting there telling me that my mum can only visit at certain times and on certain days.' I was getting very angry, 'but you can't tell me why?'

They had the grace to fidget and look uncomfortable. But they didn't seem to have any legitimate reason for their unreasonable demands.

'This is harassment,' I said standing up and pointing to the door. 'Sod off, the lot of you.'

And strangely they did.

So convinced were the constabulary by the spying locals incorrect reports that we were still plying our filthy trade from the farm, my home was raided again early one August evening, a month or so after they closed me down.

The neighbours, who all lived too far away to see anything anyway, reported seeing a group of teenage sex slaves ushered into the house. They were smuggled in under blankets from inside the blacked-out limo. Apparently, all the house lights were blazing, and passers-by noticed unusual amounts of activity in some of the rooms that looked to the dog walkers like trafficked women fighting for their lives.

The police, border control and Ms Shelby turned up in force and stormed the house to find a bunch of hyped up twelve year olds running riot in pyjamas. The Old Bill had disturbed Emilia's birthday party, frightened all her friends from school, and ruined their disco.

I told them to sod off again, and they did, looking like fools.

Work life wasn't any less tense either. The girls had for all intents and purposes split into two feuding teams, with my staff refereeing in the middle. During an evening when I was at home, feeling one of my headaches coming on, my phone rang.

'That's it!' Abi shouted at me.

I held the phone away from my ear, and grimaced at Darren.

'I've had enough. Vanessa has made Carmen cry. She's run off, and won't answer her phone, and she's got bookings all night. Vanessa is just sitting here with Mia laughing at me, and....'

'Abi! Stop!' I demanded. 'Enough already. I'm sending Darren down.'

I gave Darren his instructions and off he went. Half an hour later Abi phoned back laughing and sounding jollier than she'd done for weeks.

'Ahh! That was soooo funny Mum. You should have seen their faces. Darren walked in and just said, 'pack your stuff, Becky says you're leaving.' Vanessa and Mia started crying and begging, but he just kept saying, 'Becky says you're leaving, so you're leaving.' He just marched them out.'

One crisis averted, but another was always lurking just around the corner. I seemed to have my own built in magnet for attracting trouble.

I tended to do the phones from the farm on a Saturday night, which left the receptionist free to deal with trying to fit clients and girls into the miniscule flat. I sat in the office at the back of the farm house, paperwork spread everywhere and Dogbaby and Precious asleep on a cushion at my feet. Darren was out driving the limo for a sixtieth birthday party, and the house seemed very quiet. It was at times like that when I realised how isolated the farm was, pitch dark and silent, with no street lights for miles. Very very creepy

Under the desk, Dogbaby lifted his head and growled. Precious, my poorly formed Bichon, the size of a medium cat, with Leo Sayer hair but the heart of a lioness was also bolt upright. Totally rigid, her fluffy ears pricked, she listened to something, on full alert.

What was it? They were worrying me. I concentrated hard, trying to hear what they'd heard. I couldn't, but they knew something was out there. The phone rang loudly, making me jump, and I quickly flicked off the ringer to deaden the noise; my heart pounded.

Dogbaby growled again. Long and low. The office backed onto open fields, and the external glass door and wide window made me feel like a rabbit in headlights, perfectly illuminated, and visible to anyone who may have been watching. I switched off the desk lamp, and plunged the room into darkness - only the green power switch from the phone blinked in the thickly encompassing blackout. As soon as I'd turned off the light I could see outside. I gasped as a large shape crossed the window, heading towards the door. The handle moved, up and down, as someone tried to get into the office with me.

The dogs went insane. Dogbaby threw himself at the bottom of the door, barking fit to burst, and Precious, all mouth as always, made the most dreadful noise, and dashed in hysterical circles. I made a run for it and fled upstairs, clutching the phone. The dogs followed, still yapping furiously. I desperately tried to quiet them so I could hear if anyone had broken into the house and was searching for me. They wouldn't shut up, so over their noise I phoned T and Darren.

T was on his way, but Darren was out in the limo. I just wanted to hear his voice. He told me to lock myself and the dogs in the bathroom, so I did, and waited for T to arrive and save me.

Both boys had door keys; when I heard a knock on the bathroom door, I squeezed out from the airing cupboard to let T in. Darren stood in front of me and gathered me up into his arms. The dogs were as delighted to see him as I was, and jumped and squeaked excitedly at the surprise arrival of their dad.

'How are you here?' I asked when he let me go. 'Where's the limo?'

'Outside,' he said, taking my hand and leading me down to the kitchen.

'Where are the passengers?'

'In it.'

'What? You are joking?' I said shocked as I thought of the poor partygoers trapped in the back of a runaway stretch.

'I called T, but I was nearer, and that limo goes like shit if you put your foot down so I just floored it.' He put the kettle on. 'T was just pulling in behind me. I got it up to ninety on the road from the city centre.'

'Dear God, all those roundabouts. What about your passengers?'

'They were rolling about everywhere. I took roundabouts and bends on two wheels, I could hear them falling around in the back. I think one lady's been sick. You may have to give them their money back. It wasn't quite the outing they expected.'

'Oh Darren you arse. Those poor people.'

'You're safe,' he said, bending down to kiss me. 'Get yourself a nice cup of tea.' he looked up as T rushed into the room. 'Mr T and I'll go and have a look around out the back.'

Darren took Dogbaby to search the grounds for the intruder with T. Whoever it was, they were long gone.

Darren stayed with me while T took the well-shaken limo cargo back to their homes.

The following day Keith, the head of my covert security, came up to look around, and lectured me on my personal safety.

'You shouldn't be here Becks to be honest.' He looked out of the open office door across the fields. 'You can't secure this place. Look at it.'

He was right. It was open countryside for half a mile in each direction - not even a garden fence. The house just backed straight onto rolling farmland.

'I know you're skint, but all those little scrotes out there think you're loaded, and think you've got thousands in cash in the house. Not to mention them lot who are causing trouble.' He pointed towards the village.

'Anyone could come from across the fields and break in, it's totally exposed. It's the worst place you could be. It's not just the organised villains you need to worry about, it's all the coked up teenage tossers who shove stuff up their nose, listen to gangster rap and then wanna take on the world. The kids. They'll think this is easy. Look...' He pointed to a gap in the hedge next to the road. '...that's what I'd do. I'd drop off some randoms there, they'd come in, smash you and the place up, empty the safe, and be back out on the road and gone in under five minutes. No one would see anything.'

He shook his head. 'It would be so easy Becks.'

'What do you suggest I do?' I asked, knowing I wouldn't like the answer.

'Alarms and shit are pointless. If someone wants to get in, they'll get in. Most of the lads I know can disable any alarm system, and you're too far away for me to get to you quick if Darren's not here.'

'Great,' I sighed.

'You need a massive dog, and a cattle prod.' With his toe, Keith gently nudged Dogbaby, who was standing with us in the doorway, enjoying a chink of sunlight, and surveying his kingdom. 'Not these useless bloody things. A huge rottie or something, most people will think twice about a face-off with a rottie.'

'I'd have a different set of problems then,' I bent over and flicked Dogbaby's ears. 'This hairy blighter is one of the most dog aggressive creatures on earth, there'd be murders done if I brought a big dog into the house.' Dogbaby looked up at me, wagging his tail. Knowing he was being discussed.

'Better his murder than yours Becks.' Keith looked serious. 'You don't know who that was last night. It could have been the Old Bill, your mates in the village or just crackheads. You've pissed off a lot of people. You're a target, and an easy one out here.'

It wasn't what I wanted to hear, but I knew he was right. This was insane. The self-help books hadn't written chapters on how to stop yourself being killed if you became too successful. I'd have to give my personal safety some serious thought.

To add to the fun, the planning officers were getting desperate, and trying to make up new ways to goad me. They decided that the annex was incorrectly valued for council tax, and they would have to come over repeatedly and measure it just to be sure.

I liked Ms Shelby from the council, despite all our run-ins, and I called her up and asked her to drop by for tea and biscuits. Over a nice slice of walnut cake, she admitted that she was being pressurised by very important people, far superior to her, to cause me as many problems as possible. She was as sick of it all as I was.

I was really fed up at this stage and in truth I was feeling somewhat victimised. I believe that if you do the crime then you have to be prepared to do the time. That's why I always took raids as part of the game and never gave the police a hard time for doing their job. But this was different. We'd shut down the brothel, moved it out of the area completely, yet still they hounded us. It brought out the worst in me and I must admit I started pushing the boundaries.

Taking Keith's advice, I erected large lockable gates at the end of the drive, and invested in two enormous mastiffs, Bruce and Treacle, both trained in personal protection, to patrol the grounds.

I nailed a large sign to the front of the house, with a picture of my psychotic dogs emblazoned on it, teeth barred, it read: **'I can get to the gate in eight seconds. Can you?'**

'There you go!' I said to Darren as I stood back with my hammer and inspected my erection.

'Love me... love my dogs! Now the council chaps and our friends in the village can decide just how much they really want to come and visit me.'

A few evenings later, we sat watching the telly when the dogs informed us we had intruders. I silenced them with a word. Darren turned off the lights and peered out into the darkness. He could see at least half a dozen torches, and the garden seemed to be full of men sneaking round the bushes. A large vehicle, with huge spotlights on the roof and the front bumpers, was parked on the road, outside the locked gates of the drive, illuminating the front garden.

'There's loads of them,' hissed Darren over his shoulder to me, as I sat in the dark living room.

'It's gotta be the gypsies; they've got a big truck or something on the road.'

Both the dogs were fully focused on me awaiting instructions. I had my hand tight around Dogbaby's muzzle as I tried to stop him yapping and distracting Bruce and Treacle from the job in hand. He wriggled against me, and barked in the back of his throat, desperate to get in on the action.

'Watch 'em,' Darren instructed the big dogs - their signal to be ready to challenge the invading pikies when told. Flash light shone through my window and searched the darkened room.

'Sod this for a game of soldiers,' I said. 'This is my house, and I'm buggered if I'm sitting in the dark shitting myself.' Getting up I stomped angrily through the hallway, opened the front door, and sent the dogs out.

Men were shouting and swearing, torches bobbing about frantically in the night, while the trespassers tried to make their escape from my animals. The dogs didn't attack to harm, but they would seize and restrain and accidents happened. We were just happy for them to have chased everyone up the drive. Whoever they were, and why ever they were there, I wasn't bothered about holding travellers hostage and questioning them.

Darren flicked all the exterior lights on when we followed the dogs outside. Approaching the locked gates at the road side, we heard the doors of the truck slamming shut, and the engine rev as men jumped in and prepared to make their getaway. The spot lamps on the truck blinded us, making us unable to see anything beyond the dogs running up and down in front of the fence baying loudly. Screeching into reverse, the truck pulled backwards into the lane, was thrown into gear, and sped off.

'The sneaky bastards,' shouted Darren over the dogs barking, as the house lights picked out the word 'POLICE' in fluorescent lettering down the side of the rapidly accelerating Range Rover.

CHAPTER THIRTY ONE

'This is just the best house to have Christmas in,' Emilia said, sitting in front of the open fire in the big sitting-room at the farm.

Bruce, the male guard dog, lay on the rug and ate lumps of coal, covering the rug with black dust mixed with mastiff drool. Emilia grinned, 'I'm really looking forward to it.'

I didn't share her enthusiasm. My parents were coming to lunch, and I didn't trust the council and police not to join us sometime whilst we were pulling the crackers, or arguing over the last roast potatoes. I looked forward to the New Year more, with the foolish optimism that blights some of us, that the New Year may be somewhat better than the old one.

Christmas day lunch arrived and passed with little incident. My parents left early, and Rosie, the new lady who worked on reception, came up to the farm in the evening to play charades and talk endlessly.

We chatted about work, and laughed about how Vanessa and Mia, the trouble makers Darren had frogmarched out of the building, had set up their own flat and called it 'Love Story'. Darren re-named it Horror Story, and would phone them up and pretend to be a punter asking for details.

It seemed pointless baiting them, but he found it hilarious and enjoyed it immensely as both of them spoke hardly any English and he'd tie them in linguistic knots.

The staff had noticed how miserable I had become, and people who knew me worried about me. I spent New Year's Eve wishing I'd listened to Mr Pip and got a proper job.

I was sat in my office on the first day after the festive break, not moving, just staring into space, dreading another year of being a Madam, when my reverie was broken by the phone ringing. A professional, friendly voice announced she was the lady who booked my adverts for the local paper. I'd dealt with them for years, and had a really good relationship with her, but she sounded cagey.

'Hi Becky. How are you?'

I knew she wasn't calling for a chat, and my adverts weren't due, so I waited for her to get to the point.

'The thing is Becky...'

Here we go I thought.

'The newspaper has come under a lot of pressure from the government and the police for placing personal ads in the classified section, and so they've changed their guidelines with effect from this week.'

That didn't sound good. 'Ok, what does that mean?' I asked, knowing from her apologetic tone that it meant more trouble for me.

'Well, you can't run your personal ad in the paper anymore from this week, not like it is anyway.'

'What do you mean 'like it is?''

'Well, you have that large picture advert, with you in the cat-suit.'

I spent a fortune on the branding and imaging, with the help of Mr Pip, and we ran very expensive, very flashy adverts; the business relied on them. I didn't like what I was hearing.

'The problem is that we are not allowed to have any pictures or descriptive words anymore. It's the same for everyone,' she said. 'I'm really sorry.'

'This is ridiculous. Just like that? With no notice? What descriptive words can't we use?'

'I'm really sorry Becky.'

'I know it's not your fault, but I need to know what has to be changed. I'll have to produce new artwork,' I said, trying to keep calm and deal with the problem.

'Ok. You can't be 'Madam' anymore, or call it a 'Gentlemen's Club' or describe the business in any way.'

'So what can I be?'

A long pause... then a cough to clear her throat, then in a very subdued voice, 'just Becky's escorts, and no website, or opening times, or any locations.'

'What, you're kidding?. That's not possible! The website gets thousands of hits a week from the paper, it's vital, and how the hell will people know who and where we are?'

'I'm so sorry Becky. Everyone's shouting at me today, there really is nothing I can do about it. Poor Foxy Babes, they're not allowed to be 'foxy' or 'babes' so they're really annoyed.'

Foxy Babes was a big very professional out-call agency run by a friend of mine, and I knew they relied on their advertising more than I did. They'll be buggered I thought.

I knew that she didn't make the policy. No point shooting the messenger. I started to think that it would be impossible for me to hate 'Madam Becky's' any more than I did, but it got worse.

Fast asleep, in the busy week between Christmas and New Year, both small dogs on my bed, the phone woke me up.

'Mum, you awake?'

'Yeah, I am now Abi. What's up?'

'I've just locked up and left the flat, and I think I'm being followed, yeah, I'm sure I am.'

Sitting bolt upright, I looked at my clock radio, 4.00 am. I shook Darren awake.

'Where are you?'

'Just driving around the city,' she said, sounding petrified. 'A car's been parked outside the flat most of the evening. I just thought it was a punter who'd lost his bottle, but when I left he was behind me. I've tried to lose him, but he's still there.'

Abi was my ultra-sensible daughter, nothing of the drama queen about her. If she was worried then you knew there was something to worry about.

'Can you see how many people are in the car?' I said, trying to stop the rising panic I felt get into my voice.

'There was only one person outside the flat, but I'm sure there's two now, or maybe three.'

She sounded really shaken.

Darren sat up propped on the pillows, awake but confused.

'It's Abi,' I said to him. 'She thinks she's being followed.'

'Shit!' He jumped out of bed and started getting dressed.

'What shall I do Mum?'

'Drive to the police station. Don't come here. There are too many dark lanes on the way. Don't stop; just get to the police station. Drive right up to the front, and sound your horn. Keep leaning on it until someone comes out and finds you.' I glanced at my boyfriend, he nodded his head. 'Darren and T will meet you there. I'll find out where T is.'

'I'll take Treacle,' Darren said as he ran down the stairs. 'She'll not let anyone near Abi. I'll leave Bruce with you just in case they turn up here.'

Abi kept driving, trying fruitlessly to shake off the car tailing her. Both Darren and T arrived at the police station car park before her, so when she pulled in, with a dark saloon car a few hundred metres behind her, both men and the dog were waiting.

She pulled up, not in front of the building as she'd been instructed, but a short distance away, and a long way from Darren and T. The following car screeched to a halt and a large man jumped out and sprinted towards Abi's car, with what looked like a baseball bat in his hand.

'Fuck,' said Darren. 'That's not the Old Bill or a planning officer, who the fuck is he?'

'Why's she parked there, the stupid kid?' T started running 'We're too far away, we won't make it.'

The man was closing the distance fast, only feet away from Abi's car; he raised his weapon over his head ready to attack.

That's when Darren let Treacle go.

Darren and T had a 'talk' to the assailant after the dog had been withdrawn and put back in the car. It seemed he'd been paid by an agency from London, which had planned to move in and take over Milton Keynes using all methods at their disposal. Details were handed over, and dutifully logged by Darren. The perforated man was advised that Treacle wouldn't be stopped next time his face was seen anywhere near 'Madam Becky's' or her girls.

Rosie was on reception the next morning, so we all had a lie in to recover from the excitement of the previous night.

Abi brought me up a cup of tea late morning and told me Dave, the owner of Foxy Babes had been trying to get hold of me.

I sipped my tea and returned his call.

'Hey Dave. That's spooky. I was just talking about you a few days ago to the girl who does my ads. What a pain in the arse all that is. Jeez, this business is doing my head in. How's things with you?'

'I'm good thanks Becks, but you may have more than the papers to worry about love. My mate's a builder, and he's working on a barn conversion overlooking your house somewhere, and he's told me the police have put a twenty-four hour surveillance operation in there. The full works. They've been watching every move you make for weeks now. I didn't know if you knew.'

Maybe that's why they hadn't noticed a man with a baseball bat attacking a young girl in the police station car park, they were much too busy with the really important things in life, like setting up a pointless stakeout on a family home and watching Abi's cat dig a hole and go for a pee outside my front door.

CHAPTER THIRTY TWO

Saddened by the tedious patheticness of the Vale of Aylesbury's various departments, and their bids to remove me from within their boundaries, I decided to stage a daily cabaret for the cameras. We'd done nothing vaguely interesting from the house since we'd been shut down. If they were prepared to spend what must be a substantial sum keeping an eye on me, I felt it my public duty to give them something interesting to watch.

My big dogs fought with my little dogs, so I had to do at least two separate dog walks around the fields daily to minimise the bloodshed. I emerged from the front door dressed for the occasion in a colourful assortment of outfits from the Foo Foo rails and 'Madam Becky's' costume cupboard - PVC, rubber, skin tight and sky blue - the more bizarre the better. Red racer girl outfits, bunches and thigh boots, my Rolf Harris look or a sexy Santa. If I had it, then I wore it for the cameras, and went off through the mud with my mastiffs then out again an hour later with Dogbaby and Precious dressed as a naughty nun or a school girl.

If we ran out of logs for the sitting-room fire, out I went with a large, sharp axe, and commenced chopping wood as a pornographic pixie or bunny girl. I bent over at the waist, a perfect forty-five degrees, legs and back straight, bum pushed out. I'd erotically bury my hatchet, flicking my hair like a stripper towards my supposedly secret audience.

Darren would don a balaclava and we'd take Bruce and Treacle through their bite work and training routines on the flat piece of field right in front of the cameras. He'd attack me with a carving knife, and I'd run away shrieking theatrically in my shiny cat-suit, before setting the dogs on him.

Darren would be knocked to the ground by the beasts and held at bay by the snarling tooth-snapping canines. Delighted to have been saved, I'd jump up and down beside the fence, cheering, my boobs bouncing around for the close-up.

Various gangster friends and well known local 'faces' would visit for a nice cup of tea and a gossip, trying their best to look as shifty and deviant as possible.

I'd neglected Foo Foo, the pervy panty shop, as so much time was spent performing for spying eyes, and dealing with all the crap that came my way. So it was no great surprise that I'd booked in an eighteenth birthday limo ride and then totally forgotten about it. The Foo Foo love limo was having its MOT and was off the road. Kindly, to help me out of a spot, I was lent a stunning new bright pink stretch that had just arrived from the USA a few days previously.

The job went off without a hitch, and T, who'd been the chauffeur, brought the brand new borrowed limo back to the farm to be cleaned. He pulled off the drive and parked up on the grass. When he got back in the car half an hour later, it wouldn't budge, sunk to the axles in the mud. After fifteen minutes of manic wheel-spinning deeper and deeper into ruts filled with slime, T sent for all his brothers and cousins.

Filmed by the secret police cameras half a dozen immaculately dressed Muslim dudes arrived, swaggering out of hot hatches and pimped Japanese imports. Dressed in designer labels and shod in the most costly trainers, they proceeded to slip and slide into the farmyard filth one by one.

A beautiful two tone metallic Subaru Impreza was attached to a tow rope, and revved within an inch of its life trying to pull the big car free, but it ended up just as stuck as the limo.

The swearing and cursing was getting louder as more trainers were ruined. The borrowed car was needed back by its owners to go on another booking. Since we hadn't informed them of our awkward predicament, the limo office were expecting their pride and joy returned within the hour, cleaned, perfumed and ready to go straight out to collect more passengers.

Admitting defeat, and with time running out, a tractor was called in. Attaching a thick chain from a winch to the limo's back axle seemed like a good idea until thirty seconds after the winch was turned on it became obvious that the fibreglass body kit of the car was too long for the angle of the chain and was about to be snapped clean off.

By now I was screaming, on the verge of outright hysteria. I had no idea how much a brand new, custom-painted Lincoln town car cost, but I guessed it was more than I had, -everything was going badly wrong.

'Lads, please, I'm sure it'll work,' I keened. 'Just try. Your combined weight will force the winch chain down just far enough not to catch on the bumper. If Mr Deacon can drive the truck forwards as well as wind the winch we may have a chance to save ourselves.'

Not convinced, but desperate to save T the humiliation of having to fess up to foolish parking, one by one his family stood, in stinking, mud-soaked footwear along the length of the towing chain.

In a last ditch attempt to free the car, the boys balanced like birds on a telegraph cable along the length of the chain.

'Hold on to each other for support,' I shouted as I climbed into the driving seat of the beautiful new car, trying to keep the mud off the carpets.

'Ok Mr Deacon. Let's do it.'

And as the Pakistani boys wobbled and shuddered a foot off the ground, like an amateur circus act, Mr Deacon and I, amongst great clouds of burning oil, put every ounce of horse power we had into releasing the car. The limo leapt free and flung the balancing boys off the winch chain in one final acrobatic display flat onto their backs into the sludge. Throwing his ruined shoes and clothes in the bin, T made a mad dash to the garage jet wash station in his socks and pants to get the car hosed down. His family and Mr Deacon, hero of the hour, continued as darkness fell to extract all their other vehicles from the malevolent clutches of the Buckinghamshire countryside.

I bet they still watch the 'Madam Becky' surveillance tapes at all the Police training sessions. Very entertaining I'm sure, but what a criminal waste of my imagination, and of police time and taxpayer's money.

All the dog walking around the fields had however given me plenty of time to think about my life. I was being stalked by the police, council, angry mobs and God knows who else. I was spied on day and night, and living with the hounds of Baskervilles to try to keep my kids safe in our home. Not only that, but I just knew in my psychic handbag, that if I kept pushing my luck I was heading straight to jail. Do not pass 'go', do not collect £200. Was I mad?

I wasn't happy anymore. Upsetting the authorities and being a public inconvenience was mildly entertaining in the way that dribbling after root canal treatment is entertaining. But it had been a very long time since I had been filled with that sense of total contentment and joy that connects you with creation.

I thought about the times when I had been truly happy, and I realised that it was when I was just sitting in nature with my animals being grateful for my existence. That didn't really cost any money, unless I wanted to buy the field I was sitting in, which I didn't. So what was the point of the struggle, the threat of jail, warring with the world? It was just my bloody mindedness really - my refusal to stop fighting plus, added to the problem, having no idea what else I wanted to do.

Running MB's wasn't fun like it used to be - becoming more professional had removed some of its character and jolliness. The more successful I got, the worse life became.

Why was I providing, at great personal expense and danger, an opportunity for ungrateful girls to work safely, make money and be looked after, when they did nothing but fight and squabble? I was constantly at war, risking my life and liberty fighting for their rights, when most of them had no loyalty to me at all. Why was I doing it? For the first time in my life as Madam Becky I couldn't answer that question. I had no idea why I was doing it, and I wished I wasn't.

In January 2008 I was asked to appear on the Trisha show again. I'd been on several times in the past, and they had scheduled a show about kids growing up with strange parents, and wanted Abi to appear with me. I'd do my best to put on a good show and hoped to change one or two of the audience's long held negative beliefs.

The papers and the Labour party had wound up the British population with their myths about the wide spread abuse of sex slaves, and how every escort is a victim. I decided I'd go and stand up for all my ladies and put the record straight. Abi still worked on reception, so we made an interesting couple and they were very keen to have us.

Trisha audiences have been open-minded in the past, but the national propaganda was working well and these people now saw me as the trafficker, the peddler of human misery.

They shouted and pointed their fingers, and whereas normally I'd be up for the debate, and keen to educate, I just sat on the stage and stared at them. I was fed up with the whole sodding thing.

'You lot should be shut down! Dirty sluts,' shouted a greasy-haired, middle-aged woman with gravy stains down the front of her shapeless t-shirt.

'Yeah you should be closed down,' a boy who looked like her son, sitting beside her backed her up.

'Is this your son?' I enquired. She patted him proudly.

'Well, let's say that he has a serious car accident on the way home....'

She looked at me stunned.

'...and is profoundly injured. In a wheelchair.... unable to see to his own needs. You want to deny him the loving touch of another human being for the rest of his life?'

She stared at me. Even Trisha looked confused.

'You think our clients are all married perverts. Many are disabled, handicapped, blind or widowed. These lonely people come to us when they feel the need for human contact, for a sense of physical love.'

Trisha nodded, seeing my point

'Often...' I continued '...it is their carers who call and make their bookings. Sexual relief is not part of a carer's job, so who will do it?'

I stared her out. 'Would you?'

'You want to refuse these people any physical pleasure? In Germany, the disabled get their sexual services paid for by the state.'

The audience was silent.

The gravy lady stood up now, angry about being made to look small-minded, and thrust her pointed finger in my direction.

'We don't want your sort walking our streets,' she shouted.

I looked at her with contempt. Surely, if you knew you were coming on telly you would at least have bothered to find a clean t-shirt and a hairbrush.

'My good woman,' I addressed her sombrely, sounding a little like Queen Victoria, 'my ladies would not dream of parking their BMW's on the streets where you live,' I raised a patronising eyebrow, 'let alone ever get out and walk.'

After the shocked outcry at my condescending rudeness died down, they were out for my blood. Abi rose to the bait, and defended me, but I just sat on the stage and looked them in the eye, one by one. Aloof and stony faced.

I wasn't going to justify myself to these people. I'd had enough of explaining and fighting. I had no rights, and no one gave a shit or had any interest in what I had been trying to do for the people who worked with me. I knew why I did what I did, that was good enough for me. I had broken some antiquated, badly made laws, in a bid to keep my friends safe when they were in great need. I had some of the best times of my life, with the most incredible people. I knew how wonderful most of the women in the sex industry were. I knew how hard they worked to feed their kids, and I also knew statistically there would be several ladies in the audience who'd been escorts at one time or another. So I just sat there and ignored them.

When they attacked me I just smiled back at them or agreed with them, and told them they were entitled to their opinion.

As we left the stage Abi said, 'I don't think they'll be asking you back Mum. That really wasn't what they were paying to hear!'

'Nope. I hope not. I'm done with it Abs, I really have had enough.'

And as I said it, I realised that I really did mean it. I wanted out.

CHAPTER THIRTY THREE

Watching the Trisha show when it was broadcast a few weeks later I was horrified with myself. I'd spent thousands of pounds over the years on my personal development.

Look at me now.

Who was this bitter, defensive, objectionable witch who looked like me on the Trisha show? Was this what I'd become? I covered my face with a scatter cushion and groaned.

'Oh God. That's just too dreadful, Abi, turn it off. I can't watch. No wonder the audience hated me. I look like a right old cow.'

Abi laughed. 'You are an old cow these days isn't she Darren?'

My boyfriend looked thoughtful.

'Have I changed a lot?' I demanded. 'Since when?'

'Definitely since we left the big Bletchley flats,' Abi said. 'That's when I noticed it.'

'When we first got together you had a 'don't take anything seriously' attitude.' Darren said. He seemed a little sad, looking back on happier times. 'I remember having conversations where we both agreed that if we didn't enjoy something then it wasn't worth doing no matter how much money was involved.'

He was right, I never did anything that made me unhappy. Until now.

'Life was about having fun,' he continued, 'and not worrying about the trivia.'

'But you can't just muck about forever can you?' I argued. 'Like Mr Pip's always pointing out, you can't be a wanker all your life.'

'True, but when the business started getting bigger you changed. Setting goals and looking to be the best at what you were doing. That was great, even though no one could keep up with you.' He laughed a little grimly. 'But I think since we left Bletchley and especially since the big house got shut down you pretty much shut down with it.'

I hid behind the cushion. It all felt so pointless.

'You are definitely not having fun now baby,' Darren put his arms around me, 'and since you are no good at hiding how you're feeling, no one else is having fun either.'

I curled into him, and let my desperation flow out in hot tears.

'You do seem very bitter and pissed off about the whole thing these days. It's like you've still got your goals but know that 'Madam Becky's' isn't going to get you to where you want to be and you don't want to be connected with it anymore.'

'Can't we run the flat without Mum being so involved?'

'I'd love that!' I said blowing my nose, 'I'd happily never go near that bloody flat again if I had my way.'

'Well, maybe it's worth a thought. What do you think Darren? Anything has got to be better than letting Mum turn into a hideous old bag! You don't want to get like Grandma!' Abi said flippantly.

'If I end up half as loyal and half as supportive as your Grandmother, it won't be a bad thing,' I chided. But I knew what Abi meant. My mum was an amazing, strong, unique woman, but had an underlying rage and resentment that her life hadn't gone to plan, and sometimes it ran close to the surface.

'I think I need to go to France for a few days, and have a think. The lease is up on the farm at the end of March, so it's time to make some changes anyway.'

So off I went, still sniffing into my tissue to book some flights.

Being in France, walking in the silence of the gently rolling countryside, always cleared my head. I think God made France last, after he had loads of practice making other beautiful places, and I reckon God visited France when He had a bad day and needed a cup of tea and a nice sit down.

Staying in my friend's gite, I helped her with the gardening and spent hours in silent contemplation whilst pruning and tying back last year's roses. The time to go back home came too soon, and on the morning of my flight I woke up really anxious and distressed.

'I need to go for a walk, and see if I can calm down a bit.'

Darren was packing, and re-arranging hand luggage. He looked up at me. 'You ok?'

'I don't want to go home, I seriously feel like I'm about to have a panic attack or throw up.'

'Shall I come with you? I don't trust you to run off and not get on the plane.'

Only half joking, he looked at me.

'Would it be so bad if I didn't?'

'No. If that's what you want we'll work out a way to make it happen,' he said seriously.

I loved Darren so much. He really was the most amazingly supportive man on earth.

We went out into the early spring sunshine. I felt so much better as I walked briskly down the sun dappled lanes between the high hedges, right up until I turned around to go back to the gite. I started hyperventilating. Leaning against Darren at the side of the road, I vomited into the wild flowers and bee orchids that were beginning to bud in the weak sunlight.

Crying and shaking, I struggled to catch my breath and collapsed onto the verge. A leathery skinned farmer on an elderly tractor looked at Darren worriedly as he chugged slowly past down the narrow road.

'Ca va?' he called out, over the engine noise, asking if I was alright.

Darren lifted his free hand in acknowledgement of his concern, his other hand trying to hold my hair back as I continued throwing up in the bushes.

Somehow we got back and to the holiday home and from there on to the plane. I cried all the way back to the UK. The only thought that kept me going was the idea that I would return across the channel as soon as I possibly could.

Nothing much had changed when we got back. The kids were glad to see me back, and Abi suggested that she and I go out for the evening one night when Darren was away watching the football.

We had a nice night dancing away at several local nightclubs, and it had been great to see all my old doorman friends again. Just after midnight Abi wanted to go home to see her boyfriend. Neither of us had been drinking but half way home back to the farm, when the street lights ended, and the road became dark and winding, I realised I had a problem.

'Abi, I think my eyes are going funny.' I reduced my speed.

'Oh shit! Do you want me to drive?' She knew what I meant and I could hear the worry in her voice.

'No, I'll do my best. I'll stop if I need to, you may need to call an ambulance if I get any worse.'

She led me quickly from the car and up the stairs to my bedroom as my vision deteriorated.

'You'll have to help me get undressed, I can't see.' I started to panic. 'Call Darren for me.'

She put me into bed in the dark.

'I can't get hold of Darren, his phone's off. I'm going to see Adrian now.'

'No! Please.' I cried, 'I'm getting really bad.'

'I won't be long Mum; you've had your spazzy tablet,' she said, referring to my migraine pills. 'Call me if you want me to come home.'

I've suffered from migraine since I was a child. They've affected my life since I was about four years old and I've spent every day afraid I'd be struck down by another one.

I thought all migraines were the same, so when someone said. 'Oooh, I'm getting a migraine,' and carried on working, I'd look at them in amazement. They must be so much braver than me. I never saw a doctor about them, thinking they were normal, and I was just being a bit feeble when I was unable to function.

They were always the same. No warning then the aura, the flashing lights would start, then the numbness followed by paralysis on my left side, then the vomiting and the shocking pain in my brain. Unable to move, I'd lay in a darkened room until the main symptoms faded after four or five hours leaving me weak and confused for days afterwards.

I knew what I was in for, but this one was different. I was in the house alone and after about twenty minutes I'd gone totally blind. The aura stopped, but I had completely lost my vision and all feeling and movement down my left side. I was utterly terrified.

I knew I was losing consciousness, and tried to feel around for my mobile phone to call an ambulance, but I was unable to speak, or even move. The pain was unbearable when it started. I dropped in and out of awareness and realised at some point I'd been sick where I lay. I prayed I would die quickly. There was no help coming, Abi stayed out all night. Darren wasn't expected home till tomorrow.

I was on my own.

The first thing I was aware of was Dogbaby fretting over me. It was daylight, my vision had partly returned, and I was alive but in an awful mess. I tried to sit up, but my left side was still unresponsive. Talking to the dog, I realised my speech was slurred, and I couldn't remember what had happened.

By lunchtime when Abi returned, I was shuffling around in my nightie; she helped me clean everything up.

'Bloody migraines,' I said to Darren when he got back.

'I think you should go to hospital baby,' he was looking at me, studying my face.

'Your eye looks funny. You're sort of droopy on one side.'

'I'm ok. It was the worst one ever, and my left hand doesn't work, but I'll be ok in a day or so,' and I went back to bed.

Like the initial smaller eruption of a volcano, letting off steam before it blows its own head off, that night had been a warning. I ignored it, thinking that everyone's migraines left them with slurred speech, a paralysed arm and a drooping eye. I was lucky to be alive, but I didn't realise it at the time. I just knew I was stressed, depressed, and needed to change my life.

Getting up the following day, still weak, and unable to hold anything in my left hand, I struggled to open my post. In disbelief, I read and re-read a letter from the council - they'd started bankruptcy proceedings against me for non-payment of council tax.

My mind was still slow and almost unable to keep up with the phone call to the gloating man, whose name and direct line had been on the letter.

'Whilst I appreciate that you are up to date on your original bill, you've paid nothing for the readjusted amount we decided to charge you for your annex area.'

'You decided nothing more was owed,' I protested confused.

'Well, it seems that wasn't the case, and you owe another thirty six pounds.'

'Ok, I'll pay it now, I'll just find my card.' My head was really starting to hurt and I was getting dizzy.

'That's not possible,' the smug voice replied.

'Pardon?'

'It's not possible to clear the bill as proceedings have already started to declare you bankrupt.'

'But I never had a bill to pay! You're going to declare me bankrupt for thirty pounds?'

'A bill was issued Miss Adams, and it's now with our solicitors. That's how things stand. Good day.' He hung up.

The bastards. I knew what they were doing. They were still at it. I'd definitely never received a bill. We'd been in the house less than eight months, and they were poking around making a nuisance of themselves and measuring the annex only a few months ago. How could they bankrupt me for such a small and recent debt? A debt that I didn't know I owed but was willing to pay immediately.

Well fuck them, I was past caring. They could bankrupt me if they wanted to or chuck me into prison. They couldn't kill me, or my kids, or my animals - this was still the UK.

The lease was almost up and we were moving out anyway. People only have power over you if you let them, and I was done with giving this lot any more of my life, time or headspace. I grabbed a handful of painkillers, a glass of water and went back to bed to devise a plan.

CHAPTER THIRTY FOUR

Jack Black, in the film *The School of Rock*, says rock and roll is all about 'sticking it to the man.' Whilst I'm more rock bun than rock chick I do totally get the sentiment.

In my case the collective 'man' was the constabulary, neighbourhood watch and Aylesbury Vale council. They'd made my life as vile and unpleasant as possible and showed no signs of forgiveness.

I looked across the field and resisted the childish urge to make a rude gesture to the cameras hidden in paint tins in the nearby barn conversion.

Was I really so important? The man hours and resources dedicated to my downfall over the past six months could surely have been put to more productive use, like speed traps, or combating teenage loitering around the fried chicken shops of High Wycombe.

Ok, I accepted that during the seven days I'd entertained gents at the farm, I'd violated and affronted the members of the community. I'd upset some very important people, and the incensed posse of ladies that lunched and merlot-fuelled landowners had us removed, just like they wanted with immediate effect. It had taken the mad woman from number eight, six months of pestering the police a hundred times a day before they'd even spoken to us, yet someone from this smart hamlet whispered in the right ear, and we were dispatched in under a week. That wasn't retribution enough it seemed, the trick with the council tax and bankruptcy proceedings was just so petty, I was almost embarrassed for them. Sad they had to stoop so low.

Well it would all end soon enough. My tenancy was up, I was moving on.

I stood at the front of the house and looked all around me with sadness.

Nothing stayed the same forever and I was no stranger to adversity. I hoped the hidden cameras were correctly focused for the main event, and the pencils of the district planners were all sharpened to perfection. I'd hate for them to miss anything.

The large assortment of cars parked on the drive and frenzy of activity would have quickly alerted prying eyes, and mobilised an execution squad. All the house lights shone brightly through the open curtains, a criminal offence in Buckinghamshire as we knew, and pumping eighties disco tunes and riotous laughter shook the foundations. Through the well- lit windows I could see all types of people cavorting around in various stages of undress, hard at it with paintbrushes and wine glasses.

'There you go lads,' I muttered to myself, turning around, waving and bowing theatrically like a ringmaster in the direction of the surveillance outpost, 'get an eyeful of that you bunch of pedantic tossers.'

Lexi, the superstar escort, was at the top of a stepladder beautifully illuminated by the sitting-room light in the gathering March dusk. She was doing a poor job of applying emulsion between wall and ceiling, distracted by Wiggy in a wedding dress, who was trying to cut in under her nurse's uniform. A few punters were half-heartedly attempting to keep to the re-decorating task, but Dunky Donkey was cantering at dangerous speeds around the paint trays worrying everyone. I began to think my 'team' were more hindrance than help. They'd all been doing their best all afternoon bless them, re-painting the house to hand back to the landlord. I could see them getting bored so before it escalated or degenerated from helpful make-over, to a magnolia spattered orgy, I thought it best to go back indoors soon, and distract them with tea and gingernuts.

I could have done the painting more effectively with a team of decorators, but my main task was winding up and pissing off the natives as much as possible in the day or so before I left.

The unhelpful part of my personality, that part that enjoyed being a public nuisance, a stone in the steel-toed, jack boot of the police, wasn't going to let the locals have it all their own way.

I wasn't easily beaten, but nine months on, even I knew when to quit. I'd never been so fed up and unhappy. But I couldn't resist the final two-fingered salute to the plod and their ever watchful camera lens. Which was why I was having a moving out - painting party.

Of course, we could have revamped in dungarees, but there isn't enough controversy in coveralls. I'd give the watchers a damn good show before I made my final curtain call.

Mistress Matrix came to help, looking fabulous as a sex-crazed SS Storm trooper, resplendent in military rubber and laced jack boots. She said it was the end of an era, and she wanted to do her part. I still had a garage full of her electrocution gadgets, which I tried to flog to her, but she'd only come with her slaves to annoy the neighbours, and couldn't be parted from her deutschmarks. She'd set up on her own now and was fully equipped.

I thought it would be much more of an education to anyone watching if Matrix's shackled and gagged gimps stayed outside in the front garden, and tidied up a bit. They weren't natural gardeners, so Matrix and her black leather riding crop gave them a resounding whipping whenever they slackened, just for effect.

Wiggy splashed magnolia contract emulsion on his nuptial robes, and got quite vexed, so skulked outside and sat on the fountain with Carmen and rolled them both a spliff. Wiggy was hopeless at rolling the devil's lettuce. On the rare occasion I'd ever seen him do so, if he was feeling bohemian, the result looked more like a spider being removed from the bath in a bit of tissue. In honour of his poor performance, a joint made by Wiggy was always known as a squiff. I thought I'd allow the 'no drugs' rule to slide, as it was obviously a private party, and Wiggy was an old man in a bridal gown, obviously bonkers and needed it for medicinal reasons.

'You've really done it this time...' Keith said, coming out to stand next to me. He watched fascinated as Matrix bound a submissive slave to the front porch. 'They pay for that?'

I nodded and smiled. 'Yep. And a torturous horticultural session with Matrix is charged as an extra.'

Keith shook his head at the absurdity of it all.

'Christ, is that geeza carrying a monkey?'

'You never met Spanky at the other flats? Some of my chaps like to make love to him.'

'As you do...'

'Let's hope Dogbaby doesn't catch a glimpse of him,' I scanned the area for my mouthy little terrier 'or he'll have that chap's hand off, monkey and all.'

'People have been chatting a lot of shit about you Becky,' he sighed, getting back to his issue. 'It worries me, I'm hearing stuff from everywhere.'

'Nothing new there then Keith old bean.'

'This is different. Opening this place…..' Turning he gestured towards the house and laughed momentarily as he caught sight of Matrix feeding her captives grass.

'Some of your 'mates' in the village spend their expenses visiting the other parlours in Milton Keynes, getting their kicks.'

'Yeah, I can imagine. I can spot a punter a mile off - the hypocritical sods. It's normal don't worry.'

'You need to worry. From what I've been told, some important people out here have joined forces with two of the big parlours up the city centre and are working together to get you banged up.' I puffed out my cheeks and sagged. What was wrong with them all?

'And don't forget, those same people have got the Old Bill and the bird from the council jumping through hoops and doing their dirty work. It's all about who you know Becks. Lexi's not shagging enough MP's and judges for you to get away with it out here.'

Rival escort agencies. Why did they need to behave like that? Fighting and back stabbing? We were all in the same tricky situation, sex workers against the world, battling the hypocrites, the politicians and the criminals who frequently tried to rob us or rescue us. Now Keith was sat there telling me that I was being deliberately targeted, hounded and driven out by my peers, in conjunction with my neighbours. The other parlour owners were people who knew how difficult it was to survive in our profession. We should be supporting each other and the girls, not plotting and tearing at each other's throats. It had occurred to me that by trebling our business it would be at the expense of everyone else. Still that's competition for you. Free market economy and all that. I'd only achieved my business growth through hard work and studying. If it was me being thwarted by the competition then I'd simply up my game. Everybody in the industry bickered and gossiped as girls wandered from place to place, but deliberately trying to ruin someone's life was outrageous.

'I'd have told you sooner Becks but you've had enough stress. Me and the lads have kept an eye on the problem, but they're out for your blood, and I can't stop every little trick they try. It'll all kick off sooner or later. I know that bloke who runs girls from Aylesbury has been out ringing doorbells up and down the road.'

'That's normal Keith. I can't complain about those dirty tricks. Darren did the same thing one night to that Vanessa girl and her new place 'Horror Story', ringing the buzzers of all the other flats in their block asking for a blow job, but no one took any notice.'

'Won't you give him one then?'

'Oi!'

'Seriously Becks, that dickhead was bragging about how he'd knocked on the door of the biggest house and demanded a lap dance from a lady who turned out to be a magistrate's wife.'

'Great. That's what started all this hassle in the first place. I got into real trouble about that. The police were understandably very cross about it.'

'Yep. It's not good Becky. If you don't stop soon, between 'em they'll make sure you do time.'

I rubbed my face with my hands.

A warning from Keith I had to take seriously. It all made sense now. Although we had undoubtedly upset the locals, I never understood how or why we were such a problem so fast when we were on the edge of the village with no close neighbours. Well now I did. Sabotage. Good old fashioned sabotage. We were victims of our own success.

Part of me wanted to up the anti and go to war, but another part was totally sickened, disheartened and bored by even the mention of a massage parlour.

'Be careful and watch your back. Just about everyone's out to get you.'

Darren walked into the garden with Bruce and Treacle and shook Keith's hand. 'Alright mate?' How's it going?' Nodding towards the house he continued.

'They're all pissed in there. They've got paint everywhere.'

Lexi ran out shrieking and laughing followed by half a dozen nearly naked girls, one of whom was dressed as Rolf Harris and various punters. It was cold and getting dark, but everyone was high on fizzy drinks and illicit friendships. Wiggy held up his lace train and tried to run, giggling like a fool as his squiff took effect and toppled him onto one of Matrix's minions, upending them both onto the gravel.

Prostitutes, transvestites and punters with puppets ran round the garden drunk and shrieking, chased by a small, white, yapping dog like some acid induced Benny Hill sketch. It made me laugh for the first time in months. This was how it should be at 'Madam Becky's'. This was how it used to be. I loved these crazy, funny, sweet people. I'd had the last twenty years of my life enriched by knowing them. How could I think about walking away and giving it all up? Then I heard the sirens, the sound of several cars approaching fast.

Keith looked at me, then at Darren.

'I want to move,' I said.

'We are, back to our old house in Bletchley.'

I shook my head and looked straight at him. 'No that's it. I've had enough of this police harassment and the poke it up ya arse council bollocks.' I had to shout now over the noise of the panda cars screeching onto the drive. 'If they want me that badly, they can come and find me. Sod the lot of them, we're leaving for the south of France, now...'

CHAPTER THIRTY FIVE

I'd lived in France with Emilia for several years, before I returned to the UK, older and fatter. I stood on the softly lit stage at the All Ears story telling event and looked out over my audience of journalists. I waited smiling for the laughter and tittering to die down. My evening of brothel keeping tales had been a great success. I was holding court over a happy crowd.

I was enjoying myself, and could have stayed up there, under the spotlights for another hour chatting on, but I only had time to answer one or two more questions about my life as a Madam before the lights went up and the evening ended. I'd had an incredible if accidental journey through the sex industry. Sometimes working with the girls had felt similar to sticking your head into a bucket of bees, or spending an entire week at the dentist having your jaw drilled. Now time and distance had softened the bitterness, I could look back on it fondly and could see the funny side.

Another hand went up with a question.

The compare for the evening called from the back of the room. 'This will have to be the last question I'm afraid, but hopefully Madam Becky will come back and see us again soon.'

I nodded and waved my acceptance from the stage. 'The gentleman at the front, in the white t-shirt.' I pointed and smiled.

He stood up and was handed a mike. 'Madam Becky, knowing what you know now, would you do it all again?'

I let out a huge breath.

'Bloody hell! There's a question.'

I had to think about that one.

'I'd never re-open another place now. Times have changed too much, and I'm too old and knackered for all that excitement.'

'If I had my time again...' I paused. I didn't know the answer. Would I go through all that again?

I stood on the stage, and thought about how my life had been since I'd run off to France to hide in a field, and try to put my head back together in March 2008.

I hadn't sold up then; I'd wanted to, but we'd kept it all going, Darren dashing back and forth across the Channel, life becoming more difficult daily. I thought about how ridiculous it had been trying to run an English knocking shop from a French hospital after I suffered a stroke a few months after I'd left England, and the sadness of watching everything I'd worked so hard for be ruined and torn apart by staff I trusted and relied on, who then stabbed me in the back.

If I'd thought my life as a Madam had reached rock bottom before I went to live in France, I was wrong - the chaos had only just started. The eighteen months or so between leaving Milton Keynes in search of peace of mind, and selling out to one of my girls was the most upsetting and frustrating I'd ever lived through, but maybe that's another story...

In the last few years, 'Madam Becky's' had become a woeful millstone around my neck, and changed me for the worst. It had been fantastic fun in the beginning, but over the years the battle to keep going had made me a hard, difficult person. I suppose if you're constantly attacked you have to become defensive to survive. I had spent so long watching my back I'd forgotten what my front was like. I'd lost touch with who I was and what was important to me. The stress nearly ruined my relationship with Darren and alienated me from my friends and family. I was lucky to get out of it unhurt and with my liberty.

'I can't tell you how amazing the feeling of relief was when I eventually sold up and could stop looking over my shoulder. 'Madam Becky's' no longer exists. It was sold on several times, but was never the same. It had lost its uniqueness after I'd left it in the incapable hands of others...'

I looked into the audience. 'It was really hard to adjust to a normal life after all that madness. The business was gone but it still affected me badly. I was disillusioned, angry and bitter. I hated the world. For years all I'd thought about and talked about was prostitutes, punters and puppets. Who'd bonked who and how much they'd paid. I had no other topic of conversation. As an ex Madam, adrift in reality, I was totally lost.' I sighed to myself.

'It was the brutal murder of my daughter Emilia's school friend Adil Basharat in 2010 that shocked my sulking frozen heart back into life. It was as if his death re-set my soul and cleansed the last horrible' Madam Becky' years from me.

That tragedy made me remember who I was, who I wanted to be. The privilege of supporting my daughter and Adil's amazing family and friends through the devastation of losing a child, and the subsequent murder trial made me realise that we are all so lucky just to be alive and loved. I was heartbroken by his death, but my compassion for others had returned. I remembered that I enjoyed helping people and the important function of the early 'Madam Becky's' era had been to support vulnerable members of the community be they black, white, gay, transvestites or sex workers. Protecting and defending those who felt alienated by society was what mattered to me and something I still wanted to do.

'So would I do it all over again?'

'Financially it's been pointless. Emotionally it's been......up and down, a lot. Dreadful yet wonderful. On the whole, it was utterly bizarre. I've never laughed so much as I did every working day with Belinda, Wiggy and Spanky Monkey. I've never dressed up as Rolf Harris since to fulfil someone's fantasy, more's the pity, and I still have the beard.'

I looked across the stage at the pouting PVC younger me on the screen and smiled.

'In truth... hard, unpleasant and ugly as it was at times...

I really wouldn't have missed it for the world...'

Lightning Source UK Ltd.
Milton Keynes UK
UKOW030213010212

186433UK00001B/2/P